P9-EGM-849

# Foundations of Learning

## 3rd Edition

by

## Karl Krumsieg
Pacific Crest

and

## Marie Baehr
Elmhurst College

Pacific Crest
Corvallis, OR

# Foundations of Learning

Third Edition

by Karl Krumsieg & Marie Baehr

Copyright © 1996, 1999, 2000
Pacific Crest
875 NW Grant Avenue
Corvallis, OR 97330

(541) 754-1067

www.pcrest.com

All rights reserved under international copyright conventions. No part of the contents of this book may be reproduced or utilized in any form or by any means, electronic or mechanical, including photocopying, recording, or by any information storage and retrieval system, without the written consent of the publisher.

Process Education™ is a trademarked term for Pacific Crest. Use of this term is free but must include a citation to Pacific Crest.

*The Learning Assessment Journal*™ is a trademarked term for Pacific Crest.

Cover design by Laurie Markus

ISBN # 1–878437–96–8

## Contributing Authors

We would like to extend our sincere gratitude and thanks to those who have so willingly given of their time to make contributions to this book.

| | |
|---|---|
| Daniel Apple | Pacific Crest, President |
| Cynthia Johnson | The Westchester Business Institute, Library Director |
| Carolyn Knowles | St. Augustine's College, Director, Learning Communities Program |
| Eric Myrvaagnes | Suffolk University, Professor, Mathematics/Computer Science/Education |
| Charlotte Rakich | Purdue University Calumet, Secondary Education Advisor |
| Lee Rademacher | Purdue University Calumet, Academic Counselor and Instructor, University Division |
| Kathy Santolo | Pittsburg Adult Education, Pittsburg, CA, Instructor |
| James Seymour | St. Augustine's College, Department Head, Philosophy and Religion |
| Karyn Valerius | SUNY Stony Brook, English Department, Lecturer |
| Kathy Wendling | Kirkwood Community College, Librarian, Iowa City Center |
| Eric Wignall | Purdue University Calumet, Coordinator, Instructional Design and Media Resource Lab |

## Acknowledgments

We greatly appreciate and want to thank the following for their help, ideas, edits, and suggestions.

| | |
|---|---|
| Karen Anderson | Madison Area Technical College, Instructor of Chemistry |
| Richard Armstrong | Madison Area Technical College, Instructor of Chemistry |
| Margaret Krumsieg | School Association for Special Education in DuPage County, Vocational Coordinator |
| Nadine Shardlow | Alfred State College, Director of Learning Assistance, Freshman Seminar |
| Maurice Taylor | St. Augustine's College, Provost, Academic Affairs |
| Jan Upton | St. Augustine's College, Director, Plans and Analysis |
| Laverne Weldon | St. Augustine's College, Director, Center for Teaching and Learning |

Photographs are courtesy of Elmhurst College. A special thanks to Linda Reiselt and Mercedes Wetzel for their help and expertise.

| | |
|---|---|
| Karl Krumsieg | Pacific Crest, Educational Consultant |
| Marie Baehr | Elmhurst College, Associate Dean of the Faculty and Professor of Physics |

# Table of Contents

# List of Tables

# List of Tables (continued)

# List of Figures

# Preface

The goal of *Foundations of Learning* is to start students down the path that will lead to success in college and beyond. However, for students to be successful, they must learn not only study skills but an entire set of skills from all domains (cognitive, social, affective, and psychomotor). Recognizing that all students come to college with their own individual set of skills, an important premise of this book is that ALL students can improve the skill set they presently have—everyone has the ability to improve how they learn!

While all students would benefit from the information in *Foundations of Learning*, it is especially useful for students who are entering higher education. The first three chapters focus on helping students make the transition to college, making sure they understand their new roles and responsibilities as well as the resources available to them. Chapter Four introduces students to the concept of a "life vision" and the process of constructing a life vision portfolio while in college. The remaining chapters focus on improving the processes and skills which lead to the development of lifelong learners and self-growers.

The book can be used at almost any type of higher education institution that offers a foundations, orientation, or seminar course for incoming students. If class time is limited, the first eight chapters serve nicely as a "transition to college" course, with Chapters 5-8 focusing on basic skills (including study skills). The later chapters are intended to be a starting point for building key skills that should continue to be built and strengthened while at college (see below).

With learning as the overriding process, *Foundations of Learning* focuses on providing students with a means to improve the following key processes:

| Key Processes | |
| --- | --- |
| Chapters 4 – 8 | Chapters 9 – 13 |
| • developing a life vision | • utilizing technology |
| • learning | • personal development |
| • information processing | • teamwork |
| • reading | • communication |
| • writing | • problem solving |
| • study skills | • assessment |

Refer to page 212 in the Appendix for an entire classification of learning skills which is the focus of the book. The *Classification of Learning Skills* identifies four domains (cognitive, social, affective, and psychomotor) and then lists their associated processes, general skill areas, and specific skills. The processes of language development, assessment, and evaluation complete the classification.

To help students improve their performances with key processes and their associated skills, *Foundations of Learning* makes use of methodologies, profiles of quality performers, and a site on the World Wide Web with links to numerous additional resources.

## Methodologies

The methodologies presented in this book should not be viewed as "the only way to use a particular process," but rather as a guide or framework from which to start. Students are encouraged to look at and use the methodologies presented in this book as they would a recipe. With initial unfamiliarity, the steps are followed and studied more closely. With increasing comfort and proficiency, there is less reliance and more spontaneity. However, having a framework with explicit steps helps students understand the process and how it is most effectively implemented. With study, practice, and assessment, it is our contention that students will increase their skills associated with any process.

## Profiles

The profiles provided in *Foundations of Learning* serve as models which students can refer to and strive towards. The descriptions and behaviors associated with expert performance build understanding, assist with assessment, and provide specifics which students can seek to emulate.

The following profiles are included in the book:

- a quality student,
- a quality learner,
- a self-grower,
- an information literate person,
- a good team player,
- a good problem solver, and
- a quality assessor.

## Technology and the *Foundations of Learning* Web Site

The authors have assumed that students will have access to the Internet, either through their homes, schools, or public libraries. Several sections in Chapter Nine are devoted to explaining the Internet and World Wide Web to students.

With such a wealth of information readily accessible and available on the Internet, students should be encouraged to tap into this valuable resource. A *Foundations of Learning* web site, which is accessed from the Pacific Crest home page, exists as a companion to the text. This site provides students with links to additional information and resources and serves as a supplement to many topics presented in the book.

Whenever you see the computer icon shown at the left, this lets students know that additional information about a particular topic can be found at the *Foundations of Learning* web site.

**http://www.pcrest.com**

## Activities Book

With the exception of a few discussion questions and exercises, the authors have purposely left out specific assignments in this book. We felt that each school would have a different set of needs pertaining to the types of assignments they would want for their students.

However, for instructors who would like their students to process the content in *Foundations of Learning* in an **active learning format**, there is an Activities Book available which is designed specifically for this purpose. Each of the 44 activities corresponds to content from the *Foundations of Learning* text and specifies learning objectives with performance criteria. Various types of activity formats include: guided discovery learning, case studies, project-oriented, technology-based, and assessment-oriented activities. A few of the activity topics include time management, using a textbook effectively, assessing the quality of Internet information, and solving word problems.

We welcome your feedback. You can communicate with us by e-mail at:

karl@pcrest.com

Karl Krumsieg and Marie Baehr

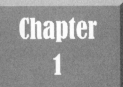
# Making the Transition to College

> No one can go back and start a new beginning, but anyone can start today and make a new ending. —*Anonymous*

## What is a Transition?

A transition is an act, process, or instance of changing from one state, form, activity, or place to another. At the moment, you are in the process of making an important transition in your life, the transition into college.

Table 1.6 at the end of this chapter presents the results of a survey of more than 250,000 college freshmen who were asked to identify the reasons they chose to go to college. Take a moment and consider how the survey results compare with your reasons for attending. Whatever your reasons for attending college, you can be certain that you will face many new challenges and additional transitions during your collegiate years.

To reach your goals as a student, you must be able to make adjustments to the new sets of circumstances you encounter. This includes a general transition to a different type of academic/learning environment, adapting to new people in academic and social settings, learning a new set of rules and regulations, and meeting specific challenges in academic, social, spiritual, physical, and financial contexts.

Knowing what to expect can help with making the transition to college. Whether you are entering college immediately from high school or at some later point, here are issues you should know about college.

*In college…*

- students experience a large amount of personal freedom.
- students must take on greater responsibilities.
- students have many choices they must make.
- time management is very important for student success.
- faculty have high expectations for student performance.
- students are expected to do large amounts of reading.
- students are required to do a great deal of work outside of class.
- challenging material is covered at a fast pace.
- performance on exams takes on greater importance.
- students typically experience increased diversity.

# Increased Responsibility

Being responsible means to think and act rationally, and to be accountable for one's behavior, including readily assuming obligations and duties. As a college student, you are now in a position where you must face new responsibilities. For many of you, these new responsibilities must be met without the benefit of significant others who have, in the past, been around to guide you and look out for you. If you are a traditional college student, your parents, relatives, and close friends may now be far away.

One of the benefits of college is the opportunity you have to grow as a person, gaining confidence from handling new responsibilities and challenges. Table 1.1 presents many of the challenges you will likely encounter. Note the connection between the items in the table and the transition into adulthood.

*Note to non-traditional students:*

You may have several advantages over traditional students because of your age and the skills you have developed in life. You may be more focused and feel more comfortable interacting with professors who may be closer to your age. You may be a better manager of time. However, you will face many of the same challenges as traditional students as well as challenges unique to your situation. For example, you may be nervous about coming back to school after being away from education for an extended period of time, feeling a sense of age anxiety when in a traditional college setting.

Table 1.1

| Responsibilities and Challenges Facing College Students | | |
|---|---|---|
| managing your time | managing your money | making decisions on your own |
| being independent | being self-reliant | being assertive |
| handling adult responsibilities | solving problems in various contexts | developing leadership attributes and qualities |
| making social adjustments | choosing mutually supportive relationships | handling peer influences and pressures |
| examining and/or changing value systems | dealing with loneliness and/or homesickness | dealing with home and family issues |
| maintaining personal wellness | making choices about alcohol and drugs | coping with stress and pressure |
| learning in large classes | communicating with professors | adjusting study habits appropriately |
| finding a role model or mentor | seeking assistance | maintaining balance |

Knowing that certain challenges lie ahead, how will you respond? What decisions will you make? As you probably realize, you are accountable for your actions and the consequences that result from the choices and decisions you make. Wise decisions will produce results that enhance your college career and promote a high level of personal control, competence, enthusiasm, and opportunities for growth. Poor choices may hinder your college experience and produce stress, anxiety, worry, and/or depression.

You have the freedom to be the person you want to be. The choices are yours to make. Table 1.2 points out some of the choices college freshmen from across the nation made in terms of activities they engaged in during their first year at college. The table presents the results of more than 250,000 students who were surveyed about their activities. *Note that because of multiple responses, the percentages add to more than 100 per cent.*

Review Table 1.2 and compare the activities with the responsibilities in Table 1.1. Consider the following questions. Generally speaking, how responsible were the students who were surveyed? And more importantly, how do you plan to engage yourself during your first year at college?

> Do what you can, with what you have, where you are.
> —*Teddy Roosevelt. 26th President 1858–1919*

## Accepting Accountability and Degree Completion

Once you have realized the vast personal responsibility that's taken on with adulthood and the great maturity that should accompany it, you will find that growing up brings many challenges and consequences that are sometimes hard to bear. According to John Bradshaw, "Part of growing up is learning to delay gratification, which helps reduce life's pain and difficulties."

Student retention is an important issue in higher education that relates directly to you. Most every student who enrolls in a degree program at college intends to graduate with a degree. Yet more students drop out of college than stay. Why is this so? Who is ultimately responsible and/or accountable for this massive exodus? A UCLA study‡ found that the number of college and university students who actually earn bachelor's degrees at the first college they attend is declining overall. This study of national degree completion rates also shows that degree attainment by African-Americans and  Hispanics falls dramatically below that of Asian-American and white students. Refer to Table 1.3 for the specific percentages.

‡Press release dated October 1, 1996, entitled "UCLA Study Finds Number of College Students Successfully Earning Bachelor's Degrees is Declining"

Table 1.2

| Activities College Freshman Engaged in During the Past Year | |
| --- | --- |
| Activity: | % |
| studied with other students | 83.5 |
| used the Internet for research/homework (2) | 82.9 |
| attended a religious service | 81.9 |
| played computer games (2) | 80.4 |
| performed volunteer work | 74.2 |
| attended a public recital/concert | 73.5 |
| used the Internet, other than research (2) | 72.9 |
| communicated using e-mail (2) | 65.9 |
| read the editorial page in a newspaper | 62.9 |
| socialized with different ethnic groups (1) | 61.6 |
| came late to class | 60.3 |
| drank wine or liquor | 54.9 |
| took part in an Internet chat room (2) | 54.2 |
| visited an art gallery or museum | 53.1 |
| drank beer | 51.6 |
| tutored another student | 47.8 |
| participated in demonstrations | 45.9 |
| was bored in class (1) | 37.7 |
| played a musical instrument | 36.6 |
| overslept and missed class | 34.5 |
| felt overwhelmed (1) | 29.6 |
| was a guest in a teacher's home | 27.3 |
| discussed religion (1) | 26.0 |
| asked a teacher for advice (1) | 21.5 |
| voted in student elections (1) | 21.1 |
| checked out a book from school library (1) | 18.7 |
| smoked cigarettes (1) | 15.8 |
| discussed politics (1) | 14.0 |
| felt depressed (1) | 9.3 |
| took prescribed anti-depressant | 5.9 |

Percentage of students who responded that they had engaged in the activity during the past year.

(1) Percentage of students reporting "frequently" only. (Results for other items in the table represent the % responding "frequently" or "occasionally.")

(2) This item included for the first time in 1998.

Source: "The American Freshman: National Norms for Fall 1998" published by the American Council on Education and the University of California at Los Angeles Higher Education Research Institute.

| Table 1.3 | Degree Completion Rates | within 4 years | within 9 years |
|---|---|---|---|
| | All students | 40% | 46% |
| | Men | 37% | 43% |
| | Women | 43% | 49% |
| | White | 43% | 47% |
| | African-American | 23% | 33% |
| | Asian | 50% | 58% |
| | Puerto Rican | 27% | 37% |
| | Mexican/Chicano | 31% | 40% |
| | Native American | 23% | 33% |

Higher Education Research Institute, "Degree Attainment Rates at American Colleges and Universities: Differences by Race, Gender and Institutional Type" (1996 CIRP Press Release).

> Only the educated are free.
> —*Epictetus, Greek philosopher 50–130 A.D.*

Why do students not complete their first year at college or fail to complete their degree? Is it the environment, teachers, or roommates? Higher education researchers are still pondering these questions. While answers may differ from place to place, it appears that a common denominator with respect to retention, centers on a student's commitment to himself or herself and an institution's commitment to its students.

Some schools of thought promote that institutions (colleges) have the primary responsibility for retention. However, others suggest that students must be responsible for their own learning. This textbook advocates and promotes the empowerment of students to gain and maintain control over their lives. While it is important to identify others to help you along the way, you must take charge of your own destiny.

## Possible Threats and Opportunities Resulting from Your Transition to College

Transitions in life involve change. When a move is made from one place in life to another, it typically has its pros and cons. For example, while support systems may not be readily available or immediately accessible for new college students, there is the opportunity to establish new relationships. With most every threat of loss during a transition, there is usually some opportunity for gain and benefit. Table 1.4 lists some examples of threats and opportunities that may occur as a result of your transition to college.

Table 1.4

| | Threats and Opportunities Resulting from a Transition to College | |
|---|---|---|
| | **Threats** | **Opportunities** |
| Family | • loss of nurturing<br>• homesickness and loneliness<br>• conflicts over adulthood | • ability to grow and mature<br>• new activities in campus life<br>• develop productive relationship with parents |
| Friends | • loss of comfortable friendships<br>• fear of meeting new people<br>• peer pressure and conflicts with friends | • choose compatible friends<br>• resolve issues by showing mutual respect |
| Personal Relationships | • isolation/loneliness<br>• loss of romantic relationship, grow apart due to distance | • identify ways to utilize time<br>• challenge the strength of a relationship through trust; create ways to remain a couple |
| Accomplishments | • no longer a big person on campus | • become a star at college |
| Environment | • loss of familiarity | • learn to survive and thrive in a new environment |

## Leverage Your Past to Optimize Your Future

Upon arrival at college, a key question to answer is, *Who am I?* However, after matriculation (enrolling in college), the focus should change to become a clarification and affirmation of the statement, *Who I am*. Build upon your strengths and accomplishments and use affirmations in the process. According to former boxing great, Muhammad Ali, he was saying, "I am the greatest" long before he actually became heavyweight champion. During your time in college, your growth and development should reflect a personal affirmation of who you are and who you want to become. Realize that once you have claimed your affirmation, you must live it, and do so with continued reinforcement.

When all is said and done, it is important that you leverage or build upon your past to optimize your future. Your past is your foundation, so continue to build upon it as you strive to become a life long-learner and self-grower. At the same time, dare to challenge yourself, set goals and dream. As you accomplish the goals you set, revise them, expand upon them, and go on to the next level. Your future is determined by the choices you make and continue to make. Reflect upon your past, relate it to your present, and take responsibility for your future.

# The Road Not Taken

Two roads diverged in a yellow wood,
And sorry I could not travel both
And be one traveler, long I stood
And looked down one as far as I could
To where it bent in the undergrowth;

Then took the other, as just as fair,
And having perhaps the better claim,
Because it was grassy and wanted wear;
Though as for that passing there
Had worn them really about the same,

And both that morning equally lay
In leaves no step had trodden black.
Oh, I kept the first for another day!
Yet knowing how way leads on to way,
I doubted if I should ever come back.

I shall be telling this with a sigh
Somewhere ages and ages hence:
Two roads diverged in a wood, and I–
I took the one less traveled by,
And that has made all the difference.

—Robert Frost

Original text: Robert Frost, *Mountain Interval* (New York: Henry Holt, 1921), p. 9

# Tools for Success

Tools are devices, implements, instruments, or utensils that serve as resources to accomplish tasks. Only with the proper tools can you turn the issues and challenges you face in college into opportunities and make the transitions necessary to be successful in college and in life.

Table 1.5 lists some of the tools that will help you have a successful college matriculation (starting toward a college degree), which will lead to your ultimate goal of graduation (completing a degree).

Table 1.5

| Student Learning Tools | | |
|---|---|---|
| Reflection and assessment | life vision plan | images and written documentation of what you would like your future self to be and methods for getting there |
| | learning assessment journal | used to document learning and thoughts |
| | self-assessment papers | papers written by individuals to measure their own performance and growth |
| People | mentors | teachers, coaches, advisors and/or fellow students who assist with an individual's personal growth and development |
| | study groups | individuals who team up to apply their minds towards understanding specific subject matter |
| | peer tutoring | the process of providing instruction to a peer by a peer |
| | peer assessments | the process of measuring performance, work products, or learning skills of peers by peers and giving feedback, which documents growth and provides directives to improve future performance |
| Technology | software tools | computer programs, routines, and symbolic languages essential to operation and maintenance of computers |
| | the Internet | virtual world wide library containing a vast storehouse of texts, sounds, images, and other resources readily available to people with computer and phone access |
| Additional tools | methodologies | frameworks or procedures used to learn processes |
| | interactive learning systems | tools that allow the acquisition of knowledge and skills of two or more systems of learning, i.e. journal writing and assessment |
| | undergraduate research | scholarly investigations at the college level |

# Why Students Go to College

The table below is a summary of the survey responses of 251,232 freshmen entering 494 two-year and four-year institutions. *Note that because of multiple responses, the percentages add to more than 100 percent.*

Table 1.6

| Reasons Noted as Very Important in Deciding to Go to College | |
|---|---|
| get a better job | 76.9% |
| make more money | 74.6% |
| gain general education | 62.0% |
| prepare for graduate or professional school | 49.0% |
| become a more cultured person | 45.1% |
| improve reading and study skills | 41.5% |
| parents wanted me to go | 39.5% |
| prove to others I could succeed | 37.0% |
| wanted to get away from home | 17.2% |
| role model/mentor encouraged me | 15.5% |
| could not find a job | 7.3% |
| because friends were going | 4.5% |

Source: "The American Freshman: National Norms for Fall 1998" published by the American Council on Education and the University of California at Los Angeles Higher Education Research Institute.

Table 1.7

## Ten Tips for Students Entering College

1. Focus on academics first, not part-time or full-time jobs.

2. Associate with people who share your values.

3. Develop a good rapport and understanding with roommates.

4. Thoroughly read the Student Handbook for your college — know the rules.

5. Properly safeguard your valuables.

6. Work very hard to "ace" the first test — the feeling of victory is contagious.

7. Keep in touch with parent(s) — they too are experiencing a void.

8. Beware of easy credit — too many credit cards are available to students.

9. Beware of drugs and alcohol — they can quickly end your college career.

10. Have fun, but don't let it get in the way of your main goal, to GRADUATE!

Contributed by Carolyn Knowles and Dr. Jan Upton, Saint Augustine's College, Raleigh, NC

## Discussion Questions

1. What are three of the most important transitions you will experience as a college student? Discuss how you plan to deal (or are currently dealing) with each transition.

2. What is your interpretation of the following statement? "*The first year at college is a real problem and a real opportunity.*"

3. What is the significance of *responsibility* and *accountability* during your transition to college life? How are they connected?

4. What actions can you take to make each tip in Table 1.7 become a reality?

# College and Higher Education

> The things taught in schools and colleges are not an education, but the means to an education.
> —*Ralph Waldo Emerson, American philosopher and essayist   1803–1882*

## Higher Education – A New Environment

You've made it! You're now in college. It's all exciting and new, but the bottom line is there still is a great deal that you don't know about this new environment called "higher education." For some students, the newness of college brings a sense of anticipation, while for others there's more of a sense of anxiety. Whatever your situation, be assured that as you learn more about higher education in general, along with the specifics of your college, you will begin to feel more comfortable and at home.

First, let's clarify what the term higher education (or post-secondary education as it is sometimes called) means. Higher education refers to formal education that takes place after high school. Colleges and universities are institutions of higher education. As you know, there are different types of colleges and universities that are distinguished or categorized in certain ways. For example, there are public and private universities, two-year and four-year colleges, and liberal arts and technical schools.

This chapter provides a framework from which you can apply the knowledge in this book to your own situation. Many new terms are explained and clarified. A variety of possible support systems, resources, and tools are identified. The general components and structure of a college are diagrammed and discussed. You will gain insights into college faculty and begin to understand the differences in behaviors that exist between different disciplines or fields of study.

As you read this chapter, use your college catalog (and possibly your student handbook) to transfer and apply what is presented here in a general context to the specific situation at your school.

## College Catalog

Every student should have a copy of the college catalog (or bulletin) published by his/her school. A catalog is an official document that serves several purposes and provides a wealth of information about a college. It can be used as a marketing and recruiting tool for prospective students. Also, by stating the specific requirements for obtaining a degree, a catalog serves as a legally binding document or contract for entering and current students.

What will you find in a college catalog? Most catalogs contain the following information:

As topics are addressed in this chapter, refer to your catalog and handbook to see what information they provide specific to your school.

- general information consisting of a mission statement, historical background, accreditation and degrees granted, buildings and facilities, and a campus map,

- student life and services including activities and organizations,

- enrollment and admissions policies and procedures,

- financial information which includes financial aid, fees and expenses, etc.,

- an academic calendar,

- academic regulations,

- programs of study with requirements for a degree, and

- a listing of faculty and staff.

Catalogs are published annually or biennial. While the most recent copy will contain information about the latest policies and requirements, you should be sure to keep a copy of the catalog from when you enrolled for purposes of clarifying your requirements for a degree. If requirements change in a new catalog, you will not usually be required to meet the new requirements but are bound by what was in effect at the time you enrolled or matriculated.

## Student Handbook

Another useful tool to obtain is the student handbook from your school. This book contains information specifically written as a guide and resource for students at your school. The student handbook contains some academic information that can also be found in the catalog, but also includes:

- student rights and responsibilities – access and privacy of your academic records, grievance policy, sexual harassment, etc.,

- college policies – substance abuse, residence hall policies, anti-hazing, governance structure, etc.,

- student services information, and

- student organizations – contacts, policies, and activities.

# Components of a College

The diagram on the next page shows how a typical college is organized. After the President, there are usually five functional areas which focus on the following: 1) academic or instructional matters, 2) financial matters, 3) public relations and marketing, 4) student affairs, and 5) admissions and enrollment. Since the titles of people in similar roles will vary from one college to another, several examples of titles within the five functional areas have been provided.

**Vice President for Academic Affairs**
also called *Provost, V.P. for Instruction*, or *V.P. for Student Learning*

> The person in charge of the faculty and areas directly related to the academic life of students. This includes general academic areas of undergraduate education, graduate programs, and continuing education (programs that enable nontraditional students to take classes without pursuing a degree). The VP for Academic Affairs also oversees issues related to teaching and instruction, curriculum, advising and registration.

**Vice President for Financial Affairs**
also called *Business Manager* or *Vice President for Finance*

> The person in charge of the financial side of the college. This includes accountants, controllers, student accounts and financial aid, human resources and the physical plant.

**Vice President for College Advancement**
also called *Director of Public Affairs* or *V.P. for University Advancement*

> The person in charge of interacting with people and companies outside of the college. This includes marketing and public relations, grant writing, keeping in contact with alumni and hosting special programs and events.

**Director of Student Affairs**
also called *V.P. for Student Services* or *Dean of Student Affairs*

> The person in charge of areas directly related to student life outside of academics. This includes areas such as athletic programs and the running of residence halls.

**Director of Admissions**
also called *V.P. for Enrollment Services* or *Dean of Admissions*

> The person in charge of recruiting and enrollment of students.

<aside>
The only thing more expensive than an education is ignorance.
—*Unknown*
</aside>

<aside>
Higher education is no longer a luxury but a necessity.
—*Anthony Celebreeze, Secretary of Health, Education, and Welfare (1965)*
</aside>

Figure 2.1

# General Overview of the Components of a College

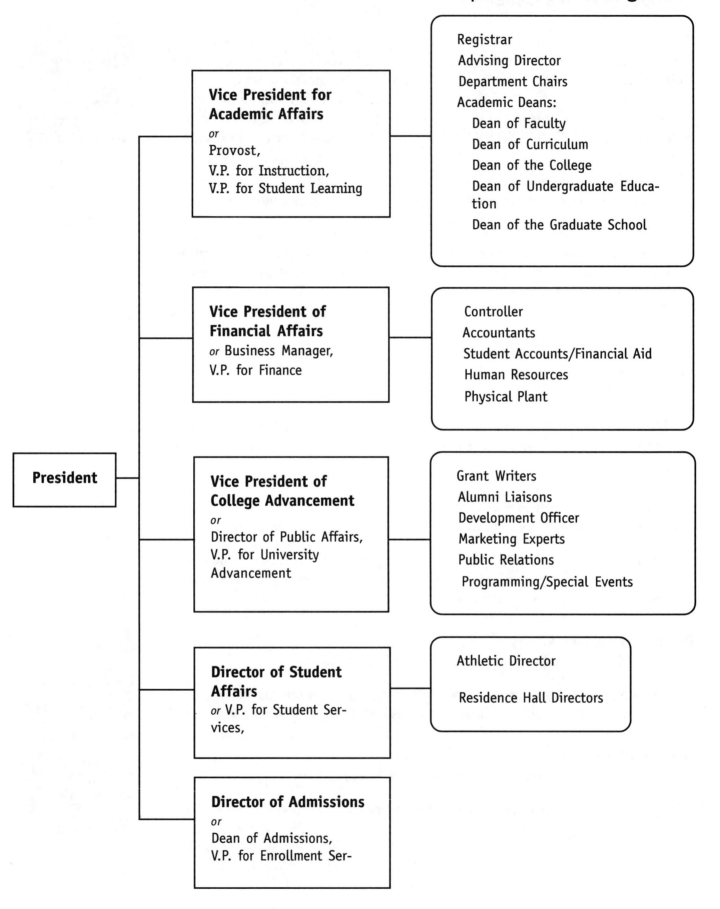

**Vice President for Academic Affairs**
*or*
Provost,
V.P. for Instruction,
V.P. for Student Learning

Registrar
Advising Director
Department Chairs
Academic Deans:
    Dean of Faculty
    Dean of Curriculum
    Dean of the College
    Dean of Undergraduate Education
    Dean of the Graduate School

**Vice President of Financial Affairs**
*or* Business Manager,
V.P. for Finance

Controller
Accountants
Student Accounts/Financial Aid
Human Resources
Physical Plant

**President**

**Vice President of College Advancement**
*or*
Director of Public Affairs,
V.P. for University Advancement

Grant Writers
Alumni Liaisons
Development Officer
Marketing Experts
Public Relations
Programming/Special Events

**Director of Student Affairs**
*or* V.P. for Student Services,

Athletic Director

Residence Hall Directors

**Director of Admissions**
*or*
Dean of Admissions,
V.P. for Enrollment Ser-

# Support Systems and Services

Colleges and universities offer a wide range of services to meet the needs of their students. These support services help students in all facets of college life including academic issues, financial and career planning, emotional well-being, social aspects, personal safety, and more. Unfortunately, many students do not take full advantage of these services even though there are usually no costs associated with them. You are encouraged to become familiar with what is available to you so that you can make use of these valuable services when the need arises.

The services common to most schools are mentioned below. The specific services offered by your college will vary depending on several factors including the type of school you attend and the students it serves.

**Academic services** help you perform better in your classes. *Academic Skills Center* or *Learning Resources Center* are the common terms used for identifying the place on campus where you can find:

- diagnostic testing services to determine your current level of ability,
- tutoring services in different areas,
- a math lab,
- a writing lab, and
- a reading lab.

**Academic Advising services** provide you with guidance and assistance as you plan and complete your academic program. There are two kinds of undergraduate advisors at a university, the professional academic advisor and the faculty advisor. See Chapter Three for more information about advising.

**Career and Placement services** assist you with deciding upon a career and finding a job upon graduation. The placement center may also help with:

- part-time employment while still a student,
- putting together a resume,
- information about internships and cooperative work,
- getting into graduate school, and
- preparing for an interview.

**Counseling services** help with your emotional and mental well-being. Counselors and psychologists can offer professional help with personal crises, depression, difficult relationships, adjusting to college, substance abuse, and addictions, to name a few. Services offered can be in the form of one-on-one sessions as well as workshops and programs.

**Disability services** facilitate learning for those who have special needs or are disabled in some way. The federal Americans with Disabilities Act of 1990 ensures that all people have access to public resources, thus eliminating discrimination on the basis of a disability. If you have a disability, look into what services are available to you.

> Education's purpose is to replace an empty mind with an open one.
> —*Malcolm Forbes, American publisher 1919–1990*

**Financial aid services** assist with the financing of college. Financial aid counselors can work to see what options might be available to you including various types of grants, loans, scholarships, and work-study programs.

**Health/medical and wellness centers** help with your physical well-being. These services vary depending on the college. Some colleges staff full-time doctors whose services are included as part of tuition while in other cases, students obtain an insurance policy at a nominal cost to cover these services. Also, some colleges provide a variety of wellness programs which focus on keeping you healthy and fit.

**Testing services** help you to perform better on national (standardized) tests and to learn more about yourself. You can take certain tests and obtain information about registering for others.

> Education is what survives when what has been learned has been forgotten.
> —*B. F. Skinner, behavioral psychologist 1904-1990*

- Students who are looking to earn college credit for previous work can take tests such as CLEP (College Level Exam Program). Many students going on to graduate school will need to take a particular national exam such as the GRE (Graduate Record Examination) or the GMAT (Graduate Management Admission Test) depending on their field of interest.

- By taking personality inventory tests, such as Meyers-Briggs Indicator and Keirsey Temperament Sorter (see Chapter Four for information about how to take this test on-line), you can gain insights and learn more about yourself.

**Campus security** services help when there are concerns for safety. For example, many schools provide an escort service for those walking alone at night.

**Student centers** or student unions are campus buildings that are often a common meeting place and center of student life. Student centers typically have recreational options, dining facilities, stores, bulletin boards, and offices for support services, and also house student clubs and organizations. You are encouraged to take time to learn more about the particular organizations of interest to you at your school.

**Campus ministries** and other religious groups support students in their spiritual life. Ministries are usually available for students of different faiths.

**International studies offices** provide information about programs to study abroad. This may also be a place for foreign students to gather and receive help, assistance, and support as they adjust to life in a new country.

Some colleges have **child care services** for students who are also parents with small children.

In addition to your school's athletic program, many schools have **intramural activities** and other forms of recreation for both men and women.

# Campus Resources

Two important resources that every student should be familiar with are the campus library (or libraries) and the campus computer center(s).

## The Campus Library

Libraries contain numerous types of information resources and tools to access those resources. Libraries provide all this in many different formats including on-line formats. Becoming familiar with the services and resources of your library enables you to take full advantage of everything the library has to offer (note that many libraries offer information/training sessions for students). Learning to effectively use library resources strengthens your information processing skills, increases the quality of your research work and places a wealth of information at your immediate disposal.

As you begin the process of learning about your campus library and its organization, it may be helpful to think of the resources in the library as being divided into three general types of resources: (1) people resources, (2) physical resources, and (3) on-line or electronic resources. People resources are the library staff, including the reference librarians and the inter-library loan coordinator. Physical resources include books, audio-visual sources, magazines, newspapers, government documents, and pamphlets that physically reside in a library. Electronic resources include book catalogs, magazine indexes, the Internet, and CD-ROM products which either contain information about what can be found in the library, or act as an access point to this information inside or outside the walls of your library.

Understanding how information is organized is key to developing effective library skills. First, it is important to realize that there are different kinds of libraries. Each type of library specializes in collecting and accessing information useful to its particular audience. For example, a hospital library collects medical information for health professionals and those using the hospital, while a law library contains information and resources devoted to law and legal matters. A historical library collects matters of historical interest such as journals, letters, photographs, and other memorabilia associated with a certain period, person, or place in history.

Second, it is important to understand that information and materials are alphabetized for easy access (think of how an encyclopedia is organized) or classified into different subject areas with an indexing system. Similar to a textbook index that points you to a particular page location(s), a library indexing system points you to where the information is physically located. Examples of materials arranged alphabetically in a library include periodicals (magazines and journals), newspapers, and subjects within a pamphlet file. Books and audio-visual resources are classified into subject areas using either the Library of Congress Classification System or the Dewey Decimal System.

> Getting lost in a library should be by choice.
> —*Unknown*

The **Dewey Decimal System** is used in public libraries, K–12 school libraries, small academic libraries, and some specialized libraries. Under the Dewey Decimal System, knowledge is divided into 10 categories using numbers 000 through the 900's. The classifications of the Dewey Decimal System are as follows:

| | | | |
|---|---|---|---|
| 000 | General works | 500 | Natural Sciences and Mathematics |
| 100 | Philosophy and Psychology | 600 | Technology and Applied Sciences |
| 200 | Religion | 700 | Fine Arts |
| 300 | Social Sciences | 800 | Literature and Rhetoric |
| 400 | Language | 900 | Geography and History |

The **Library of Congress Classification System** was developed by the Library of Congress to handle large research collections. The Library of Congress cataloging system provides a more detailed breakdown of the areas of knowledge. It uses letters of the alphabet and thus allows for the creation of more categories. The classifications of the Library of Congress System are as follows:

| | | | | | | | |
|---|---|---|---|---|---|---|---|
| A | General works | H | Social Sciences | N | Fine Arts | T | Technology |
| B | Philosophy & Religion | I | *not used yet* | O | *not used yet* | U | Military Science |
| C | History (sciences of history) | J | Political Science | P | Language and Literature | V | Naval Science |
| D | General and Old World History | K | Law | Q | Science | W | *not used yet* |
| E,F | History of America | L | Education | R | Medicine | X,Y | *not used yet* |
| G | Geography, Anthropology, Sports | M | Music | S | Agriculture | Z | Bibliography and Library Science |

Libraries have tools to help you locate and find the information you need. Electronic library catalogs and card catalogs serve as an index for books and media resources. Catalogs give you a call number that you then use to find the physical location of the information you are seeking. Periodical indexes, which can be in either paper or electronic format, give you the location within a periodical title of the information you are looking for.

## Computer Centers

Computers are such a part of everyday life that it is imperative that you become proficient with various computer skills. You can be certain that your professors will require work that involves using a computer. Regardless of your major or career plans, you will be expected to have some basic level of computer proficiency.

Even if you have your own computer, you should learn what computer facilities your college has to offer. Campus computer systems can provide you with access to the Internet and e-mail, and make available a variety of different software programs for you to use.

## Higher Education Degrees

The following section provides a brief discussion about the types of degrees offered by colleges and universities.

### Associate's Degree

A degree that is granted after successful completion of a two-year course of study in the arts is an Associate of Arts (A.A.). In the sciences, the degree is an Associate of Science (A.S.). Community colleges and technical schools offer associate degrees as do some, but not all, four-year colleges and universities.

### Bachelor's Degree

A degree that is granted after successful completion of a four-year course of study in the arts is a called a Bachelor of Arts or B.A. degree. A degree in the fine arts is called a B.F.A. In the sciences, the degree is called a Bachelor of Science or B.S. degree. The number of credit hours required for a bachelor's degree will vary depending on the specific major or field of study. In some cases, students may complete a bachelor's degree in less than four years while in others, students may take more than four years.

*Note*: some states have "articulation agreements" between two-year and four-year state schools whereby classes satisfactorily completed toward an associate's degree will count toward a bachelor's degree.

### Master's Degree

A degree granted after two or more years of study beyond a bachelor's degree in the arts is called a Master of Arts or M.A. degree. A Masters in Business Administration degree is called an M.B.A. In the sciences, the degree is called a Master of Science or M.S. degree, while a M.Ed. is a Masters in Education. Students may continue to study in the same discipline as their bachelor's degree or study a different discipline. A master's degree may require comprehensive exams, a thesis or long paper, or an internship.

### Doctoral Degree or Doctorate

A doctorate is the highest degree awarded by a university and requires study beyond a master's degree for at least three years. A dissertation or extended writing (often the length of a book) is required. A doctorate degree in an academic philosophy is a Doctor of Philosophy or Ph.D. while a Medical Doctorate is an M.D. A doctorate degree given in the field of education is an Ed.D.

## Faculty Responsibilities

In general, college faculty have four main duties or responsibilities. These are teaching, learning, service, and research. Within each of the four main areas are numerous performance requirements or expectations. Some examples are presented below.

**Teaching** — includes classroom teaching, conducting office hours, designing curriculum, assessing and evaluating students, mentoring, and attending faculty development events to improve teaching processes.

**Learning** — includes reading professional papers and journals, attending professional conferences, dialoging with colleagues, reviewing the work of others, and learning new professional tools.

**Service** — includes advising, attending meetings, serving on committees or task forces, participating in professional societies, involvement in community service, and professional consulting.

**Research** — includes grant writing, performing research to build new knowledge, publishing papers, and writing books or textbooks.

Different colleges and universities emphasize or require different responsibilities. Also, each faculty member has individual preferences as to how his or her time is spent.

Note, *tenure* signifies a person has achieved a lifetime faculty position at an institution by meeting specified requirements for length of service and quality of performance. Tenure can be terminated only under select conditions. At many colleges and universities, a high percentage of full-time faculty are tenured.

## Faculty Rankings

Colleges and universities have titles or ranks they give to faculty. These titles are based on various performance criteria as they pertain to teaching, learning, service, and research. The rankings in descending order are as follows:

- *professor emeritus* (retired professors who bring expertise and prestige to a college)
- *professor* or *full professor*
- *associate professor*
- *assistant professor*
- *instructor, part-time instructor* or *lecturer*
- *graduate assistant* (a student who teaches courses, typically introductory courses, while he or she is working on a master's or doctorate degree)

> The mediocre teacher tells. The good teacher explains. The superior teacher demonstrates. The great teacher inspires.
> — *William Arthur Ward, U.S. author and columnist*

# Ways of Being for Different Disciplines

Each academic discipline has a particular language or set of terminology through which it defines itself. In addition, disciplines have particular methods and skills that are used to advance learning and knowledge in that field. Different disciplines ask different types of questions based upon what is studied. For instance, a mathematician may be concerned with proving a particular theorem, while a political scientist studies voting behavior. Thus, within each discipline, there is a "way of being" which encompasses:

- a shared system of values and beliefs of what is important,

- a specific language or jargon, and

- specific skills and methods associated with study in that particular field.

In college, there are differences in every discipline of study. There are certain traits, skills, and ways of thinking that are more suited to one discipline than another. For example, care-giving is important to nurses while mathematicians value persistence. Artists greatly utilize visualization skills while chemists are good modelers. These differences do not imply that these skills and behaviors are limited solely to one group but rather that there are certain distinguishing characteristics that are common to that group. This helps explain why your professors choose their particular fields of study. They went into an area in which they enjoyed the content, "the culture," and performed well with regard to the most frequently used skills.

The concept of ways of being has relevance to you as you consider a discipline area as your major. You can narrow down your choices of a major by being aware of what academic areas intrigue you, hold your interest, and bore you. You can also observe your instructors and what is important to them with regard to their discipline areas. You may even want to meet with an instructor to discuss more about your interests. By doing so, you can begin to develop the skills that are most needed in a specific discipline area. However, even though you are interested in a particular discipline, without proficiency in the most commonly used skills, you will have difficulty performing well.

Note that tools such as the Strong Interest Inventory (Consulting Psychologists Press, Inc.) are available to help you become more aware of how your interests match the interests of people in various careers.

In summary, learning more about the ways of being for different disciplines provides you with:

- insights into possible majors to consider as well as those to avoid,

- ideas for interesting courses to take outside your major,

- an opportunity to match your strong skills to a discipline where they are well suited,

- knowledge about different expectations faculty have for their students in different disciplines, and

- knowledge to lessen the frustration when performing in a course that relies heavily on skills that are not your strengths.

For example, consider a student who lacks persistence. Rather than being negative about a math class which requires persistence to work through problems, the student can instead channel his or her efforts toward coping, adjusting, or best of all, working to improve the situation with respect to his or her skill at persistence.

## Classroom Learning Environments

You will encounter a variety of different classroom learning environments during your time in college. While the lecture may be the most common, it by no means is the only environment or the best environment (especially for developing a variety of skills in all areas of learning). This section briefly describes some of the classroom environments you may encounter in college.

### Lecture

The lecture is a common learning environment you are familiar with. In a typical lecture, students (passively) listen while the instructor (actively) talks. The lecture is an efficient means to communicate information from an expert to enhance the information base of students. However, the effectiveness of a lecture is reduced over time due to peoples' relatively short attention span. Unless students think critically about what is being said as they take notes (requires active listening), learning is not effective. Finally, the lecture builds only a small number of skills in the cognitive (thinking) domain without requiring skills in other areas (e.g., social and emotional).

### Interactive Lecture

In an interactive lecture, a student is more involved and active than in a traditional lecture. In this type of learning environment, the instructor can do any of the following to make the lecture more interactive:

A teacher is one who makes himself or herself progressively unnecessary.
— *Thomas Carruthers*

Some people talk in their sleep. Lecturers talk while other people sleep.
—*Albert Camus, French novelist and philosopher 1913-1960*

- give a quiz at the end of class,

- provide a set of critical questions that are to be answered during the lecture,

- ask students to work on discussion questions with another student(s) every 15-20 minutes, or

- use the last 5-10 minutes to have students write down what they have learned along with any questions they may still have.

In an interactive lecture, students are accountable for understanding the class material at the time it is presented rather than waiting until after class to digest and study the material.

## Group Discussion

In a group discussion, the topic or new knowledge becomes the focal point for a discussion among a team of students. Questions provided by the instructor and/or generated by students serve to stimulate and guide the discussion. Discussions work best when there is a facilitator or moderator to control tangents, provide summaries at periodic points, and require group members to contribute.

## Laboratory

A laboratory environment allows students to learn and create knowledge in a manner similar to the way a scientist would. Used in a variety of disciplines, laboratories build a wide range of skills including collecting data, making hypotheses, designing experiments, analyzing data, validating conclusions, and communicating results.

## Cooperative Learning

When working in cooperative teams, students have an opportunity to develop skills in the social and affective domains (especially the processes of teamwork and value development). Many times team roles are used so that each team member is accountable for an aspect of the team's overall performance. Learning to work with others and achieve more as a team than as individuals will be of great benefit to you in college and beyond.

## Guided-Discovery Learning or Activity Learning

When placed in a guided-discovery learning environment, students must work with various types of models, make use of background information, and answer questions to arrive at new knowledge. In others words, rather than being told about something, students work to discover it. Typically, guided-discovery is structured so that students work in teams on a particular activity. This builds students' learning skills at the same time the content of the activity is learned. Key components of an activity are the performance criteria and the critical thinking questions which guide the learner in his or her thinking. *Foundations of Learning* has an accompanying book of activities which contains numerous examples of guided-discovery activities.

How do you
explain school
to a higher
intelligence?
—*from the
movie E.T.,
The Extrater-
restrial*

### Student Communication/Presentations

Presentations provide students with an opportunity to gain confidence and build communication skills. While a speech is a common form of communication, other speech communication opportunities include explaining problem solutions, orally answering quiz questions, presenting a summary of a reading assignment, or giving a peer assessment (providing feedback to a fellow classmate to help improve his or her future performance).

### Problem Solving

Working to solve a problem is one of the most challenging classroom learning environments. It requires that a student and his or her team members apply knowledge to new situations and integrate relationships with prior knowledge. Students must be time conscious and use a problem solving methodology (see Chapter Twelve) to effectively meet the given performance criteria. This type of learning environment is suited particularly well for competitions and games.

## Web Resources

**http://www.pcrest.com**

The World Wide Web is a resource that you are encouraged to use as a supplement to the information presented in this text. To help you find relevant information on the web, a *Foundations of Learning* web site has been designed (organized by chapter) that provides links to useful sites. The site is accessed from the Pacific Crest home page at **http://www.pcrest.com**.

For more information about colleges and higher education refer to Chapter Two of the *Foundations of Learning* web site. Links take you to directories for the homepages of colleges and universities throughout the United States and the world. The *Yahoo Guide to University Home Pages* has links categorized according to American tribal colleges, historical black colleges, men's colleges, women's colleges, private colleges by state, public colleges by state, and community colleges. A site called the *College Locator* has links to college newspapers and educational magazines in addition to a directory (by state) of universities and community colleges in the United States.

A site called the *Internet Scout Project* (from the University of Wisconsin at Madison) is a particularly useful site for people in education, especially students doing research. Information and resources are divided into categories including Business and Economics, Science and Engineering, and Social Sciences. A paragraph from the home page describes the site:

> *Surf smarter, not longer. Let the Internet Scout Project show you the way to the best resources on the Internet – then you can choose what's best for you. Librarians and educators do the filtering for you, reading hundreds of announcements each week looking for the on-line resources most valuable to the education community.*

# The Role of a College Student

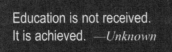

Education is not received.
It is achieved. —*Unknown*

## Preparing for a Career

According to the survey responses from more than 250,000 college freshman (found in Table 1.6 on page 9), the top two reasons students attend college are (1) to get a better job, and (2) to make more money.

These survey results support the fact that many students perceive college as a means to getting a better job with more pay than would be possible without a college education. However, while a college degree does open doors to new and exciting opportunities, it does not automatically guarantee a person a job upon graduation. Therefore, if you will be pursuing a career after college, a couple of key questions you should ask are:

- What specifically are employers looking for when interviewing and hiring potential employees?

- What can I do during my college years to put myself in the best position to get the job I want upon graduation?

A 1991 Report from the Department of Labor addressed the first question by asking employers, in all contexts, what they felt were the most important considerations with respect to the employees they were about to hire. Take a moment and think about how you would respond before turning to page 30 to find a summary of the results.

## Getting an Education

"Getting an education" was the third-most popular reason for attending college listed in Table 1.6. However, an education cannot be obtained like a car, a house, or a computer. Getting an education requires your active participation and involvement in a process that you control and for which you are responsible. In other words, you and only you are responsible for doing what it takes to earn a college degree. In a nutshell, this is what it means to be a student.

## Your Role as a Student

Your time as a college student should provide you with many wonderful experiences and contribute to your goals and dreams. College should also be a time for growth and development; an opportunity to develop skills and acquire knowledge that you can use throughout your entire life.

However, making the most of your college experience depends on how you perform as a student. The focus of this chapter is to provide insights about the attitudes and behaviors that are common to quality students as well as to provide a model for how to perform as a student.

## Profile of a Quality Student

The following discussion looks at common characteristics and behaviors of highly successful college students. Many of the areas mentioned are expanded upon either later in this chapter or in other parts of this book (with references provided).

**Highly successful students take college seriously.**

*Quality students realize the differences between high school and college.*
They don't make the mistake of thinking the two educational environments are the same in terms of their requirements for student performance. See page 40 for an exercise which gets you to compare college and high school.

*Quality students allocate an appropriate amount of time for academics.*
They realize that even though nonacademic activities are a part of a well-rounded college experience, performing well in class is a much higher priority. See page 35 for more about time management.

*Quality students realize that they are part of an academic community which has certain rules, regulations, expectations, and responsibilities.*
They make an effort to learn about their college and develop relationships with people at various levels in the community (e.g., peers, instructors, and administrators). The first three chapters of this book help you better understand college and your role as a new member in an educational community.

*Quality students value academic honesty.*
They have a deep sense of personal integrity as well as for the integrity of their school. See page 31 for a discussion about academic honesty.

**Highly successful students take responsibility for their learning and perform at a high level in class.**

*Quality students make it a point to attend and actively participate in all their classes.*

If they are unable to attend class, they let the instructor know ahead of time and explain their reason for being absent. They understand that they are responsible for making arrangements to obtain notes, information, and assignments as well as make up any work that is missed. They make connections with peers who can help out in these situations.

*Quality students come prepared for every class.*

They do the required homework and readings, review their notes (from class and the assigned readings), develop questions to be clarified in class, know what will be covered in class, and relate new material to what was previously learned.

*Quality students know where they stand in each class they take.*

They effectively utilize the syllabus (identifying important dates for exams, projects, and papers) and plan their time accordingly. They are able to accurately predict their grade in a class at any point in the semester or term. They make use of tools such as the Course Record Keeper (see Table 3.5 on page 37) to collect data and stay organized.

*Quality students make effective use of faculty office hours.*

They realize that the purpose of faculty office hours is not for an instructor to do the work, but rather to guide or assist student learning. See page 33 for information about making effective use of faculty office hours.

*Quality students understand that grades are earned rather than handed out by an instructor.*

They avoid the misconception that an instructor gives them a grade on an exam or in a course, and take ownership and accountability for their preparation and performance.

*Quality students are good at accepting both evaluation and assessment feedback.*

They do not make excuses and become defensive about criticism of their work. They understand that evaluating and critiquing course work is part of an instructor's job. They realize that an instructor is not judging students, only their work product.

*Quality students seek to develop positive relationships with their instructors.*

They ask for details or examples when they don't understand feedback they have received. If a problem or conflict develops with an instructor, they set up a meeting to identify the problem and express their concerns clearly (which are the first steps toward negotiating an effective and acceptable solution).

> Teachers open the door, but you must enter by yourself.
> —*Chinese Proverb*

**Highly successful students have a life vision which includes an educational plan.**

*Quality students work with their advisor to develop an effective and efficient plan for earning a degree.*

They use the college catalog to identify the general education requirements as well as the requirements for their major area of study. They are efficient at the registration process and know the associated policies (add/drop, electronic registration, etc.). See page 31 for more information about academic advising.

*Quality students begin creating a life vision portfolio when they enter college.*

They understand the importance of establishing a portfolio which can be used to document their progress and growth while at college. Refer to Chapter Four for a detailed discussion of life vision portfolios.

*Quality students set goals for college as well as other areas of their life.*

They realize that goals do help to focus their efforts and achieve higher outcomes (see page 52 for a set of guidelines for goal setting). Quality students have academic goals which include a target or desired grade point average. See page 34 for information about calculating a GPA.

*Quality students have a plan for financing their college education.*

They are fully aware of what options are available to them and make the best use of available resources in order to meet their financial needs and obligations. See page 38 for information about financing a college education.

**Highly successful students have strong self-management skills.**

*Quality students have developed good study habits and skills.*

They are good at note-taking, highlighting, preparing for exams, and test-taking strategies (see pages 87-101 for more information about these topics).

*Quality students have strong time management skills.*

They know how to schedule their time and stick to their plan. They overcome procrastination with action. They properly allocate their time between academics and extra curricular activities. See page 35 for more information about time management.

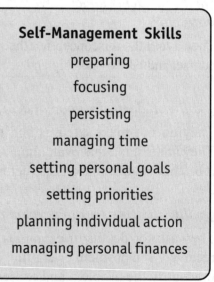

**Self-Management Skills**

preparing

focusing

persisting

managing time

setting personal goals

setting priorities

planning individual action

managing personal finances

*Quality students are able to manage their personal finances effectively.*

They are able to manage day-to-day finances and avoid getting dangerously in debt (especially with credit cards).

**High performance students enjoy learning and work hard at developing their learning skills in all areas.**

The last nine chapters of this book are devoted to various learning skills that are important for success during and beyond college. The table below identifies characteristics associated with quality students and where that topic or skill is discussed in this book.

Table 3.1

| Characteristics of Quality Students | |
|---|---|
| Quality students... | |
| • work to improve their learning skills by utilizing tools such as methodologies. | *Chapter 5*<br>*Improving Your Learning Skills* |
| • are information literate and have good study skills. | *Chapter 6*<br>*Information Literacy & Study Skills* |
| • are good readers and writers. | *Chapters 7 & 8*<br>*Reading & Writing Skills* |
| • use technology and tools to assist and enhance their learning. | *Chapter 9*<br>*Utilizing Tools & Technology* |
| • are focused on growth and personal development. | *Chapter 10*<br>*Personal Development* |
| • work at developing communication and people skills. | *Chapter 11*<br>*Relating and Working with Others* |
| • are good problem solvers in a variety of contexts. | *Chapter 12*<br>*Problem Solving Skills* |
| • use their skills at assessment to keep improving their performance as students. | *Chapter 13*<br>*Assessment & Evaluation Skills* |

The remainder of this chapter goes into more detail about several of the topics mentioned in Table 3.1. These include the skills that employers want, academic honesty, academic advising, utilizing faculty office hours, calculating a grade point average, time management and financing a college education.

# What Employers Look For When Hiring

The 1991 SCANS Report from the Department of Labor presented the findings from more than a year's worth of talking to employers (in all contexts) about what they desired most in their employees. An excerpt from this report is as follows:

> Their message to us was the same across the country and in every kind of job: good jobs depend on people who can put knowledge to work. New workers must be creative and responsible problem solvers and have skills and attributes on which employers can build.

The report highlighted five competencies and a three-part, set of foundation skills and qualities essential for students to develop. The results are presented in the tables below.

Table 3.2

| Foundation Skills | | |
|---|---|---|
| **Basic Skills** | **Thinking Skills** | **Personal Qualities** |
| reading | ability to learn | individual responsibility |
| writing | ability to reason | self-esteem |
| speaking | ability to think creatively | self-management |
| listening | ability to make decisions | sociability |
| mathematics | ability to solve problems | integrity |

Table 3.3

| Competencies | |
|---|---|
| Effective individuals can productively use... | |
| resources | They know how to allocate time, money, materials, space, and staff. |
| interpersonal skills | They can work on teams, teaching others, serve customers, lead, negotiate, and work well with people from culturally diverse backgrounds. |
| information | They can acquire and evaluate data, organize and maintain files, interpret and communicate, and use computers to process information. |
| systems | They understand social, organizational, and technological systems; they can monitor and correct performance, and they can design or improve systems. |
| technology | They can select equipment and tools, apply technology to specific tasks, and maintain and troubleshoot equipment. |

The Secretary's Commission on Achieving Necessary Skills, U.S. Department of Labor, June 1991

Note how the qualities desired by employers (for a quality worker) match up very closely with those of a quality learner. In both cases, responsibility and pride in performing at a high level are important. If you want to put yourself in the best possible position when seeking a career job, the challenge is to use your college experience to develop the skills and qualities mentioned in Tables 3.2 and 3.3.

## Academic Honesty

Most schools have academic honesty codes or policies which outlaw cheating, plagiarism, and other forms of dishonest behavior. Since a large part of the learning and writing done in college involves "processing" ideas and material originally conceived by others, it is important to understand the difference between using the work of others (in constructing your own knowledge) and reproducing other people's work as if it were your own. The adage "honesty is the best policy" goes a long way. Adherence to academic honesty and maintaining your reputation and integrity is always in your best interest.

The reputation of any school is the shared responsibility of its administration, faculty, and students. Students are expected to observe the same standards of scholastic integrity as their academic and professional counterparts.

Students who take shortcuts and cheat to get ahead can take no pride in their work and unearned accomplishments. By cheating, the learning process is bypassed and the quality of one's education suffers. For example, the use of commercially prepared essays in place of a student's own work essentially destroys the purpose of a university education. In the end, what has a student learned from this type of action?

Take a moment to look at cheating as a process. Students who opt for this method or approach usually spend extra time and effort in order to avoid getting caught. But what is the objective? The vast majority of cheating is done to get a good grade and save time and effort. If the subject matter is important, the student will have to go back again and learn it all anyway at some point. That's more than twice the effort it would have taken to do the work honestly.

## Academic Advising

Advisors provide valuable guidance as you progress through your academic program. Guidance typically comes in four main areas: guidance about appropriate courses and a major, guidance about the academic institution and its policies, guidance about life issues that occur while in college, and guidance about opportunities after college.

Advisors have knowledge of the "big picture" and can offer advice that is not found in a college catalog. An advisor can help with sequencing of courses using his or her knowledge of course requirements, the difficulty of course content, and when courses are offered during the academic year. As you build an academic schedule that is right for you in your current situation, be sure to take advantage of the expertise of your advisor.

There are two types of undergraduate advisors, the professional academic advisor and the faculty advisor.

**Professional academic advisors** are either generalists or specialists. Generalists are knowledgeable about most or all of the majors available to students at the freshman-sophomore level. Specialists typically work within a particular department and are knowledgeable about all of the programs within a particular major or school within the university. Usually professional academic advisors are available to see students throughout the calendar year, even when classes are not in session.

**Faculty advisors** take on advising in addition to their teaching duties. They are knowledgeable about the majors within their department and are excellent guides for students who have decided on a major. They are usually available only a few hours each week during the academic year. Often faculty advisors are available via e-mail as well as during their office hours.

## Advising Tips

From an advisor's point of view, a good advisee:

- takes time to read through program and course descriptions as well as the requirements in the college catalog before visiting with an advisor.

- visits the advisor before the registration period to discuss and clarify questions.

- understands that the responsibility for registering is that of the student, and that the role of the advisor is to give advice, not to mandate.

- checks the advice given by an advisor before taking final action; realizing that advisors can occasionally make mistakes, especially during hectic periods (e.g., your advisor suggests you register for a course that you've already taken because he or she doesn't have your transcript handy).

- takes responsibility for choosing his or her classes at registration time after consulting with an advisor regarding the advisability of those choices.

- lets his or her advisor know when something is going wrong or awry.

# Faculty Office Hours

In addition to time in the classroom, your instructor sets aside time each week in the form of office hours to meet with students. Faculty office hours are usually listed in the course syllabus. Since this time is limited, it is important for both you and your instructor that this time be well utilized.

While your instructor is a resource you should not ignore, realize that the purpose of office hours is not for your instructor to do your work for you but rather to guide or assist you with your learning.

Below are some tips for making effective use of faculty office hours.

*Don't wait until just before a test or exam to try and meet with your instructor.* You should review and study on a regular basis and avoid last minute cramming. However, since many students do not heed this advice, you will find that other students will be competing for limited office hour time with your instructor just prior to an exam.

*If you have missed a class, before asking questions of the instructor:*

- make every effort to obtain notes and information from other class members,

- and be sure to have thoroughly read the required material.

If you are confused or "stuck" with a concept or certain information, before visiting your instructor write down the following:

- what you think you understand,

- where you are getting stuck and what you have done to try to get "unstuck,"

- what particular materials you find confusing and the reasons why you find them confusing, and

- what particular materials you find ambiguous and the various ways you could interpret the ambiguous materials.

Often by writing down this information, you will discover the solution to your problem. Even if you don't find the solution, your instructor will be aware of the effort and critical thought you are using while studying.

## Calculating a Grade Point Average

Grade point average, or GPA, is a numerical calculation based on the letter grades given to students for the courses they take. A GPA is one of the most common measures that schools and potential employers use to evaluate academic success. An understanding of a GPA and how it is calculated helps you set academic goals and assess your progress through college.

The following illustrates one way to calculate a GPA. Create a five-column table with column headings that look similar to the example table below. Before doing any calculations, enter the appropriate course data in the first four columns. Table 3.4 shows the numerical equivalents for grades based on a four-point grading scale (the highest numerical equivalent being 4.0). Note that various grade equivalents are provided since different schools use different grading schemes. Note that you can calculate a GPA for courses you have taken for any given semester (or quarter), or for the entire time you have been in college.

Table 3.4

| Numerical Equivalents |
| --- |
| A = 4.0 |
| B = 3.0 |
| C = 2.0 |
| D = 1.0 |
| F = 0.0 |
| |
| AB = 3.5 |
| BC = 2.5 |
| |
| A⁻ = 3.67 |
| B⁺ = 3.33 |
| B⁻ = 2.67 |
| C⁺ = 2.33 |
| C⁻ = 1.67 |
| D⁺ = 1.33 |

| Course | Credit Hours | Letter Grade | Numerical Equivalent | Grade Points |
| --- | --- | --- | --- | --- |
| History | 3 | A | 4.0 | 12.0 |
| Biology | 4 | B | 3.0 | 12.0 |
| Economics | 3 | C | 2.0 | 6.0 |
| Foundations of Learning | 3 | A | 4.0 | 12.0 |
| Computer Applications | 2 | B | 3.0 | 6.0 |
| Total | 15 | | | 48.0 |

Grade Point Average = total grade points divided by total credit hours

Calculations to obtain a GPA:

1. Multiply the number of credit hours by the corresponding numerical equivalent to obtain the "grade points." Place this value in the appropriate cell.

2. Sum the values in the "credit hours" and "grade points" columns.

3. Divide the total number of grade points by the total credit hours.

$$\text{Final GPA calculation} = \frac{48}{15} = 3.2$$

**Discussion Questions**

1. What information is needed to begin calculating a GPA?

2. What are grade points and how are they calculated?

3. What is meant by *average* in a grade point average?

4. What is the significance of a numerical equivalent when calculating a GPA? Why is it necessary?

5. In which class will a letter grade of "A" more greatly affect a person's GPA, in a 5-credit course, or a 3-credit course? Why?

6. Which grade will more greatly affect a person's GPA, an "A" or an "F"? Explain why.

## Time Management

Time management refers to how you plan, control, regulate and schedule your time. In the context of college, good time management skills help you to complete all your course work in a timely manner while maintaining balance in your life outside of academics.

Time management is an important factor in determining student success in college. High performing students tend to make a conscious effort to plan and manage their time. Perhaps the main reason more students don't focus on time management is that it's not trivial and takes effort.

The following ideas and guidelines will help you to manage your time more effectively.

**Determine how you currently spend your time.**

The first step in time management is to become aware of how you are currently spending your time. Once this determination is made, regardless of your current situation, you can take action to make improvements.

A good tool to monitor your time is a day-planner that breaks down each day into certain time increments. Day-planners are readily available in bookstores or you can easily create your own day-planner.

Be diligent in recording your activities throughout the period of a week. Break down how you spend your time into various categories (such as in-class time, studying, sleeping, eating, time with friends, recreation, e-mail and Internet, television, etc.). Don't be too general in your use of time category headings.

At the end of a week, sum the totals in the various time categories. Analyze the time data you collected. Assess your strengths and areas for improvement with respect to time management.

> Nine-tenths of wisdom consists of being wise in time.
> —*Theodore Roosevelt, 26th President 1858–1919*

**Develop a time management plan.**

Begin with a blank weekly schedule that lists the days and hours during the day. Start by filling in your committed times or fixed commitments. These include items such as your scheduled classes, work commitments, meal times, travel time (for commuters), sleep, organized sports or activities. If your committed times change from week to week, it is important that you adjust your time management plan on a weekly basis.

Once you have accounted for the committed times, you should begin to see patterns or blocks of available free time. Your next consideration should be allocation of study time. *A general guideline for out-of-class study time is that for every hour spent in the classroom, you should spend two hours studying out of the classroom.* For more challenging courses, you should allocate three or more hours outside of class for every classroom hour. Another factor that influences study time in a course is your skill set compared to the demands of a particular course. For example, if you are a slow reader taking a history or literature course, you should adjust your study time accordingly. Keep track of the time you spend studying for each course. Record how long it takes you to complete problem sets, to read chapters in particular textbooks, etc. This information can be used to help you revise and adjust your time management plan.

When considering allocating or designating study times, consider times when you are physically and emotionally ready to study and perform at a high level. Try to match the times of the day when you are sharpest with times you can study. Also, realize that for many people, it is more effective to study in one-hour blocks of time than to study for three or four hours at a time. If you do study for longer periods of time, be sure to take breaks.

With your committed time and study time allocated, fill in the rest of your plan with other activities based on how you usually spend your time.

**Organize your time for different time intervals.**

*On a monthly and semester basis*
The Course Record Keeper presented on the next page is an ideal tool for staying organized in all of your courses. Use the Course Record Keeper along with a monthly calendar (you fill in) and the syllabus from each course to keep on top of important deadlines and dates associated with your courses. Refer to these tools on a regular basis and update the information accordingly.

*On a weekly basis*
Fill in a schedule for the week with committed times, study times, and other uses of your time.

*On a daily basis*
To-do lists are helpful for prioritizing tasks on a daily basis. Label or categorize the items in order of importance.

Table 3.5          **Course Record Keeper**

| Course | Tests | Quizzes | Homework & Assignments |
|---|---|---|---|
| Course 1 | | | |
| | | | |
| | | | |
| | | | |
| | | | |
| | | | |
| | | | |
| Course 2 | | | |
| | | | |
| | | | |
| | | | |
| | | | |
| | | | |
| | | | |
| Course 3 | | | |
| | | | |
| | | | |
| | | | |
| | | | |
| | | | |
| | | | |
| Course 4 | | | |
| | | | |
| | | | |
| | | | |
| | | | |
| | | | |
| | | | |
| Course 5 | | | |
| | | | |
| | | | |
| | | | |
| | | | |
| | | | |

# Financing a College Education

Education costs money, but then so does ignorance.
—Sir Claus Moser, British educator

Every student must deal with meeting the financial obligations associated with college. For many students, the main source of funding for college comes from themselves and their families, with other possible sources being the federal government, state governments, colleges, private foundations, and employers. Unfortunately the processes for obtaining funds are not always easy, and they are complicated by the fact that college expenses are incurred for several years with typically higher costs each year. Knowing your financial options can save you money as well as give you more peace of mind as you plan for your remaining years at college.

Attending college requires planning from both an academic and financial perspective. What options do you have in paying for a college education? Financial resources to pay for college come from three main areas:

- a student's assets and income earnings,

- a student's parents and/or family member's assets and income earnings, and

- various forms of financial aid available from government, military, colleges, employers, and private foundations.

Financial aid accounts for less than half of the money students spend on their college education. In general terms, while students can obtain financial aid, the majority of the financial burden falls on the students and their families.

However, the more resourceful you are at obtaining financial aid, the smaller the personal and family burden will be. Financial need is the main factor used to determine the amount of financial aid offered to any particular student. Something called the "expected family contribution" may limit or exclude you from receiving certain types of need-based financial aid. The rules pertaining to calculating expected family contribution are fairly involved (your financial aid office can assist you with the details). A needs analysis form called the *Free Application for Federal Student Aid* is what the federal government requires in order to compute an expected family contribution.

Discuss with your school's financial aid officer what possible options you may have for financing your education. Options for students include:

- the **financial aid offerings at your school**. These could include low cost loans, installment programs, middle-income assistance programs, and work-study programs.

- **academic scholarships** which are given regardless of a student's financial need.

- money that the **military**, ROTC, and the National Guard have for college students.

- **state aid** that is available to students who stay in their home state.

- **athletic scholarships** given to those athletes who are not the superstars.

- **cooperative education** (co-ops) programs or internships which offer work experience before graduation.

## Financial Aid Information on the Web

For more information about financial aid, refer to Chapter Three of the *Foundations of Learning* web site accessed from **http://www.pcrest.com**.

**http://www.pcrest.com**

There you will find links to useful sites for students looking for ways to finance their college education. Included is a government site called *The Student Guide, Financial Aid from the U.S. Department of Education.* The Student Guide is a comprehensive resource about student financial aid from the U.S. Department of Education. It covers the Department's major aid programs, including Pell Grants, Stafford Loans, and PLUS Loans. About 70% of all student aid comes from the programs discussed in the Guide.

Another link is to *FinAid, The Smart Student Guide to Financial Aid.* FinAid was established in the fall of 1994 as a public service. This site has grown into a comprehensive annotated collection of information about student financial aid. The site is a good place to get information and guidance about securing financial aid.

# Exercise – Comparing College and High School

Generate a list of the similarities and differences between high school and college. Think of the things that make high school and college different and then think about how they are the same. To the adult learner, compare college to the work environment or your home environment.

| Differences | Similarities |
| --- | --- |
| | |

After completing your lists of similarities and differences, answer the following two questions.

1. Which are the two most important differences and how will you make sure that these differences do not inhibit your learning?

2. What two similarities do you feel will be most helpful with your transition to college?

# Chapter 4

# Creating a Life Vision Portfolio

Vision – it is essential for survival. It is spawned by faith, sustained by hope, spawned by imagination, and strengthened by enthusiasm. It is greater than sight, deeper than a dream, broader than an idea. Vision encompasses vast vistas outside the realm of the predictable, the safe, the expected. No wonder we perish without it.
— *Chuck Swindoll, pastor, speaker, President of the Dallas Theological Seminary*

## What is a Life Vision?

A life vision involves looking forward and establishing a map for your life. When setting a course or direction to follow, realize that as your life unfolds, you will take many highways and byways. You will encounter pastures, swampy lakes, and/or beautiful rivers and streams. The journey will encompass many hills and valleys as well. However, it is not important that your life exactly follow the path you envision, but rather that you have an idea of where you would like to be at certain stages of your life. If you meet all of your goals and objectives along the way, GREAT! If not, continue to revisit, revise, and/or renew your vision.

## What is a Life Vision Portfolio?

In general, a portfolio is a collection of representative works. Perhaps you have seen artists carrying their portfolios—large flat cases that contain a collection of their works. Nowadays portfolios are being used in a variety of different contexts. Also, what is in a person's portfolio is more than just a collection of his or her work products. A portfolio is an excellent tool to document growth and highlight the development of skills.

Higher education is an area where portfolios are being used more and more frequently. Many college faculty use portfolios as a key resource during the tenure and promotion processes. It is becoming more common for students to use portfolios when presenting themselves to potential employers. Student portfolios can include grades and transcripts, past employment, a list of skills, areas of strength and expertise, and important credentials.

A *life vision portfolio* is a special type of portfolio that combines a life vision with the concept of a portfolio. In its entirety, a life vision portfolio is a comprehensive collection of items that intimately describes a person and tells his or her life story.

# Why is it Important to Develop a Life Vision Portfolio?

*If you have a vision, do something with it.*
*— Anthony J. D'Angelo, The College Blue Book*

While anyone can create and benefit from having a life vision portfolio, it is an especially appropriate tool for students. Because a life vision portfolio goes beyond recording or documenting to include reflective thoughts and narrative, it is an excellent means to gain insights about learning and the development of learning skills. This is true for both the student who creates the portfolio and the person who reads the portfolio.

A life vision portfolio documents growth over time. For this reason, a life vision portfolio should contain many examples of *assessment* items, including self-assessments. These assessment items focus on providing feedback to improve future performance and aid in the development of learning skills. While your grades are a permanent entry on your college transcript and can be included in your portfolio, they are an example of an *evaluative* item. For more discussion of assessment and evaluation, refer to Chapter Thirteen.

By developing a life vision portfolio, you are afforded the opportunity to assess yourself continually and have others assess you. Assessment is a process that represents a positive, win-win situation. You receive feedback that identifies and promotes your strengths while identifying your areas for improvement and providing suggestions on how to help you make the most of those improvements. This can be especially beneficial because for many students it is difficult for them to determine or measure their progress in areas such as reading, writing, critical thinking, and problem solving. Throughout this text, there are many opportunities for you to improve your skills in these areas and document your growth.

A portfolio serves many purposes including:

- encouraging you and your instructors to regularly reflect on your work in a positive and constructive manner.

- encouraging you to take on greater responsibility by actively planning your education and your life.

- encouraging you to produce quality work and communicate with a high level of proficiency.

- allowing you to see growth in a wide range of learning skills and contexts through the use of assessment and self-assessment.

- allowing you to use evaluative items to demonstrate your strengths rather than weaknesses.

- helping you to gain self-confidence as you see growth and improvement in your abilities.

- allowing you to reaffirm who you are and what your values are.

- providing you with a greater sense of empowerment as you make progress on goals and objectives.

# Factors that Promote Commitment to the Development of a Life Vision

**Being comfortable with self-disclosure and exploration.**

Self-disclosure involves dealing with the good, the bad, and the ugly—about YOU. It is very important to be true to yourself as you reflect upon your personal history. Many times we are willing to share only those things we are proud of. As you take time to reflect upon past events, activities, behaviors, and people in your life, you must make honest assessments. As you explore new challenges and opportunities, you must learn from the past and apply those lessons to the present and the future. You must stretch your mind, body, and soul to increase knowledge and level of performance. Having a level of comfort with self-disclosure prevents cover-ups and promotes growth.

**Valuing the process of developing a life vision.**

The previous section dealt with why it is important for you to have a life vision portfolio. However, you must accept this, if it is to work for you. "Peak performers develop powerful mental images of the behavior that will lead to the desired results. They see in their mind's eye the result they want and the actions leading to it." (*Charles Garfield*) When you choose to value this process, you choose to value yourself enough to take the first step on a journey of self-acceptance, self-confidence, self-discipline, self-love, and self-actualization. You will then be more prone to "love your neighbor, as you love yourself" and be a happier, more productive member of society.

**Having a mentor who supports you and the process.**

A mentor is a teacher, coach, advisor, or perhaps a fellow student who can assist you in reaching your goals and dreams. "Nobody, but nobody can make it out there alone." (*Maya Angelou*) As a student, you should develop relationships that are mutually supportive. A mentor can serve as that liaison, who points you in the right direction for success in your college career and in other areas of your life thereafter.

**You must have a plan to deal with the serious "negative hits" of life.**

There is an old adage which says, "Into each life, some rain must fall" or putting it another way, "in life, stuff happens." Receiving *negative hits* is a part of growth. It does not matter how many blows or hits you receive. What does matter is how you respond to those blows (i.e., being able to pick yourself up, dust yourself off, and continue on). Making a commitment early to positively deal with the negative hits of life can be the difference between destructive and constructive behaviors in your moments of distress.

> Our lives improve only when we take chances — and the first and most difficult risk we can take is to be honest with ourselves.
> —*Walter Anderson, Mississippi artist, writer, and naturalist 1903-1965*

# Example Components of a Life Vision Portfolio

A life vision portfolio can have many components that get added over time. There is no set format or structure that must be followed. Examples of components that can be included in a life vision portfolio are mentioned below.

## An exploration into who you are

**Pre-assessment** — Before building a portfolio further, the first item should be a three to four-page "Who Am I" paper. Use this paper to establish a benchmark as to where you are at this point in time. By doing so, it will be much easier to see growth and development as it occurs.

**Self-analysis** — Analyze or inventory your likes and dislikes. Discuss your areas of interest and disinterest. What do you like to do? How do you most enjoy spending your time? Clarify your top ten to fifteen *likes* and then do the same for the things you *dislike* most.

**Passion exploration** — A passion is more than an area of interest or something you like to do. A passion brings on strong emotional feelings and represents something you care about deeply. Discuss and rank the five things you are most passionate about in the format of a two to four-page paper.

**Values analysis** — Seriously reflect and identify the values you feel most strongly about. Discuss and rank your most important personal values.

**Meaning of life** — Another possible component of the portfolio that incorporates your values is a two to four-page paper discussing your views and insights with respect to the question "What is the meaning of life?"

**Processing life's difficulties** — Being able to respond to negative life experiences and learn from them is an important life skill. Describe the two or three most significant negative experiences in your life along with what you learned and how you grew from those experiences.

**Personality inventory tests** — Tests of this kind can help you learn more about yourself and can be included in a life vision portfolio. The Meyers-Briggs Indicator and the Keirsey Temperament Sorter are two well-known examples.

*There is a link from Chapter Four of the Foundations of Learning web site to the Keirsey Temperament Sorter, which has an on-line version of a personality questionnaire that you can take.*

**http://www.pcrest.com**

## Plans, goals, and ideas for the future

**Educational plan** — Determine which major or majors are of interest to you. Identify the General Education courses you are required to take along with the courses in your major and their prerequisites. Include a timeline, semester by semester, for the courses you plan to take.

**Career plan** — Reflect on how you want to make a living. Respond to "I would enjoy the following career because…" Describe the differences between a job and a career and why you feel a career is important. Note that the career and placement service on campus is a good source for information including career interest surveys which can help with this component of the portfolio.

**Reflect on personal life issues** — In a free-writing format, respond to, "I would like the following in my personal life and relationships…" A suggestion is that the term "personal life" be broken into four areas: family, recreation, social, and spiritual.

**Legacy or "rocking chair analysis"** — Imagine you are celebrating your 90th birthday. The front page of your local newspaper is featuring a story about you. Write the leading six paragraphs for this article. Identify what aspects of your life you feel will continue beyond your life.

**Synthesis paper** — Identify how various aspects or components of your life relate. Write a three-page paper that addresses the following issues: (1) the relationship between your career, work, avocation, personal and spiritual life, (2) the relationship between your likes and dislikes, as well as your values and passions, and (3) balancing the trade-offs in life to produce the desired legacy for yourself.

**Time analysis** — Consider the value of time in your lifetime. How much time will you spend on a career as compared to time with your family, or other aspects of your life? The purpose here is to gain new perspectives for the value of time. Begin by answering the following questions. How long do I expect to live? How many hours are in a year? How many hours are there in my projected life? How many hours will be spent working (on a career), sleeping, and on other important aspects? Do the estimations and calculations and write about your insights.

## Other possible components

**Resume** — Create a resume that identifies your career path and past accomplishments. Include an analysis of your skills as part of the resume.

**Role model exploration** — Identify five people who are your role models (whether dead or alive). Provide a one-page write-up for each which includes an explanation as to why the person was chosen. Autobiographies are one source of information about role models.

> Self reflection is the school of wisdom.
> —*Baltasar Gracian, Spanish Jesuit philosopher 1601-1658*

# Using a Life Vision Portfolio Throughout One's Life

While a life vision portfolio is an excellent tool for students to create and maintain during their college years, many components of the portfolio should be revised and revisited throughout one's lifetime.

In order to appreciate the usefulness of creating a life vision portfolio, let's first look at the phases one typically goes through in a lifetime. A person's life can be separated into different stages or phases based on time. Table 4.1 identifies five phases and the corresponding time frame in terms of age. The source of the population data is the U.S. Census Bureau.

| Table 4.1 | Phases in One's Lifetime | Time frame (in years) | % of 1998 U.S. population |
|---|---|---|---|
| | the beginning years | birth to 18 years old | 28% |
| | the early adult years | 19-32 years old | 17% |
| | the middle-age years | 33-51 years old | 30% |
| | the pre-retirement years | 52-64 years old | 11% |
| | the senior years or bonus years | 65 years and up | 14% |

**The Beginning Years (birth – 18)**

It is during the beginning years that various factors contribute to shape your life and influence who you are. Recall that an entire section of a life vision portfolio involves reflecting, analyzing, and exploring who you are (e.g., a self-analysis, passion exploration, values analysis, and processing life's difficulties). Three factors that are important during the beginning years are genes, environment, and behavior.

A gene is a functional hereditary unit located at a particular point on a chromosome that controls or acts in the transmission of hereditary characteristics (Webster). When doing a self-analysis, realize that some of your personality traits and tendencies can be attributed to genes and heredity.

Environment is the combination of external physical conditions affecting the growth and development of organisms (Webster). A common adage says, "People are products of their environment." The people you live and associate with do influence who you are, and what you believe and value (and you influence those around you as well). As you develop your life vision plan, realize that your surroundings will influence the choices you make.

Behavior is the way you act, react, or function in a particular manner (Webster). One's values, morals, and ethics, as well as societal laws, rules, and regulations influence behavior. Once set, changing a behavior can be difficult, requiring an emotional event to stimulate the change. In developing your life vision, past behavior as well as current behavior play a major role in the opportunities that are made available to you.

The process of creating a life vision portfolio ideally should start during the *beginning years*. Those who have the guidance and insight to plan and set goals while in junior and senior high school can enter the early adult years with a greater degree of confidence and sense of direction.

## The Early Adult Years (19 – 32)

If a person hasn't started working on components of a life vision portfolio during his or her beginning years, it is important that work begin at the start of the early adult years. As a college student, this is an ideal time to develop your personal life vision; documenting the mental images (dreams) of what you would like your future self to be and methods for getting there. In other words, take the time to explore who you are and to make plans, goals, and generate ideas for the future.

Performing a time analysis and developing an educational plan which translates into a career plan are especially important as you begin college. When developing your career plan, consider expected trends related to demographics, the workforce, economics, and work/life events. These trends are currently playing a major role in the way we do business in this country and will continue to do so in the future. Also, note that a table from the U.S. Bureau of Labor Statistics is included in the Appendix of this book to help you better understand the projected makeup and trends of the U.S. workforce. The table shows employment figures by occupation for 1996 and employment projections for the year 2006. In general, realize that the demand for skilled workers is growing significantly and work teams are expected to be the most important format for high performance work.

If you haven't used journal writing much up to this point in your life, you should be aware of how powerful a tool journaling is for documenting and recording personal growth. You are encouraged to practice and develop your skills at journaling (see the section about journal writing later in this chapter).

## The Middle-Age Years (33 – 51)

A life vision portfolio should be a dynamic product that is created and developed over time and then revisited and revised on a regular basis. Personal reflection, including reflecting on life issues, can help to keep a person focused and in balance avoiding a "mid-life crisis" that affects some people. For while the earning power of individuals can be especially productive during the middle-age years, it is also a period when people are most affected by the trends of corporate down-sizing, out-sizing, and early retirement.

Workplace trends you can expect during your middle-age years are that employers will continue to recognize the need for childcare to accommodate working parents, single parents, and two-income families. Also, the physical work environment will continue to change. Casual dress policies are spreading and more people will be able to work from their homes. Treating workers well by enriching their work environment will be a high priority.

### The Pre-retirement Years (52 – 64)

The pre-retirement years are a period when those who have properly planned and invested can look forward to a comfortable retirement; working only if they choose to rather than continuing to work out of necessity. They can look back on a legacy that has been well-developed (with time still to add to it). They can reflect on how they have handled life's good times and difficulties, and on how they have influenced the lives of others.

For some, economic issues, such as the cost of living, medical care, and retirement planning will play a major role in the decisions they make with their time and money. As you near completion of this phase of your life, what will your situation be? Will the choice be up to you as to whether or not you will continue working, or, will your circumstances dictate the answer to this question?

As a final note, realize the following trend. In general, older people are staying in the workforce longer. Some reasons for their bigger role in the workplace include:

- the lack of interest of younger persons in some of the more mundane jobs in the service sector, especially in the food service and retailing industries;
- employers are offering fewer early retirement incentives than in previous years;
- the insecurity of many of today's jobs inhibits workers in their ability to build up financial resources;
- child bearing at older ages extends the greatest family and financial responsibilities to later years;
- aging parents are living longer than earlier generations requiring more care; and
- the Social Security system is gradually increasing the retirement age to receive maximum benefits to age 67.

### The Senior Years or Bonus Years (65 and up)

As the life expectancy table (Table 4.2) illustrates, most people can expect to spend time in their senior or bonus years. These years represent a time to reflect upon the challenges and opportunities that life brought, as well as the wisdom gained. It is a time to revisit the life vision plan and fill in gaps. Having a life vision that is strategically planned, continuously updated, and aggressively executed, ensures enjoyable senior years and an obituary that leaves a great legacy.

Life itself is a blessing, but for those who experience these years in good health, the senior years truly can be considered bonus years. Live, love, and continue to learn until it is time to leave this earth.

All growth depends upon activity. There is no development physically or intellectually without effort, and effort means work.
—Calvin Coolidge, 30th President 1872-1933

| United States Life Expectancies at various times during the 20th Century | | | | |
|------|------|------|------|------|
| Year | White | | Non-white | |
| | Male | Female | Male | Female |
| 1930 | 59.7 years | 63.5 years | 47.3 years | 49.2 years |
| 1940 | 62.1 | 66.6 | 51.5 | 54.9 |
| 1950 | 66.5 | 72.2 | 59.1 | 62.9 |
| 1960 | 67.4 | 74.1 | 61.1 | 66.3 |
| 1970 | 68.0 | 75.6 | 61.3 | 69.4 |
| 1980 | 70.7 | 78.1 | 65.3 | 73.6 |
| 1990 | 72.9 | 79.4 | 67.0 | 75.2 |
| 1995 | 73.4 | 79.6 | 67.9 | 75.7 |
| 1996 | 73.8 | 79.6 | 68.8 | 76.2 |

Table 4.2

Source: National Center for Health Statistics

## Criteria Lists for a Quality Life Vision Portfolio

Table 4.3

| Criteria for putting together a Life Vision Portfolio | Criteria for a Life Vision |
|------|------|
| • requires full engagement | • describes your key personal and family values |
| • produces full disclosure | • describes the value of the social aspect of your life (including family) |
| • requires a plan for life | • identifies the spiritual meaning of your life |
| • requires self-awareness | • identifies your planned accomplishments |
| • requires clarification of values | • clarifies the historical context for your vision |
| • inventories likes and dislikes | • clarifies your own personal development plan |
| • inventories current skills (self-assessment of performance ability) | • gives structure and connectivity to life issues |
| • inventories life accomplishments | • explains the legacy you plan to leave |
| • allows for dreaming | • articulates your attitude towards service to society |
| • encourages one to "story-tell" the future | • provides a clear description of who you are |
| • requires the development of a legacy | |

Table 4.4

| Criteria for an Education Plan | Criteria for a Career Plan |
|---|---|
| • analyzes the General Education Requirements | • inventories a list of current skills |
| • analyzes the requirements for a given major | • inventories likes and dislikes |
| • includes a schedule of classes for each term | • inventories a list of ten potential jobs |
| • provides a tracking system to measure progress toward completion of the plan | • includes job descriptions and requirements |
| • links courses to the development of specific skills | • describes a profile of a high performance professional |
| • analyzes the plans to finance a college education (includes the role of summer jobs and internships) | • includes educational development |
| • seeks opportunities to grow outside educational/classroom contexts | • provides an analysis of jobs against preferences |
| • identifies performance goals for each class | • includes notes from interviews with three professionals |
| • includes a time management plan | • illustrates what a suitable resume would look like |

*Do things outside of the class*

# Life Vision Work Sheet

## Questions that Help Define a Life Vision

1.  Who am I?

2.  Who do I want to be?

3.  What do I need to do to get from where I am to where I want to be?

4.  What are some of the things I like?

5.  Do I like working with my hands?

6.  Do I like working indoors? outdoors?

7.  Do I like to travel?

8.  Do I like being around people?

9.  Do I prefer working with inanimate objects?

10. What are some of the things I dislike?

11. What are my skills? talents? abilities?

12. Do I plan to start a family? If so, when?

13. What are my spiritual aspirations?

14. Do I believe in life long learning? If so, what is the highest degree I wish to pursue? If not, how will I stay current?

15. What are my social goals?

16. What are possible career choices?

17. Where do I want to live?

18. What are the descriptions of those careers?

19. What salary options am I pursuing?

20. What types of benefits are important to me?

21. Where do I plan to be professionally in the next 5 years, 10 years, 20 years?

22. Do I want to retire early or do I want a regular retirement?

23. Am I a team player?

24. Are there any past incidents in my life that may hinder me from obtaining my goals?

25. What other areas would I like to include in this life vision?

The aim of education is the knowledge not of facts but of values.
—*William Ralph Inge, English religious author 1860-1954*

# Goal Setting

There is only one corner of the universe you can be certain of improving, and that is your own self.
*–Aldous Huxley*

You most likely have heard about goal setting and its importance at one point or another. Perhaps you are even familiar with phrases such as, "a person without goals is like a ship without a rudder," or "not having a goal is like trying to hit a target you can't see or reach a destination you don't have." However, you may not be familiar with the process of goal setting and the specifics that help you improve your use of the process. The following criteria are meant to serve as guidelines as you set personal goals.

1.  Goals should be *written down* and not simply kept as thoughts in your head. You are much more accountable for keeping to your goals if you write them down and review them regularly.

2.  Goals should be *specific*. The more specific the goal, the more likely you are to accomplish it. Notice how a vague goal such as "I'll study tonight" can be changed to the more specific goal "tonight I'll read a chapter in biology, and do the ten math problems assigned from Chapter Four."

3.  Goals should be *measurable*. A goal is measurable if you can verify or confirm that you have reached it. A goal such as "I want to do well in psychology" cannot be measured (how do you measure "doing well") as compared to "I will get at least a B in psychology."

4.  Goals should be *action-oriented*. You can daydream, speculate, and fantasize about what you want, but unless your goals translate into specific actions for the here and now, more than likely your goals will simply stay creations of your mind.

5.  Goals should be *realistic*. Goals which are unrealistically large and not attainable quickly lose their meaning and motivational impact. Ask yourself if the goal is realistically achievable from the standpoint of time, skills, and resources.

6.  Goals should have *time limits or constraints*. There must be some accountability in terms of meeting goals by some deadline. Otherwise, meaning and motivation are lost and it becomes too easy to keep putting things off. However, it is very important to have both short-term and long-term goals. Long-term goals let you look at the big picture, farther into the future. Short-term goals provide continued motivation as a result of meeting and accomplishing goals/objectives on a more frequent basis.

7.  Goals should be *self-chosen and not imposed* upon you by others. Goals must be worthwhile to you and have the potential to give you a sense of accomplishment. They should be something you value and not what somebody else wants for you.

8.  Goals should be *written in a positive manner*. Avoid using phrasing such as "I won't fail ...," or "I can't do... until I do ...," "I won't do any worse than....". Although they may seem positive, avoid using words such as *try, hope,* and *think* in your goal statements. Starting goals with *I will*... is better because the other types of words give you a way out and an easy justification for not accomplishing a goal.

# Journal Writing

Journal writing is a process by which you write and record many different types of things including thoughts, ideas, feelings, experiences, important information, things learned or discovered, assessments, notes, terms, pictures, and drawings, to name a few.

Journal writing gives you an opportunity to reflect on what you have learned, articulate and generalize concepts, learn from problems or difficulties, and know yourself better. Keeping a journal of this growth is a powerful tool.

Different types of pages in your journal can be designed to serve different purposes. Consider the following *forms* or pages for use in your journal. (Note that these forms are available in *The Learning Assessment Journal* published by Pacific Crest.)

**Free Writing** pages are for reflecting on experiences and expressing yourself both in words and various other forms including sketches, drawings, mind maps, figures, and formulas. These pages are a place to capture the "ah-hahs" and significant thoughts.

**Collection Points** are for collecting information from discussions, meetings, and lectures. The space in this form can also be used for "to do" lists, outlines, and documenting research efforts.

**Self-Assessment** pages are for assessing your performance on a regular basis. Self-assessments allow you to better understand what you are learning and how much you are growing. A good model for self-assessments is the *SII Method* which involves looking for **S**trengths, areas for **I**mprovement, and **I**nsights. See Chapter Thirteen for more information about assessment.

**Reading Logs** document your critical exploration of texts and assigned readings. A reading log has three sections: (1) before you read, (2) while you read, and (3) synthesis and analysis after you read. The purpose of the reading log is not to replace highlighting and writing in the book, but rather to provide a place where new discoveries and important data can be recorded as well as analysis to help you, the reader, make greater sense out of the reading.

In summary, journal writing is a powerful process you should use to facilitate the creation of your life vision portfolio. Journaling allows you to become better at processing information, recording development, and assessing learning as it occurs in and out of the classroom. The resulting journal becomes a working document that records your growth and literally grows as your learning skills grow.

> The wise man will always reflect concerning the quality, not the quantity of life.
> *—Lucius Annaeus Seneca*

# Where Do I Go From Here?

Dreams are the start of your life vision. According to Napoleon Hill, "Whatever the mind can conceive and believe, it can achieve." If you have no idea of where you want to go in life, you probably won't get there.

**Reflect** on the past....

**Live** in the present....

**Plan** for the future....

**Assess** yourself every step of the way.

Developing and maintaining a life vision portfolio requires major effort from you, but it gives major benefits to you. Become the master of your destiny and empower yourself to take control of your life. Make it the best life possible!

> While it is true that without vision the people perish, it is doubly true that without action the people and their vision perish as well.
> —*Johnetta B. Cole, Former President, Spelman College*

# Improving Your Learning Skills

> Learning is what most adults will do for a living in the 21st century.
> — *Bob Perelman, American author and poet*

## Learning and Learning How to Learn

If you stop and think about it, perhaps the most powerful and beneficial skills a person can possess are those associated with learning. Imagine the possibilities available to those who are not intimidated by new challenges because they have confidence in their learning skills. Good learners can adapt to different situations knowing they are capable of learning what it takes to be successful. Whether it's learning difficult concepts in a college classroom, using new software packages on the computer, utilizing market information to make investments, or developing new skiing techniques on the slopes — there is no limit!

What do you think of when you hear that someone is a "good" learner? Does it mean that he or she simply has the ability to quickly learn new information? Webster defines "learning" as the process of gaining knowledge or skill by study, experience, or instruction. The key words we wish to emphasize from this definition are *process* and *skill*.

### Process

Learning is a process. A good learner is not only fast and efficient within the context of a single learning situation, but most importantly, a good learner is proficient at the process of learning. In other words, he or she can "learn how to learn." Later in this chapter you will be introduced to a tool called the Learning Process Methodology that can be used to better understand the *process* of learning.

### Skills

Learning requires using existing skills to improve or build new skills. Another valuable tool is the *Classification of Learning Skills* (found in the Appendix) which presents a comprehensive listing of an entire set of learning skills. This tool helps you identify key skills fundamental to learning and is a resource you can refer to as you develop, improve, and assess your learning skills.

The focus of this book is to help you become a quality learner by providing you with the knowledge, skills, and attributes that will enable you to succeed in college and in life. Let's look more closely at a model of a good learner and at how *Foundations of Learning* is developed to support this model.

# Profile of a Quality Learner

Below are many of the attributes and characteristics that are associated with people who excel at learning.

Table 5.1

| | Quality learners... |
|---|---|
| Role of a Student Chapter 3 | • focus their energy on the important task at hand.<br><br>• exhibit learner ownership, taking responsibility for the learning process and their own learning. |
| Creating a Life Vision Chapter 4 | • have a vision for their life and can articulate goals and objectives with measurable outcomes in various areas of their lives.<br><br>• engage in learning experiences having clarified their own values and maintaining an appreciation for other people's values. |
| Learning Skills Chapter 5 | • focus on improving and developing their learning skills by modeling the learning process itself.<br><br>• use inquiry, questioning, and critical thinking to be more efficient with time and gain new insights about how concepts can be applied. |
| Information Literacy Chapter 6 | • access information quickly and are able to distinguish relevant from irrelevant information. |
| Reading Skills Chapter 7 | • engage all their senses to access information; with a special emphasis on listening and reading. |
| Writing Skills Chapter 8 | • clarify, validate, and assess their understanding of a concept through verbal and written means. |
| Using Technology Chapter 9 | • make regular use of appropriate tools and technology and invest in learning new ones. |
| Personal Development Chapter 10 | • are willing to take risks and experiment; they are secure in their emotions and can accept failure as a frequent and productive event on the road to success.<br><br>• utilize their self-esteem and self-confidence to successfully meet new and challenging learning situations, building upon successes to improve future performance. |
| Relating with Others Chapter 11 | • demonstrate strong social skills, easily interact with other people, and are valued members of productive teams. |
| Problem Solving Chapter 12 | • are strong problem solvers who are able to visualize, model, transfer, and synthesize concepts.<br><br>• demonstrate interest, motivation, and desire to seek out new information, concepts, and challenges so they can apply them to new situations and problems. |
| Assessment Chapter 13 | • are good at the process of assessment and seek to continually develop their self-assessment skills. |

# Levels of Learner Performance

Let's now look at a range of levels or abilities with respect to a person's performance as a learner. An examination of this kind allows you to assess where you are currently and provides a progressive path to follow. Five levels of learner performance are presented below beginning with *trained individuals* and progressing up to *self-growers*.

**Trained individuals** have developed a specific knowledge base, with specific skills for a specific context. Most college students want their college education to be much broader than simply being trained for a job.

EXAMPLE CHARACTERISTIC: *must have explicitly defined rules, procedures, and policies.*

**Learned individuals** have acquired a broad base of general knowledge and can apply it to related contexts. Traditionally, colleges and universities have had mission statements that focused on producing "learned" individuals. Creating learned individuals can be viewed as a process where professors "fill" their students with knowledge, similar to filling a container with water.

EXAMPLE CHARACTERISTIC: *are willing to accept challenges within their area of expertise.*

**Lifelong learners** have developed the skills and motivation to facilitate their ongoing learning (of knowledge) and are able to apply learning to a variety of contexts. It is common today for colleges to have missions that state a desire to develop lifelong learners thereby acknowledging that learning continues in both personal and professional contexts beyond college and throughout one's life.

EXAMPLE CHARACTERISTIC: *seek out new challenges in related areas of knowledge.*

**Enhanced learners** have developed higher levels of learning skills in all areas including cognitive, social, affective, and psychomotor domains (see the *Classification of Learning Skills* in the Appendix). Enhanced learners are active learners who seek new knowledge and contexts for learning. In addition, they work to build greater proficiency with skills from several domains (cognitive, social, affective, and psychomotor) including assessment. Typically a mentor helps with the growth and development of an enhanced learner.

EXAMPLE CHARACTERISTIC: *seek to push the boundaries of their performance.*

**Self-growers** represent the highest level of learning performance. In addition to having the skills of a quality enhanced learner, they possess especially strong self-assessment skills which enable them to continually grow and improve after each performance. Rather than requiring a mentor, self-growers typically serve as a mentor to others.

EXAMPLE CHARACTERISTIC: *take control of their own destiny – there are no boundaries.*

---

**Levels of Learner Performance**

Trained individuals

Learned individuals

Lifelong learners

Enhanced learners

Self-growers

---

One's mind, once stretched by a new idea, never regains its original dimensions. —*Oliver Wendell Holmes, U.S. poet, physician, and essayist 1809–1894*

# Improving Your Learning Skills

Learning is a
treasure that
will follow
its owner
everywhere.
—*Chinese
Proverb*

How do you rate yourself in terms of the five levels of learner performance? Regardless of where you evaluate yourself, it is important to realize that everyone can improve his or her learning skills. Even self-growers can improve! In fact, it's in their nature to want to improve, drawing upon their self-assessment skills to learn from the past to improve performance in the future.

What can you do to improve your learning processes and skills, and how can you move closer toward becoming a self-grower? In a general sense, this book is devoted to helping you become a self-grower. In more specific terms, this book can help you:

**Gain a better understanding of the learning process.**

The Learning Process Methodology (LPM) presented on the next few pages is a tool that you can apply to learning situations in all contexts. It can be used to better understand what should take place (1) as you prepare to learn, (2) during a learning experience itself, and (3) after a learning experience.

**Regularly assess your performance against the Learning Process Methodology when in learning situations.**

Familiarize yourself with the steps in the Learning Process Methodology and regularly assess your performance against the methodology. The processes of assessment and self-assessment are explained in Chapter Thirteen.

**Identify specific skills you need to use for particular learning situations.**

The *Classification of Learning Skills* found in the Appendix helps you to identify general skill areas and specific skills for certain processes. As you familiarize yourself with this classification, you can select the most appropriate skills to focus on during a particular learning activity. *Note: activities in the accompanying book identify two or three "focused learning skills" for you at the beginning of each activity.*

**During learning activities, self-assess your performance with the skills you identified.**

Assess against criteria established by you or a mentor. Note that Chapter 13 provides details about the process of assessment and establishing criteria for assessment.

**Identify and learn about your preferred learning style.**

Knowing more about learning styles allows you to make discoveries about your strengths and areas for improvement as a learner. If maximum performance is needed in a very challenging or difficult learning situation, you can use your preferred learning style. In other situations you can work to improve and build skills associated with other learning styles. A discussion of learning styles with references to web sites for further information can be found later in this chapter.

## Methodology

A methodology is an orderly arrangement of steps or procedures.

In the context of this book, a methodology is the key tool for helping a person learn how to perform a new process.

# Methodologies – Tools to Help You Get Better at a Process

A process is a sequence of steps, events, or activities that result in a change or produces something over a period of time. Our everyday lives are filled with processes we perform, ranging from simple and mundane to very complex. Simple processes such as tying a shoelace or connecting to the Internet don't require much, if any, thought. They have become second nature to us. However, to a small child or a first-time computer user, these processes have not yet become so trivial.

Simple processes are not the issue here. The key issue is learning how to get better at the more challenging and difficult processes such as writing a research paper for a psychology class, or solving a set of word problems in a math or physics course, or preparing for a presentation in a speech communication class — in a broader sense, improving your writing, problem solving, and communication skills.

An excellent tool or resource to help with learning a process is a *methodology*, or an orderly arrangement of steps or procedures. A methodology serves as a model by listing a set of steps which describe how to best perform a process in an effective and efficient manner. In the case of this book, methodologies for important processes are presented for you. In other cases, you may need the help of an expert or someone who is good at the process to create a methodology for you to follow. Better yet, have the expert serve as a mentor or coach to give you feedback as you first learn the process.

*Consider a methodology to be like a recipe.* For example, if you are preparing a lasagna for the first time, the recipe serves as a guide that you constantly check to make sure you are doing things correctly. However, with each subsequent time you prepare the lasagna, you rely less and less on the recipe and become more free and spontaneous to make adjustments that suit your tastes (just like an expert chef might do).

The same is true when using a methodology to learn a process. The more unfamiliar you are with a process, the more closely you will want to follow the methodology in a step-by-step manner. Then as you become more proficient, you become less reliant and more flexible with respect to how you follow the methodology, in some cases skipping steps or making adjustments to suit your needs.

When using a methodology in a situation that is not complex or difficult, it is a good idea to think through all the steps even though you may choose to skip certain steps that are not necessary. By doing so, you will reinforce the methodology and become more familiar with it. The better you know and understand a methodology, the better you will be able to apply it in more challenging and difficult situations.

**A methodology is like a recipe.**

A beginning cook is well advised to follow the recipe closely for best results. With more experience, the cook may dare to vary the recipe, or even depart from it significantly.

The seasoned cook will pay little or no attention to the recipe, because the principles underlying it are by now second nature.

Nevertheless, the expert cook will always remain faithful to the spirit of the recipe, even while improving it.

Likewise, with experience, you will develop your own instincts to tell you how closely to follow any step-by-step process.

## The Most Efficient Way to Learn a New Process

The table below describes the most efficient way to learn a new process.

Table 5.2

| **How to Learn a Process** |
| --- |
| 1.  Obtain an effective methodology or set of procedures for the process. |
| 2.  Closely follow the steps to acquaint yourself with how the process works. |
| 3.  Practice the process on a regular basis. |
| 4.  Assess your use of the process after every performance or practice. Identify your strengths and acknowledge your progress. Look for areas for improvement and determine what you can do the next time to get better. |
| 5.  Find a mentor who has expertise with the process who can help you. Have your mentor give you feedback as you do steps 1- 4. |

How might you describe the five steps mentioned above? They are a methodology! In this case, the methodology above is a procedure to help you effectively learn any new process.

Throughout the remainder of this book you will find many valuable methodologies. However, the value of a methodology comes not from knowing it but *applying* it. You will gain the most from this book if you follow the steps in Table 5.2 with new processes that you want to learn, and processes that you want to improve upon.

## The Learning Process Methodology

Let's look at the process of learning — a process used continually as a student and one you will use throughout your entire life. While learning is not a new process, it is a process that has its complexities and is not easily understood.

The Learning Process Methodology has components that cover three main areas: (1) preparing to learn, (2) performing a learning activity, and (3) assessing and building new knowledge. Each area can then be broken down further as follows:

**Overview of the LPM**

*Preparing to learn*

- set the stage for learning,
- set goals and criteria for learning, and
- obtain relevant information for learning.

*Performing a learning activity*

- implement action for learning and
- apply what has been learned.

*Assessing and building new knowledge*

- assess performance at learning, and
- construct new knowledge.

> The mind is not a vessel to be filled but a fire to be kindled.
> —*Plutarch, 1st century Greek writer*

The Learning Process Methodology (LPM) can be used as a resource to gain insights into your current learning process. Realize that everyone's learning process can be improved, and the LPM is a useful tool for this purpose.

As you increase your ability to learn, your self-esteem and confidence will grow, and you will become a person with broader horizons. You will also increase your opportunities for personal growth, leading to life experiences that become more rewarding and enjoyable.

Table 5.3

| **LPM** | **Learning Process Methodology** |
|---|---|
| Preparing to Learn | |
| 1. Why | Identify and explain your reasons for learning. |
| 2. Orientation | Develop a systematic overview of what is to be learned. |
| 3. Prerequisites | Identify necessary skills and background knowledge needed to perform the learning. |
| 4. Learning Objectives | Set appropriate goals and objectives for the learning activity. |
| 5. Performance Criteria | Determine specific desired outcomes used to measure and gauge performance. |
| 6. Vocabulary | Identify and learn key terminology. |
| 7. Information | Collect, read, and study appropriate resources. |
| Performing a Learning Activity | |
| 8. Plan | Develop a plan of action to meet the performance criteria. |
| 9. Models | Study and review examples that assist meeting the learning objectives and performance criteria. |
| 10. Thinking critically | Pose and answer questions that stimulate thought and promote understanding. |
| 11. Transfer/Application | Transfer knowledge to different contexts; apply knowledge in new situations. |
| 12. Problem solving | Use knowledge in problem solving situations. |
| Assessing and Building New Knowledge | |
| 13. Self-assessment | Assess use of the learning process and mastery of the material learned. |
| 14. Research | Create and develop knowledge that is new and unique. |

Table 5.4

| | | The Learning Process Methodology — A Simple Example |
|---|---|---|
| | | Scenario: You just received a new digital watch as a birthday gift. The watch is not currently set with the correct time and date. You want to start wearing your new watch and need to know how to set the time and date. |
| 1. | Why | You want to start wearing and using your new digital watch. |
| 2. | Orientation | Look over the contents of the package, the watch, and printed materials. |
| 3. | Prerequisites | Includes reading skills, ability to tell time, and fine motor skills. |
| 4. | Learning Objectives | You want to learn how to set the watch to the correct time and date. |
| 5. | Performance Criteria | Set the watch to the correct time and date within five minutes. |
| 6. | Vocabulary | Terms to know: LCD screen, functions. |
| 7. | Information | The operating instructions booklet. |
| 8. | Plan | Read instructions for three minutes. Refer to the watch while reading instructions. Set the time and date according to the instructions - within two minutes. |
| 9. | Model | The diagram of the watch included with the instructions. |
| 10. | Thinking | Which buttons control which functions? What is the correct time and date? Does the watch need to be set according to A.M. and P.M.? Does a button need to be pressed more than once? |
| 11. | Transfer/Application | You should be able to adjust and change the time correctly when changing time zones. |
| 12. | Problem solving | The watch needs to be used as a stopwatch and as an alarm. |
| 13. | Self-assessment | Is the time and date set correctly? Did you meet the criteria? |
| 14. | Research | Look at improving the design of digital watches. |

# Overview of The Learning Process Methodology

PREPARING TO LEARN

**Set the stage for learning:** *Why, Orientation, and Prerequisites*

A person will perform better at the beginning of the learning process if the following occurs. The learner:

- feels that what is to be learned is important and worthwhile,

- sees how what is to be learned fits into a "big picture" or builds on what he or she already knows, and

- has the necessary prerequisite skills and knowledge to start the process.

In general, the learner should have some motivation to learn, some understanding of what is being learned and the basis to determine if he or she has the appropriate knowledge and skills for learning the new material.

**Set goals and criteria for learning:** *Learning Objectives and Performance Criteria*

The next two steps of the LPM provide a clear statement about what is to be learned (learning objectives) and what is expected of the learner at the end of the process (performance criteria). By determining learning objectives, the learner clarifies the general purpose of the learning activity. The performance criteria provide specifics as to what is expected of the learner in terms of outcomes or performance.

**Obtain relevant information for learning:** *Vocabulary and Information*

These two steps provide the learner with the terminology and background information necessary to begin the process of learning something new.

PERFORMING A LEARNING ACTIVITY

**Implement action for learning:** *Plan, Models,* and *Thinking*

The process of building new knowledge (learning something new) involves constructing and following a plan with a set of tasks which results in meeting the learning objectives and established performance criteria. The plan should include the use of the obtained information, models, and questions which require critical thought. Models and examples help the learner to explore and build understanding about what is being learned. New knowledge is constructed by thinking critically which involves asking and answering key questions.

> I cannot teach anybody anything, I can only make them think.
> —*Socrates, Athenian philosopher 470-399 B.C.*

**Apply what you have learned:** *Transfer/Application & Problem Solving*

A measure of true understanding and learning is exhibited when a learner is able to transfer what has been learned to new contexts and apply knowledge in new and different ways to solve problems.

ASSESSING AND BUILDING NEW KNOWLEDGE

**Assess the learning process:** *Self-Assessment*

The learning process can be improved if a learner becomes good at self-assessing his or her performance while he or she is learning. By focusing on strengths and areas for improvement, a person can use this information to improve his or her performance in the next learning situation. At the very least, a learner should be able to determine (self-assess) the quality of his or her performance.

**Construct new knowledge:** *Research*

A learner becomes a "self-learner" when he or she continues the learning process to conduct research and construct new knowledge which builds upon prior knowledge. This includes applying knowledge in new contexts, creating new methodologies, and making new interpretations or understanding things in a new way.

# Discussion of the Steps in the Learning Process Methodology

**Why**

The process of learning begins with identifying the need or motive for learning (acquiring knowledge). The reasons for learning vary based upon the context, whether it be getting more enjoyment from life, obtaining a college degree, performing a job better, or learning about something to solve a problem. Also, when the objectives are clear and the motivation for learning is strong, the learning process becomes more enjoyable and productive.

However, unless there is some justification that learning will be personally beneficial, most individuals are not willing to invest their time and effort. When it comes to learning something new, people tend to choose how they spend their time based on personal needs and goals. It is common for people to ask, "is this worth my time and is this relevant to meeting my personal, educational, career or life goals?"

**Orientation**

The orientation provides a systematic overview of what is to be learned. This information helps you to prepare for a learning activity by showing how the new knowledge fits into a larger picture, similar to knowing how a single chapter fits within the context of an entire textbook. Your ability to see the "big picture" helps you to stay focused and improve your learning effectiveness. An orientation involves first reviewing all the parts, and then looking to see how the parts are connected and work together as a whole.

**Prerequisites**

A prerequisite is defined as something required beforehand; a necessary condition for something to follow. As it pertains to the LPM, prerequisites identify the skills and/or knowledge required at the start of the learning process. In other words, the learner needs to identify necessary background information or prerequisite skills before going any further in the activity or learning process. Taking personal responsibility for preparing yourself for a new learning experience increases your confidence and self-esteem as a learner.

**Learning Objectives**

Learning objectives help you focus your efforts to be more productive by providing a clear statement about what is to be learned and accomplished during the activity (learning process). Learning objectives are typically action-oriented statements written to support one's reasons for learning. Effective objectives are personal, relevant, valuable, motivating and support your overall learning objectives.

Learning is the indispensable investment for success in the "information age" we are entering.
— *National Commission on Excellence in Education (1983), A Nation at Risk*

## Performance Criteria

Performance criteria provide a standard to measure your performance during a learning activity. Criteria should be measurable, observable, fair, and reflect high expectations. These criteria help you focus on what is important and allow you to gauge the quality of your performance. The assessment process relies on set criteria. Furthermore, self-assessment is key to improving any process you perform.

## Vocabulary

Learning can be very language dependent. The process of learning something new often involves being introduced to new and unfamiliar terminology. Without an understanding of new terminology (near the beginning of the learning process), you can easily become lost and frustrated. It is important to take time to identify and define new and important terms used during the learning activity. This is best accomplished by using a variety of sources such as glossaries, dictionaries, textbooks, and the Internet to write a brief description of how each key word fits within the context of the learning activity.

## Information

The learning process uses prerequisite knowledge (third step of the LPM) and introduces new information. It is important to have a solid base of information when learning or acquiring knowledge. Certain factors affect the quality and usefulness of information. Learning is most productive when the information used is comprehensive, drawing from various sources such as textbooks, lectures, discussions, libraries and the Internet. Information should also be relevant and appropriate, accurate, accessible, and cost and time effective. *(Note that Chapter Six provides more detail about information and information literacy.)*

## Plan

The first seven steps of the LPM are preparing you for the learning activity. In this step, you implement a plan of action for learning. The Plan is a sequence of steps or tasks you follow in order to accomplish the objectives and criteria. A good plan defines necessary tasks and puts them in a sequence. It also allocates time and other resources and serves as a management tool to guide and assess your performance.

## Models

Models are tools to assist you in the learning process. Depending on the learning situation, different types of models are used to explore, identify, understand, and build relationships among information. For example, when learning about a concept or topic, using diagrams, graphs, simulations and mathematical and physical models are beneficial. When learning a process, using a methodology or sequence of steps is an extremely useful model.

Contextual learning uses analogies, experiences of others, and role playing as models. Learning to use tools is best modeled by simulations, demonstrations, tutorials, and instruction booklets. Models should be flexible, easy to use, comprehensive, and accurate.

### Thinking

The process of learning and acquiring knowledge requires *critical thinking*—the use of a quality thought process. Thinking critically involves both asking and answering "key" questions that stimulate thought, and promote greater understanding of what is to be learned. The (critical thinking) questions you answer should be logically sequenced whereby information is clarified. Questions should provide links which produce new understanding and require you to expand, extend, and generalize your thinking. The answers to these questions should make use of models, methodologies, relevant information, and prior knowledge. Strong critical thinking skills significantly enhance your learning process, particularly the rate of learning and the level of understanding.

### Transfer/Application

An outcome of learning is the ability to apply or transfer what you have learned to new situations and different contexts. Doing homework exercises is an example of transfer and application. Your ability to transfer, generalize, and apply what you've learned to different contexts will take you to higher levels of thinking, learning and problem solving.

### Problem Solving

Problem Solving requires you to combine your ability to use new knowledge with a (problem solving) methodology to develop or create a useful solution to a problem. Being able to generalize the solution to one problem so that it can be used in other contexts greatly enhances your performance when problem solving. An intended outcome of learning is the ability to apply what you have learned to solve actual problems. *(Note that Chapter Twelve is devoted to the process of problem solving.)*

### Self-assessment

The ability to self-assess is key to knowing when you have accomplished objectives and met the criteria for a learning activity. Being able to self-assess allows you to distinguish between "thinking you know" (needing someone else to tell you) and "knowing you know" (knowing for yourself). Good self-assessment skills are essential for you to become a self-grower.

The *Learning Assessment Journal* is a resource to assist you with self-assessment. This journal allows you to document information during the learning process that you can later review, analyze, and use for assessment purposes. *(Note that Chapter Thirteen is devoted to assessment and self-assessment.)*

> I hear and
> I forget.
> I see and
> I remember.
> I do and I
> understand.
> —*Confucius,
> Chinese teacher
> and philosopher
> 551-479 B.C.*

**Research**

The learning process does not stop with current knowledge. You are encouraged to become a researcher, one who discovers or constructs "new" knowledge. This includes applying your expertise to come up with new ideas, create new methodologies, make new interpretations, and see things in a completely different way—to stretch your mind to new heights.

## Beyond Knowledge to Skills

It shouldn't surprise you to know that you will need to continue learning after college. With a lifetime of learning ahead of you, doesn't it make sense to spend time in college working to improve your ability to learn to learn? Yet some students come to college with the expectation of being "spoon-fed" knowledge from a professor in the belief that knowledge or information is the key to preparing for a future career or life after college.

In the process of meeting requirements to earn a degree, you will gain a great deal of knowledge. However, you cannot expect to retain all that you have learned. Even if you could retain all the information you learn, it still would not be enough. Today's employers are looking for individuals who are able to think critically, solve problems, work in teams, communicate effectively, utilize technology, and effectively process information.

> Spoon feeding in the long run teaches us nothing but the shape of the spoon.
> —*E. M. Forster, British writer and novelist 1879-1970*

## Classification of Learning Skills

How does one go about developing the skills that are essential for learning and are desired by employers? The first step is to identify what skills we are talking about. In other words, classify or list the skills that encompass learning in all contexts. The *Classification of Learning Skills* was created to be a resource that both students and faculty can use to identify key processes and skills fundamental to learning. It also provides a framework for making quality assessments of performance.

The *Classification of Learning Skills* (found in its entirety in the Appendix) consists of a listing of skills in four main areas or domains.

- The skills associated with the **cognitive** domain deal primarily with the intellect and with attaining knowledge.

- The skills within the **social** domain involve interactions among people.

- The **affective** domain contains skills that deal with emotions and feelings.

- The skills in the **psychomotor** domain deal with one's physical development and well-being.

Each domain has certain key processes associated with it. The table below shows the processes within each domain in order of increasing complexity.

Table 5.5

| Domains and their Associated Processes | | | |
|---|---|---|---|
| **Cognitive** | **Social** | **Affective** | **Psychomotor** |
| Information processing | Communication | Value development | Wellness |
| Critical thinking | Teamwork | Personal development | Motor development |
| Problem solving | Management | Esthetic development | Tool usage |
| Research | | | |

Each process, such as information processing, consists of general skill areas which can be broken down into specific skills. A listing of all the general skill areas and specific skills are presented in various chapters throughout this book.

Language development and assessment are two processes that are common to all domains. Language development, in the broad sense, is the foundation from which skills in all domains are built. Assessment is the most complex process requiring skills from the other domains. The four-sided pyramid shown below illustrates the domains and their processes. Note that language development forms the base of the pyramid and that assessment is the capstone process located at the top of each domain.

Figure 5.1

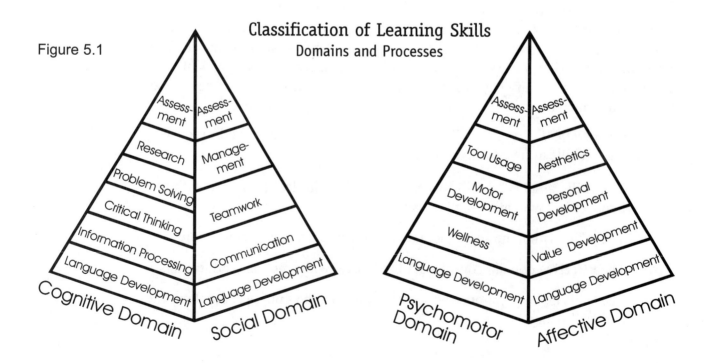

Classification of Learning Skills
Domains and Processes

## Learning Styles

All people have preferred methods of approaching a learning situation and processing information. There are numerous theories and models concerning learning styles which describe a preferred manner in which a person learns. Learning styles can take into account both personal and environmental factors in describing how people are most comfortable and capable when performing in learning situations.

How we learn determines what we learn.
—*Unknown*

Some models emphasize **personality dimensions** that influence the way we acquire and integrate information. The Meyers-Briggs Type Indicator is a well-known tool which has scales measuring extroversion versus introversion, sensing versus intuition, thinking versus feeling, and judging versus perception.

Other models, such as Kolb's, focus specifically on the way in which we **process information**. Still other models look at the way in which we interact with others. Anthony Grasha and Sheryl Riechmann developed a **social interaction** model which identifies learners who are either independent, dependent, collaborative, competitive, participant, and avoidant. Finally, other models stress the importance of identifying and addressing a person's **individual preferred environment** for learning.

## Information about Learning Styles on the Web

For more information about learning styles, refer to Chapter Five of the *Foundations of Learning* web site.

Links from the George Washington University site describe more than fifty theories relevant to human learning and instruction. Each description includes an overview, scope or application, an example, principles, and references.

**http://www.pcrest.com**

Other links include a section devoted to learning styles from the student handbook at the University of Minnesota at Duluth and learning style links from pages at Virginia Commonwealth University and Metropolitan Community College.

# Bloom's Taxonomy

In 1956, Benjamin Bloom classified types of learning, ranging from basic to complex, into six levels known as Bloom's Taxonomy. The six levels are as follows: recall, comprehension, application, analysis, synthesis, and evaluation. The table below summarizes Bloom's Taxonomy.

Table 5.6 can be used to determine an instructor's expectations for individual assignments or tests. Many times true-false, multiple choice and matching tests are written with expectations for student learning at the recall or comprehension level. Short answer, essay and problem-based tests usually require learning at the application level or problem solving level. Larger projects, typically given in higher-level and graduate courses require learning at highest levels in Bloom's Taxonomy.

Table 5.6

| Levels | Bloom's Taxonomy | Requires skills from: |
|---|---|---|
| Recall | Learning pieces of information such as facts and definitions enough so that you are able to repeat them. | Information processing |
| Comprehension | Understanding enough about a topic so that you are able to explain it to someone else. | Critical thinking |
| Application | Putting what has been learned into practice; applying what you know. | Higher order critical thinking |
| Analysis | Breaking a topic into specific parts and studying the interaction of the parts. | Problem solving |
| Synthesis | Integrating prior knowledge and creativity to gain insights into a topic. | Research |
| Evaluation | Knowing a topic so well that you can judge its quality according to established criteria. | Assessment |

Bloom, B. 1956. Taxonomy of Educational Objectives, McKay, New York

Learning is its own exceedingly great reward.
—*William Hazlitt, English essayist and literary critic 1778-1830*

# Gardner's Theory of Multiple Intelligences

Another theory associated with learning styles is Gardner's Theory of Multiple Intelligences. In 1983, Harvard Professor Howard Gardner hypothesized that there are seven independent ways in which we process information for learning. They are summarized in the table below.

Table 5.7

| Gardner's Multiple Intelligences | | |
|---|---|---|
| *Intelligence type* | *Descriptive words* | *Typified by a person who...* |
| Verbal-linguistic | reading, writing, and speaking | is good with language and words |
| Logical-mathematical | numbers and problem solving | likes to ask questions, think, experiment and explore |
| Spatial | art and architecture | enjoys drawing and designing; using pictures |
| Musical | sounds, harmonics, and tones | enjoys music, sounds, and melodies; has rhythm |
| Intra-personal | feelings and a sense of self | enjoys working alone; follows instincts about himself/herself |
| Interpersonal | relationships, interacting with others | enjoys socializing and trying to understand people |
| Kinesthetic | physical action and body movement | enjoys being active and in motion; uses the body to express ideas |

Gardner, H. 1983. Frames of Mind: The Theory of Multiple Intelligences. Basic Books, New York

## What Does This Mean for You?

Everyone has a preferred learning style(s). An advantage to knowing your learning style is that in certain situations you may be able to choose the style that best suits you. You can use information about how you learn to more efficiently manage your time, study for tests, complete your reading and communicate with peers and instructors.

While accommodating your preferred learning style can make you feel more comfortable in learning situations and increase your productivity and creativity, does this mean you should always try to learn in your preferred style? Most educators would say no, preferring not to teach each student according to his or her preference but instead using a variety of methods. The result is that students are taught partly in their preferred manner and partly in a manner where they must practice skills that need improvement.

In an article titled, Matters of Style, Richard Felder wrote...

> If professors teach exclusively in a manner that favors their students' less preferred learning style modes, the students' discomfort level may be great enough to interfere with their learning. On the other hand, if professors teach exclusively in their students' preferred modes, the students may not develop the mental dexterity they need to reach their potential for achievement in school and as professionals.
>
> An objective of education should thus be to help students build their skills in both their preferred and less preferred modes of learning. Learning style models that categorize these modes provide good frameworks for designing instruction with the desired breadth. The goal is to make sure that the learning needs of students in each model category are met at least part of the time. (ASEE Prism, 6(4), 18-23 December 1996)

It should be noted that having a learning preference does not always mean that you are good at it or that you are necessarily weak at doing something you prefer not to do. However, it is important to realize that when you are learning or working outside the comfort of your preferred learning style, you have the greatest opportunity for personal growth and skill development. It has been argued that a sign of maturity is being able to perform outside of your learning style preference.

In summary, set your sights high as a learner. Strive to become a self-grower. With practice, assessment, and persistence you will grow and improve as a learner regardless of current abilities. Challenge yourself to keep growing, for as Will Rogers put it, "Even if you are on the right track, you'll get run over if you just sit there."

# Information Literacy & Study Skills

> Ultimately, information literate people are those who have learned how to learn.
> — *American Library Association's Presidential Committee on Information Literacy*

## Living in the Information Age

We live in an "age of information" where satellites, personal computers and computer networks such as the Internet provide us with convenient access to staggering amounts of information. Consider a few examples of what we have come to accept as common place:

- viewing near-instantaneous media reports of events as they happen from around the world,

- buying personal computers with hard drives containing "gigabytes" of space,

- using CD's that contain the equivalent of entire volumes of books on a single disk, and

- browsing and purchasing an ever-increasing array of products and services over the Internet.

With all the changes and benefits of the information age come a new set of challenges and problems. This includes "information overload" which represents the gap between the volume of information we encounter and our ability to handle it or make sense of it. The following paragraph from the Information Literacy Project of Tri-County Technical College (South Carolina) summarizes the situation nicely:

> Virtually no change in American society has presented greater challenges than the emergence of the "Information Age." Dealing with the overabundance of information now routinely available seems at best overwhelming and, at worst, unmanageable and uncontainable. Futurists estimate that the amount of information in the sciences doubles approximately every five years. Academic curricula cannot be revised often enough, or expanded enough, to keep current with that rate of change. For students to be able to cope with this rising volume and to be able to maintain a knowledgeable control over any significant portion of the information necessary to their personal and professional success, they must gain special skills and understanding, the acquisition of which is called Information Literacy.

Source: http://www.tricounty.tec.sc.us/14a.html

The focus of this chapter is to address the issues associated with becoming an information literate person and the building of skills associated with information processing.

## Information Literacy

Information literacy refers to the ability to apply methods for collecting, retrieving, evaluating, organizing, and storing information. Being information literate involves knowing:

- what information is available,

- when the information is needed,

- where to find relevant information,

- how to gain access to information,

- which information is useful and should be kept, and

- what to do with the information once you've got it.

An information literate person processes information, thinks critically, solves problems, and performs research. These are the four key processes associated with the cognitive domain (from the *Classification of Learning Skills*). Note that these processes build upon each other. Information processing skills are a foundation for critical thinking skills, which are important for problem solving. Finally, there is research which is the most demanding and complex of the four processes.

The more you understand and use information processing, the less overwhelmed you will be by the vast amount of information available to you, and the more effective you will be at using information to your benefit. By working to become information literate and a skillful information processor, you become empowered with greater confidence to apply and use information for problem solving and decision-making purposes.

## Information and Knowledge

*Information* can include any of the following: facts, data (words, numbers and symbols), lore, news, intelligence, and something told or read.

Knowing, understanding, and deriving meaning from information requires critical thought. James Billington, from the Library of Congress, recently commented about the difference between *information* (what is made so abundant by digital technology), and *knowledge* (the insights gained when you have a chance to sort through things and figure them out). His advice for attaining knowledge when there's too much information, "Turn off the computer. Even shut the book on occasion. And let your mind flourish and work."

Let's now look at a profile of an information literate person and the specific skills that are associated with information processing.

---

Processes from the cognitive domain

*Information processing*

*Critical thinking*

*Problem solving*

*Research*

---

We're drowning in information and starving for knowledge.
—*Rutherford Rogers, librarian, Yale University*

# Profile of an Information Literate Person

Christina Doyle, in a national Delphi study, defines *information literacy* and creates a list of characteristics of an information literate person. An adaptation of her list follows:

Table 6.1

---

### Profile of an Information Literate Person

An information literate person *accesses* information:

- recognizes the need for information,

- recognizes that accurate and complete information is the basis for intelligent decision making,

- formulates questions based on information needs,

- identifies potential sources of information,

- develops successful search strategies,

- accesses print and technology-based sources of information, and

- is a competent reader.

An information literate person *evaluates* information:

- establishes authority,

- determines accuracy and relevance,

- recognizes opinion from factual knowledge,

- rejects inaccurate and misleading information, and

- creates new information to replace inaccurate or missing information as needed.

An information literate person *uses* information:

- organizes information for practical application,

- integrates new information into an existing body of knowledge, and

- applies information in critical thinking and problem solving.

Other characteristics include:

- being a resourceful and independent learner,

- being confident in his or her ability to solve problems,

- being able to function independently and work equally well in groups, and

- being creative and able to adapt to change.

---

## Skills Associated with Information Processing

The basis for being information literate starts with building the skills associated with information processing. The general skill areas associated with information processing along with their specific skills are presented in the table below.

Table 6.2

| Information Processing Skills | | | |
|---|---|---|---|
| **Collecting Data** | **Generating Data** | **Organizing Data** | **Retrieving Data** |
| sensing | predicting | outlining | reading |
| listening | experimenting | categorizing | remembering |
| memorizing | estimating | translating | reviewing |
| recording | surveying | systematizing | utilizing information systems |
| skimming | brainstorming | sorting | |
| observing or recognizing | | | |

## Highlighted Information Processing Skills

The following information processing skills will be discussed or presented in more detail *listening*, *brainstorming*, *memorizing*, and *skimming*.

Chapter Seven is devoted to *reading* while *outlining* is discussed in the study skills section of this chapter under note-taking.

## Listening

Listening is not the same as hearing. You may hear a conversation but that doesn't necessarily mean that you were listening. Without making this distinction, it's easy to take the skill of listening for granted and assume that we are all at the same level of skill. However, as with any skill, some are better at listening than others. Why is this so and what can you do to improve your listening ability?

Listening is the receiving and decoding of messages from others. Listening includes hearing words and sounds and noticing non-verbal cues to ascertain the meaning that others are trying to convey. Listening also involves the recall of what has been presented. A listener identifies his or her purpose and tries to understand the sender's purpose. Good listening results in effective feedback to the sender.

Table 6.3 contains ten criteria that provide some insight into what distinguishes different levels of listening ability. Five levels of listener performance are described in detail at the end of the chapter. The terms used to identify these levels are: novice listener, survival listener, maintenance listener, effective listener, and quality listener.

Table 6.3

| Criteria that Affect the Quality of Listening | |
|---|---|
| concentration | focusing on the message |
| comprehension | interpreting meaning accurately |
| perception | understanding the sender's nonverbal cues and hidden meaning |
| motivation | wanting to learn new material/knowledge |
| background knowledge | relating prior information/theories to the current context |
| classifying | organizing current information into an existing framework |
| targeting | sampling key words and phrases |
| empathy | willingness to understand underlying issues & values of others |
| paying attention to details | inventorying important specifics |
| compare and contrast | using prior knowledge to evaluate and differentiate ideas |

# Brainstorming

Brainstorming is a group process which involves generating ideas or solutions (to a problem) in a rapid manner without judgment or criticism. The premise is that the more ideas that are generated, the greater the likelihood of finding a good solution or idea. Brainstorming has three phases, (1) generating ideas, (2) discussion and evaluation, and (3) planning for future action.

During the **idea generation** phase there are some common rules to consider.

- Define the problem or task; typically stated in the form of a question.

- Set a time limit.

- Identify a recorder to write down the ideas/solutions; recording can be in the form of lists or sentences, or by drawing a map or "tree."

- Write so that all can easily see what's being recorded. Use a flipchart, overhead projector, whiteboard or blackboard.

- Generate and collect as many ideas as possible; all ideas are welcome.

- Be creative; no idea is too silly or wild.

- Build upon other's ideas.

- Don't criticize or judge; all ideas are equally valuable at this point.

- Don't spend time discussing individual ideas.

- Don't spend time wordsmithing ideas.

There is no *right way* to do the **evaluation** phase. The following are some general guidelines:

- Determine criteria to be used for selecting the "best" ideas or solutions.

- Modify the list by combining, consolidating, amending, and deleting ideas; allow for open discussion at this time.

- Reduce the list further to include no more than one third of the total ideas; each person votes or ranks the ideas.

- Once again, vote or rank (on a scale of 1-5) the ideas to determine the best idea(s). Note that there may not be one best solution or idea.

Finally, the **planning** phase involves taking the chosen idea(s) and creating an action or implementation plan. Outline the steps to be taken and identify factors which may effect the implementation of the plan.

## Memorizing

Memorizing involves both putting information into memory and getting it out again at some point later in time. As a student, having a good memory can be very helpful when taking certain types of quizzes and exams.

However, memorizing is not the same as learning. For example, you could memorize the quadratic formula for a math class. However, knowing the formula doesn't necessarily mean that you have "learned" the formula well enough to use it and apply it in different situations. Also, as you know from Chapter Five, learning is a complex process with many steps in the Learning Process Methodology. Memorizing, on the other hand, has three main components.

### Encoding

Encoding is making information meaningful. Be aware of encoding errors. These include misreading, misinterpreting (what you see, hear, or read), and not understanding information correctly.

### Storing

Storing involves organizing and placing information in short-term and long-term memory. The goal is to move information into long-term memory for easier retrieval.

### Retrieving

Retrieving involves getting back information so that it can be used in some way. *Mnemonics* are methods, devices, or even mental tricks or games that help with improving memory; especially aiding the retrieval component of memory.

## Information about Memory and Mnemonics on the Web

For more information about memory and mnemonics, go to Chapter Six of the *Foundations of Learning* web site.

There is a link to an article about mnemonics entitled, *Improving Your Memory Skills*.

**http://www.pcrest.com**

Note the site from Nottingham Trent University in England. This link has information and resources for a cognitive psychology course on memory. There are also links to many other memory sites including other courses, document archives, research labs, Scientific American articles, and commercial sites.

Another link is to the site for The Center for the Neurobiology of Learning and Memory. The Center was founded in 1981 on the UC–Irvine campus by three professors in the Department of Psychobiology. The Center is a research institute dedicated exclusively to the investigation of the basic brain mechanisms responsible for learning and memory.

## Skimming

Skimming involves looking at printed material or written work without reading every word; passing over the text lightly and quickly to pull out the main ideas. Unlike scanning, with skimming you don't know exactly what you're looking for and don't have a specific goal in mind. Skim when you want to get the gist of things without taking the time to read the material in full. You can skim both to preview new material as well as rapid review of long text assignments you have already read. Some tips for skimming include:

- Familiarize yourself with the reading (author, title, subtitle, headings, and source) before you start skimming.

- Read the first sentence (topic sentence) of each paragraph to get the main idea. Then glance through the rest of the paragraph looking for bold type, italics, digits, or capitalized words.

- Key into the main idea and a few facts such as names of people, dates, places, things, and numbers.

- Ignore extra words, articles, prepositions, and conjunctions.

- Read the last paragraph in more detail as it contains a summary or conclusion.

- Move quickly.

- At the end, you should have a grasp of the main ideas.

# Information Processing Methodology

The Information Processing Methodology is a key tool in helping you become better at collecting, organizing, and retrieving information. Everyday you must make decisions that require information processing—which mail to read, what radio station to listen to, what magazine articles or newspaper sections to read, or what to watch on television. This includes information presented to you and that which you must seek out.

The ability to use the Information Processing Methodology reduces the anxiety associated with "information overload" and gives you confidence about finding important information when you need it. It is important to note that every other methodology in this book includes a step that requires information to be processed.

Table 6.4

| Information Processing Methodology | |
|---|---|
| 1. Perform a needs analysis. | Analyze who needs the information, why it is needed, when it is needed, what the user will do with the information once it is received. |
| 2. Create a collection plan. | Create a plan to collect the information from various sources. |
| 3. Assess the resources. | Create a method to assess the quality of the information. |
| 4. Organize the information. | Develop a plan for storing and organizing the information that is collected. |
| 5. Retrieve the information. | Search and collect the information. Provide it where and when it is needed. |
| 6. Assess and review. | Assess the process and the outcomes. Determine if the needs have been met. If not, determine what more is needed and repeat the process starting at Step 2. |

## Discussion of the Information Processing Methodology

### Needs Analysis — Identify the Need for Information

As you begin any process, it is important to first identify the purpose for the process and understand why it is necessary. In your work as a student, the need for information often comes from an assignment or an engaging problem. In this context, you need to know what the parameters of the assignment are and how the process and the product will be evaluated.

Table 6.5

| Information Processing Methodology — A Simple Example | | |
|---|---|---|
| **Scenario**: You have three young children who enjoy cereal for breakfast. You are at the grocery store looking at breakfast cereals which are high in fiber and low in sugar. You need to process the information printed on the cereal boxes to determine which ones to buy. | | |
| 1. | Needs Analysis | You need information about the grams of fiber and sugar per serving. This information is the primary basis for choosing a cereal. |
| 2. | Collection Plan | Look at the nutritional information printed on at least ten different boxes of cereal known to be not high in sugar content. Write down this information. |
| 3. | Resource Assessment | Look at the size of the serving to determine if it is reasonable, based on what the children normally eat. If too small, increase the fiber and sugar values. |
| 4. | Information Organization Plan | Create a three-column table which includes the name of the cereal, number of grams of fiber per serving, and the number of grams of sugar per serving. |
| 5. | Information Retrieval | After looking at the boxes and recording the information, sort the cereals in order of low to high sugar content. You determine that you will only buy cereals in the top third of the sorted list. |
| 6. | Asssessment and Review | Keep track of those cereals in the top third of your list that your children enjoy. Eliminate those cereals that they won't eat. |

One of the most challenging aspects of the research process is the analysis of the problem and the related need for information. In the case of information processing, you should analyze who needs the information, why it is needed, where and when it is needed, and what the user will do with the information once it is received. By asking these questions, you can clarify the type of information needed and what you will do to obtain the appropriate information.

**Collection Plan**

Having a plan for gathering and obtaining information before you start searching makes the information retrieval step of the methodology far more efficient. A collection plan should identify what information is needed, when it is needed, and identify possible options for finding it.

A common question is "where can I find the information I need?" Knowing which sources are available and where to find them is a key part of a good collection plan. Main sources of information available to you are textbooks, the library and the Internet.

In your thirst for knowledge, be sure not to drown in all the information.
—*Anthony J. D'Angelo, The College Blue Book*

### Libraries

Libraries are sources of detailed global information, available in minutes. To a beginner, it may be confusing. The "mother" of all libraries is the Library of Congress. It carries listings of all the  books, magazines, and journals published in the United States. Other libraries carry only the materials that best meet the needs and wants of their patrons. Public libraries serve a diversified clientele, where most colleges have a more extensive library to meet the specific classroom and research needs of the students and faculty.

There are special purpose libraries specific to an industry or business such as law, business, or engineering libraries. Any collection of books becomes a library (through its definition) by being organized. A collection of information resources cannot be considered a "library" unless it is organized in a manner such that information can be retrieved. Most libraries use either the Dewey Decimal or the Library of Congress system for cataloging their holdings (see Chapter Two for more information).

### The Internet

The Internet is also a source of detailed global information, available in seconds. To a newcomer, it may also be confusing. The Internet is a collection of information resources but cannot be considered a library. Even though information can be retrieved, there is no organization system for information on the Internet.

Instead of classification systems through which information can be retrieved, search engines have been designed to assist in the retrieval of information. But there are no  guarantees of finding information on the Internet. In many cases, information is not classified and if it is classified, it may not be in a manner that you know how to ask for it. For example, information may be classified, indexed and even cross-indexed, but you don't know what these classifications are and they are not universal for all informational searches on the Internet. Also, the unregulated nature of the Internet raises issues concerning the quality of the information you find (this is dealt with in the next step of the methodology).

### Other sources

Everyone has had experiences with a broad range of resources that are of potential use in exploring information or solving problems. Think about the information resources you have used in the past for personal or educational or business-related projects.

Other information sources include dictionaries, almanacs, encyclopedias, newspapers, magazines, maps, movies, videos, television, radio, books, and friends. This is not a complete list but rather just some examples, there are many more!

Finally, if information is to have meaning, you must make connections between new information and previous experiences or knowledge. The first step in orienting yourself to an unfamiliar subject is to find one or more existing connections that give the subject meaning.

## Resource Assessment

The information you collect (later in the methodology) is not of equal value based on your needs analysis. The credibility and reliability of the sources also varies. For these reasons, it is important to develop a set of standards or criteria for evaluating and assessing the quality of the information you obtain. These standards serve as the basis for determining which information you choose to use and how to use it.

As you locate potentially useful bits of information, a screening process takes place. First, the information must pass the test of relevance and then it can be scrutinized in terms of how current, objective, thorough, consistent, and clearly understood it is. The level of understanding depends on your personal learning style and familiarity with the subject.

A piece of information that is useful to one person may be of limited value to another working on the same question. There can be no understanding of information that does not relate to what is already known. As you progress, you gain skills in applying these and other tests of usefulness.

Every source needs your personal assessment as to its value and its validity. In many cases, you make assessments just in the physical handling of the source. For example, the following give you a sense of validity for a source: a familiar author is noted, the publisher is well-known to you, the source was reviewed in *The New York Times*, or a work is in its 5th printing.

There are other times when great care is needed to insure that an assessment is made of the information. For example, an Internet source may be here today, gone tomorrow; where did the brochure in your mailbox, or the e-mail message, or the bulletin board posting come from? Verify your sources.

## Develop a Plan for Organizing Information

After you determine which information meets the criteria set in the previous step, you must develop a plan for storing and organizing this information. It is important to know what information you already have and where to find the information you need. Refer to the needs analysis for insights which might influence how you choose to organize the information.

> It's amazing that the amount of news that happens in the world everyday always just exactly fits the newspaper.
> —*Jerry Seinfeld, television actor*

Information sources are rarely organized in ways that exactly match your end use of the content. As notes are created, they are classified in a way that meets your original need. This classification scheme may evolve during the quest and probably will closely approximate the final structure or outline. While the original questions led to the desired information, they might also lead to much repetition if used in a presentation of the findings. In some cases, it may be advantageous to create a new structure or outline.

You can benefit from a variety of experiences in applying information; written reports are only one of them. You need to reach conclusions and to prepare for activities that are the outcomes of your quests for information. Presentation formats can include papers, dramatizations, panel discussions, multimedia presentations, models, demonstrations, or school-wide projects. Each application has its own set of skills required for success. Interpersonal skills are as important as language skills; visual skills are as important as verbal ones.

## Retrieve Information

Gather and obtain the needed information while at the same time make evaluations as to the usefulness of the information you collect. Interpretation skills are important as you retrieve information.

Interpretation skills start, but do not end, with reading. A good reader makes use of context clues, discerns the structure of a piece of writing, draws inferences, and perceives relationships. Such skills are also essential to such diverse activities as reading maps, interpreting tables of statistical data, reading schematics, studying photographs, and viewing films or videos. During any information quest, you must have the interpretation skills required by each format to retrieve the useful pieces of information or else the whole process becomes meaningless.

Organize and integrate the fragments of information into a comprehensible whole to create personal meaning. With practice and assessment of your performance, your knowledge of sources will grow, the plans you create will improve, as will your searching and organization skills.

## Assess and Review

Assess what you have done up to this point to determine if you have adequately met the needs analysis stated in Step 1. Determine if more or different (useful) information is needed. If so, repeat the steps of the methodology starting with Step 2. Incorporate the new useful information with the information found the first time through the process.

# Research Tips

**Using primary resources**

Whenever possible, your first step in the search process should be using a primary source. Primary sources provide information via first-hand experience; whether you or someone else collects the data/information. Examples of primary sources are interviews (in-person, survey, or e-mail), experiments, or direct observations.

You, yourself, should be the first primary source in the research process. Ask yourself the following three questions:

1.  What do I know? (activates previous knowledge)

2.  What do I want to know? (provides a purpose for investigation)

3.  What have I learned? (summarizes what has been learned)

To expand on your use of primary sources, step back and review the possible "people" sources immediately available to you. These include friends, family, faculty, business people, etc. As you focus in on the central research question, broaden your research arena by contacting and interviewing those people at hand who are good sources of information.

**Pre-search techniques: brainstorming, clustering, and mapping**

There are several pre-search activities such as brainstorming and clustering that can be used to help establish the scope of research and to develop related areas of inquiry. When brainstorming, searchers ask, "What comes to mind when I think about this topic?" All possibilities are written down in individual words or phrases, and all ideas are acceptable; evaluation of the ideas comes at a later stage. The purpose of brainstorming is to generate a wide range of possible approaches (see the section about brainstorming presented earlier in this chapter).

After brainstorming, the next step is to place the ideas into logical clusters. These are organized into a *map* to which you can refer during the research process. Mapping is an organized visual representation of ideas that are viewed graphically as a whole. The map becomes the guide to locating significant information.

**Formulating a central search question**

Whatever the impetus for seeking and using information, there is an advantage to formulating a central question as the first step of the quest. Thinking in terms of a question to be answered rather than a "topic" provides focus for the search.

Develop a preliminary central question or thesis statement by using a variety of questioning strategies such as yes/no, open-ended, and probing to create possible questions related to the identified need for information.

A research question should meet the following criteria. The question should be:

- specific,
- focused,
- manageable,
- measurable,
- meaningful, and
- have limits (where an "end" is visible).

**What do I already know about the topic or question?**

The process begins with thoughtful consideration of what is already known that is related and useful. Begin to make notes of key words, concepts, and names related to the search question. Focus on the research question.

After that, there may be a need to consult general sources and knowledgeable people to add to the list of key words and concepts. It is important to distinguish this step from the beginning of the search itself so that attention is focused on relationships and key terms, rather than on factual detail.

**Gathering information**

Select the most useful parts of the gathered information. By scanning and skimming, you can avoid wasting time with bits of information that are not useful in answering the central question.

One reliable test, again the best test, of your understanding of a piece of information is your ability to paraphrase it accurately. Developing habits of summarizing and paraphrasing in taking notes makes you think about and interpret information at the time it is accessed, not later when context clues are missing.

In emphasizing the essence, rather than the form, of note taking, it is important to teach the organizing or indexing of paraphrased notes according to the search questions (or working outline). In some cases, drawing diagrams, making audio recordings, or collecting artifacts may be used, rather than notes, as important means of preserving information.

**Evaluating information**

- Read, view, or listen to sources, identifying main ideas, opinions, and supporting facts. Inconsistencies are noticed and questioned.

- Interpret graphic sources for information: maps, charts, pictures, diagrams, graphs, tables, etc. Inaccuracies are discovered and rejected.

- Derive valid inferences from information sources. Substitute new ideas when information is inaccurate.

- Summarize and paraphrase important facts and details that support the central question. Compile notes/information according to the outline previously developed. Create new conclusions from facts using different perspectives. Review compiled information to bring personal meaning and understanding to the original problem, topic, or question.

# Study Skills

In this section of the chapter, topics related to effective study habits and techniques are discussed in detail. Topics include note-taking (including note-taking from written texts), preparing for various kinds of exams, and strategies for taking different types of tests and exams.

## Note-taking

Note-taking is a common activity that most students do during class (especially lectures) or when reading a textbook. However, note-taking is rarely taught or practiced. Consider your note-taking ability and the notes you take. How complete are your notes? Do they capture the main points in a way that helps you clarify, simplify, and understand what you've heard or read? Would they help you pass an exam on the material? Could you use the outline created from your notes to teach someone else the information captured in it?

For many students, note-taking is simply copying information from the blackboard, trying to get down every word the instructor says, or directly rewriting sentences from a textbook. Not surprisingly, poor note-taking often leads to poor performance on exams. It is important to realize that effective note-taking should always include active listening, thinking, learning, and questioning. Good note-taking techniques require you to be active and engaged in the learning process. You must concentrate on what you are hearing or reading, organize and rephrase ideas, and distinguish between important and unimportant information. Also, writing and putting information in your own words increases comprehension and understanding of the material.

There is no one correct way to take notes but the following are some general guidelines to follow.

**General suggestions for good note-taking**

*Distinguish between reading notes and lecture notes.*

By taking your reading notes on yellow pads of paper, you can easily distinguish them from lecture and discussion notes typically taken on white paper. This allows for your notes to be filed together and remain easily distinguishable. You'll always know the difference between your "yellow pages" and "white pages."

*Take notes on only one side of the page.*

This gives you the option of spreading out your notes to see all that you have, without having to turn over pages and check for material.

*Write legibly without too much information on a page.*

Your notes will be of little value if you are not able to read and make sense of what you have written. Also, avoid using a pencil that tends to smear more easily than a pen.

*Use headings to identify main points.*

Topic headings organize the material in your notes and make it possible to quickly find and identify the four or five most important ideas or pieces of information. Make use of indenting to visually identify the relative importance, ordering, and structure of information. (See the section in this chapter on outlining for more discussion.)

**Table 6.6**

| Common Abbreviations | |
|---|---|
| & | and |
| e.g. | for example |
| i.e. | to say |
| w/o | without |
| w | with |
| pg | page |
| ex | example |
| vs | versus |
| esp | especially |
| fig | figure |
| info | information |
| sq | square |
| ft | foot |
| km | kilometer |
| oz | ounce |
| F | Fahrenheit |
| C | Celsius |
| yr | year |
| hr | hour |
| k | thousand |
| = | equal |
| # | number |
| > | greater than |
| < | less than |
| $ | dollar |

*Write complete notes.*

This does not mean that you should take down everything from your source word for word, although you will occasionally want to record an especially well-worded or stimulating phrase or quotation. It is usually best to paraphrase as much as possible. This will help reduce dependence on the source and encourage your own analysis of material. However, even when paraphrasing, make sure to preserve the original intent of your source.

*Use abbreviations to save time and extra writing.*

Become familiar with standard abbreviations that can save you extra writing. Abbreviating can also help you keep up with your instructor during lecture situations. Some common abbreviations are shown in Table 6.6 to the left. Many more abbreviations exist and can be used depending on your particular needs. You can invent your own abbreviations. However, make them obvious to you so you do not forget what they mean.

*Leave space for a "recall" column.*

Leave an inch or two of empty space at the left side of your notes to use when you go back and review your notes. Use this space for writing key terminology, predicting possible exam questions, noting material about which you are unclear, as well as other writing notations which will remind you of something or stimulate your thoughts. Refer to this column when preparing for an exam.

*Put the date, main topic(s), the source and page number at the top of your notes.*

By putting this information at the top of your notes, it will help keep your notes better organized and make it easier when you review and study the material in the future. When you have many pages of notes, it is helpful to number and date the pages. If you are taking notes from materials other than your textbook, you should clearly identify the source. In the case of other books, identify the title of a book, author, publisher, place and date of publication. In the case of a journal or magazine article, identify the title, author, and name and date (including number) of the journal.

*Organize your notes according to the topic rather than the source.*

When you reread your notes, all the material about a topic should be in one place. This is especially useful when your notes come from several different sources such as lectures, textbooks, magazine and journal articles, and Internet sites.

*The Learning Assessment Journal can be used for note taking.*

The Collection Point form in the *Learning Assessment Journal* can be used for notes from lectures, meetings, and presentations. Use the Reading Log form when you are reading new text material.

## Note-taking from Written Text

The process of note-taking from written material (as compared to notes taken from a lecture) directly parallels the process of reading. Since so much of note-taking involves reading, you'll notice that the Reading Methodology presented in Chapter Seven can be applied to the process of note-taking.

### Skim

Before starting to take notes, skim the pages to get an overview of what is being presented by the author. By looking for the subheadings, you can obtain a mental outline of the reading. Notice items printed in bold or italic, for they may give you cues to important information you should know. Using these cues helps you focus on the most important information and avoid copying too much material from a text. (See the section about skimming presented earlier in this chapter.)

### Outline Basic Structure and Complete the Outline

Many people find using an inset system for outlining major and minor points works best for them. With this method, the main heading, often in uppercase capital letters, is placed at the margin. The next subheading(s) is (are) indented or inset away from the left margin. The less important the subheading, the further away it is from the left margin. The next main heading is placed back at the margin and the system follows the same pattern for the next subheading(s) and so on.

Two common methods of inset outlining are the *dot-dash method* of outlining and a method using *Roman and Arabic numbers along with upper and lower case letters*.

The example in Table 6.7 illustrates the dot-dash method of outlining. The outline is for a chapter in a text about an educational philosophy called Process Education. Note that you can start the outline with either dots or dashes. Many public speakers who present from notes tend to use the dot-dash method, along with a larger than normal typeface making it easier to read the information and keep their place when glancing down.

Table 6.7

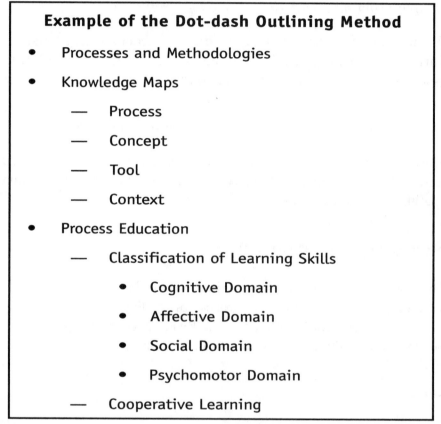

**Example of the Dot-dash Outlining Method**

- Processes and Methodologies
- Knowledge Maps
  — Process
  — Concept
  — Tool
  — Context
- Process Education
  — Classification of Learning Skills
    - Cognitive Domain
    - Affective Domain
    - Social Domain
    - Psychomotor Domain
  — Cooperative Learning

The pattern for using Roman and Arabic numerals, and upper and lower case letters is presented in Table 6.8. Main headings use Roman numerals. The capital letter "A" identifies the first sub-heading, "B" the second sub-heading and so on. The Arabic number "1" identifies the first main point under a sub-heading, "2" the second main point and so on. The small letter "a" identifies the first supporting detail of a main point.

A final word about outlining. Be sure to include enough information in your outline to make it meaningful. One-word notes are much less valuable than meaningful phrases when it comes to studying and reviewing material.

Table 6.8

**Roman Numeral, Letter and Number Outline Style**

I.    Main Heading

      A.    First sub-heading

          1.    First main point

              a.    supporting detail

              b.    supporting detail

          2.    Second main point

              a.    supporting detail

              b.    supporting detail

      B.    Second sub-heading

II.    Second Main Heading

## Read and Question

Think of questions you would like answered as you read and take notes. It is also a good idea to jot down questions when you skim a reading. By asking questions, it helps you focus your note-taking on material that you find worthwhile and reliable. Questions you raise during your reading can be used to assure that your notes are accurate. Note that the words *what, who, where, when, why* and *how* can help trigger questions you might want to ask in connection with a reading.

Compare your notes taken from a reading with those of someone in your class. You may be surprised at the differing opinions (reflected in what is written) about what was important. You can often improve your notes by sharing and combining notes with another person. This allows you to clarify points and add any important omissions.

## Highlighting

Highlighting can be an effective study technique which makes it easier and quicker to reread and review written material. You can focus your study and review time on the most important material, spending less time on or completely skipping unmarked sections. This can be especially valuable when many chapters of material are covered for an exam. Highlighting keeps you alert as you read. Highlighting requires that you make decisions continually about what is important, and should be highlighted, and what is not important. Effective highlighting involves a balance between highlighting too much and not highlighting enough. Since it is much faster and easier to highlight material (than to write notes), many readers make the mistake of highlighting too much text. If you are not careful, entire sections that could be summarized in one or two sentences can become bright blocks of ink.

The following are a few suggestions for highlighting.

- Read a paragraph first before doing any highlighting. Try to avoid highlighting a sentence as you are first reading it. Read and then assess what should be highlighted.

- Highlight meaningful phrases and the most important parts of sentences.

- As a general rule, if the material is important enough to be in your notes, then it should also be highlighted.

- Highlighting should include key words, lists, definitions, formulas, and examples.

Try these suggestions and decide what works for you. Whatever you decide, if you highlight, you must be prepared to read and reread the highlighted lines to help you learn the material.

### Note Cards

A good method for organizing information is to write your notes on file cards. Note cards provide a flexible way of organizing and recording information because they can be easily sorted. Note cards are especially useful for learning new terminology. Limit the amount of information on any one card. When applicable, identify the source on each card including the name and the page number. Regularly compare your notes to your outline to determine where you have accumulated enough support and where you still need to find more.

### Evaluate Your Notes

Periodically assess your notes. A good time to assess your note-taking is after a graded exam is returned. Check to see how many answers to exam questions can be found in your notes. You can do this for notes taken from lectures and those from reading the textbook. This process of assessment is how you improve your note-taking skills and your future test scores.

## Preparing for Tests and Exams

Exams and tests are a common means of evaluation used in college. Although exams may not always be the best way to demonstrate what you know, it is important for you to take your performance on exams seriously because for many courses in college, exam results are the main contributor to a final grade. Also, final grades are used by graduate schools and potential employers as a main  component in their evaluation of your abilities. Proper preparation is the best way to ensure good performance. Table 6.9 outlines a useful methodology for preparing for exams and tests.

The process of preparing for exams has many parallels to the Information Processing Methodology. This should not be surprising since exam preparation involves gathering and learning information. An abbreviated and modified version of the Information Processing Methodology leads to a simple model for preparing for exams. While specific preparation varies depending on factors such as the type of exam and the individual preparing for the exam, the methodology provides some general guidelines to follow.

Table 6.9

| **Methodology for Preparing for an Exam** |
| --- |
| 1.  Gather information. |
| 2.  Assess resources. |
| 3.  Plan your time. |
| 4.  Monitor and assess your performance implementing the plan. |
| 5.  Review performance. |

## Gather Information

*Mark on a calendar the dates for the exams in all your courses.* You may want to highlight these dates. The syllabus for each course should provide the dates, and, in some cases, information about the exam itself. Marking a calendar in this manner gives you an idea of how frequently exams occur and helps you be aware of situations when several exams are scheduled very close together, or perhaps even on the same day.

*Find out information about the exam.* The more you know about an exam, the better you can prepare. You should try to know what type of exam you will be given, the amount of time you will have to complete the exam, the range of possible material covered, the total number of questions, and how the points are distributed among the questions.

The most common types of exams are multiple choice, matching, true-false, completion, short answer, essay, and problem-based. While general study strategies apply to all exams, the factors mentioned above influence how you prepare. For example, preparing for an essay exam is quite different than preparing for a true-false or problem-based exam. *Your preparation should take into account a self-assessment of exam preferences. Assess which types of exam you typically do well on and which types you have more difficulty with.*

The more time allowed, and the greater the number of questions on the exam, the greater the likelihood that you will see more "picky" details. On the other hand, if the amount of material covered is extensive and the number of questions asked are few, the exam will more than likely cover primarily main ideas and concepts.

**Assess Resources and Develop a Plan**

Develop a plan to manage your study and review time, and then follow through on your plan. A key component to your plan is allocating time to prepare adequately for an exam. Students who manage their time well, spread out their learning and take an organized approach to studying and exam preparation. In other words, they treat exam preparation as an ongoing process rather than something that is accomplished "the night before" the exam date. In contrast, students who don't effectively manage their time are often in situations where too much is left to the last minute and the result is panic, work overload, and poor exam results.

Note that good time management takes into account dealing with and scheduling (or rescheduling) other responsibilities which might interfere or converge with exam preparation.

The following are some **guidelines to help you develop a plan.**

1. *It is more effective to study over a longer period of time rather than all at once immediately before the test.* The more frequently you review material (daily), the more familiar you will become with it and the less time you will have to spend preparing at the last minute. Soon after a class, try to review material presented in that class because after 24 hours, what has been covered and learned is more rapidly forgotten. Summarize and regularly review key concepts and terms (before class starts, while doing laundry, at the end of study sessions) to improve your familiarity, mastery, and recall of the material.

2. *Look at how many chapters and topics are covered on the exam.* Divide the material that must be studied and reviewed and *allocate the time appropriately.* Allow more time for older material that may not be as familiar to you and to material which gave you difficulty in the past. Realize that with practice your study time estimates for chapters and topics will improve. In general, the more you assess your performance, the more your performance will improve.

3. *For most people, their effectiveness begins to drop after an hour or two without any type of break.* You should assess your own study effectiveness over time. Plan to study the most difficult material when you are most alert and not at the end of a long study session. Avoid marathon study sessions because there are limits to your ability to concentrate.

4. *Understand the differences between important (major) themes and concepts in a course and minor or supporting themes.* The material in a course can be viewed similar to a map or a puzzle with many pieces (major and minor themes or topics) fitting together. Your time is best spent making sure you first understand the major concepts before going on to the minor or more focused topics. In many cases, unless you fully understand the main concepts, you will have difficulty comprehending the sub-concepts.

**Assess and Monitor Plan and Performance**

*Your growth and improvement are dependent upon your willingness and ability to assess your performance.* The "SII Method," which involves looking for strengths, areas for improvement, and insights gained, is a useful model to follow (see Chapter Thirteen for more information). The following are some questions to ask during the assessment process. How effective was your study plan? How closely did you follow the plan? Did you adapt and change the plan as needed during the time you were preparing for the exam? What did you learn from the experience that you can apply to future situations?

**Study Strategies and Techniques**

*Use more than one method or study strategy when preparing for an exam.* The more actively engaged you are in learning and preparing for an exam, the better will be your understanding of the material and the more likely you will be to do well on the exam. In other words, your exam preparation needs to go beyond simply "reading over" the material.

Below are some strategies for preparing for exams. Obviously, you won't use all of these techniques for any one exam. You may find that some strategies work well for one class or type of exam but not for another. Experiment and try these techniques. Assess what works best for you in the different situations you encounter.

1. *Study in a group* and utilize the benefits of cooperative learning. Form a study group for a particular class and put to use what you have been learning in this course about working in teams. Make use of team roles, and agree to hold each member accountable.

2. *Create a study checklist as part of your plan.* This list should include all the tasks you need to accomplish that are associated with preparing for the exam. Check off the items as you do them and use the list as a device to keep you on track.

3. *Create summary sheets.* Rewrite, condense, and summarize the information for each topic. Refer to your class notes, the textbook, and other resources when constructing a summary sheet. Go back through the material and write a summary outline. This requires you to think critically, organize, and assess your understanding of the material.

4. *Create vocabulary lists* or cards as a course progresses, not just prior to an exam. Each subject area has its own terminology which you must learn to correctly use. Often, definitions are part of the exam. Even if there are no questions requiring a definition, you are expected to know the meaning of terms, and this understanding is necessary to answer questions which appear on the exam. As you encounter new terms, add them to a vocabulary list (or a separate card for each term) with definitions that you can regularly review and refer back to. (*Note: there are designated glossary pages in the Learning Assessment Journal*).

5. *Create concept maps.* Concept maps are tools that present a visual picture or map of a single concept or idea, or show the relationship between several concepts within a subject area. Concept maps are useful in making distinctions between major and minor points. The use of concept maps also accommodates various learning styles, especially visual learners.

6. *Take practice tests.* The idea here is to get practice taking the type of exam you will face as well as test your understanding of the material. You can create your own exams by writing questions or problems you think your instructor will ask. Sometimes old exams are available to first practice and then study from. If the test you will be taking is problem-based, you can get practice by doing additional problems in your textbook or going to the library and getting another textbook which has new problems in the same subject area. Some students find study guides that accompany a textbook or a course helpful.

7. *Use practice charts, diagrams, and maps.* For tests that require you to fill in a diagram or a map, the best way to prepare is to start with a blank diagram or map, and then work to fill in the answers. You may have to recreate the diagram, in some cases several times. However this method is far more effective than simply staring at a diagram and trying to learn what goes where.

8. *Write down questions to go over with your instructor.* Remember that your instructor is a resource to help you, whether you make an appointment during his or her office hours, use part of the class time, or send a question via e-mail. While your instructor can't do the learning for you, your instructor probably can help when questions still remain after using other resources.

**Preparing for Essay Exams**

Essay exams require you to write paragraph-style answers to questions. The following are some general ideas for preparing for essay exams.

1. Sometimes professors will give a list of questions or possible questions ahead of time. This allows you to focus your preparation in certain subject areas. In situations where you don't know the questions, it's best to predict the questions yourself. You should predict and prepare for several more questions than will actually be on the exam. The more questions you prepare for, the more likely you will do well on the exam.

   Knowing the amount of material covered and the number of questions on the exam should help you in preparing for exams. When more material is covered, and fewer questions are asked, you can expect to find broad questions. Refer to the section on *Test-Taking Strategies* to become familiar with the key task words commonly found in essay questions. It is to your advantage to predict and then practice with challenging questions.

2. After predicting questions, you must use your information processing skills to gather and organize information which will be used in response to the question. Make sure the information you are gathering actually answers the question. The key task word in the question (e.g., compare, discuss, evaluate) determines how the answer should be constructed. When preparing an answer, it is best to start with outlines or lists rather than use sentence/paragraph form.

3. Study and learn the information you have gathered and organized so that you can reproduce it on the exam. Review your outline frequently to learn the main points you want to communicate. Practice writing out your answers in sentence form, especially for the more difficult questions. This helps you to overcome the common problem of not being able to start writing something.

## Test-Taking Strategies

Most courses in college require you to take exams or tests of some kind, whether it be multiple choice, essay, problem solution, matching, or short-answer. While good preparation is the most important criterion for good test performance, a person's test-taking ability also influences the overall score. By learning and applying basic strategies and techniques along with proper test preparation, you can improve your test-taking skills, build greater confidence, and achieve higher test scores.

### General advice when taking any exam

1. *Pay attention to the oral directions given by the instructor, and carefully read the written instructions on the exam.* By simply following the correct instructions, you put yourself in a position to avoid unnecessary and costly mistakes which can hurt your score. Note that instructions or directions may not be the same for the entire test.

2. *Once you receive the exam, take a moment to scan it.* Look at the form or formats (essay, multiple choice, problem solution, etc.). You should have some idea of this before taking the exam, but verify what the instructor has included. Also, check how many questions or problems there are as well as the point value for each section or question.

3. *Budget your time and pace yourself based on the number of questions and their point value.* Allocate your time according to the point value for the questions or sections of the test. In other words, if the essay questions account for 75% of the total score and multiple-choice questions account for the other 25%, then you should spend approximately 75% of the total exam time on the essay questions. Allow some time at the end for review. Be sure to wear a watch.

4. *Do not always answer the questions in the order they are written on the test.* Answer the questions you know first. At the beginning, don't spend too much time on questions you don't know the answers to. Mark the questions that you are unsure of so that you can come back to them later. By answering the questions you know first, you will be sure to get credit for what you do know, should time run out. Also, this helps to build your confidence early on. In general, make notations on the pages (if permitted) to assist you when you go back through the exam.

5. *Be on the lookout for information presented in other questions* that might help you answer questions that you don't know, or are unsure of.

6. *Before turning in your exam, review the entire exam.* Rethink through the problems or questions and verify your answers. Review to find questions you may have misread or misinterpreted. When computation is involved, check for careless errors and look to see if your answers make sense or are realistic. Don't be in a rush to leave immediately. It is well worth your time to take these few extra minutes.

7. *When using a computerized answer sheet, periodically check to make sure the number of the question matches the number on the answer sheet.* Also, be careful not to place any extraneous marks on the answer sheet.

**Tips for taking MULTIPLE CHOICE exams**

1. Carefully read the directions to make sure only one answer/choice is correct per problem. In a few cases, multiple choice exams are created where more than one answer per question may be correct.

2. Answer the obvious or easy questions first. Mark the questions you don't immediately know so that you can quickly return to these questions after answering the questions you do know. Also, remember that material in the exam may give you clues that help you answer or eliminate responses to earlier questions.

3. Read all the answers/choices before selecting the one you feel is correct. Sometimes two answers may be similar with just a slight modification making the difference between right and wrong answers. Also, one answer may be more complete or more correct than another.

4. Eliminate answers that are clearly wrong. This allows you to make a better guess if needed, increasing the chances you will select the correct answer. Check to make sure that the scoring of the exam does not penalize you for making guesses. If there is no penalty for guessing, you should always make a guess rather than leave the question blank.

5.  Read carefully when questions and/or answers contain words such as *always, never, not, except,* and *but.* Careful interpretation of these words can often make the difference between getting the question right or wrong.

6.  Sometimes multiple choice exams will include "none of the above" and "all of the above" choices. Realize that if you can eliminate even one answer, then "all of the above" can also be eliminated, and that if at least one choice is correct, you can eliminate "none of the above" also.

**Tips for taking TRUE-FALSE exams**

1.  Carefully read the directions to determine how you are to mark the exam (T or F, True or False, 1 or 0). Also, note if the instructor requires that false statements be corrected to make them true.

2.  Realize that for a question to be true, every part and detail within the question must be true.

3.  Statements containing absolute words such as *always, all, never, none, only,* and *every* are many times false, while statements that include less definite terms such as *frequently, may, can, sometimes, rarely, some, many,* and *few* suggest that the statement may be true.

4.  Reread sentences which contain a double negative to eliminate the negative, and then determine whether the statement is true or false. Double negatives generally include the word "not" along with another word which contains a negative prefix (in, un, ir, or il). Simply drop the word "not" and the negative prefix. For example, "not incomplete" is the same as "complete," "not irreversible" is the same as "reversible."

5.  Don't spend too much time on true-false questions since each individual question is usually not worth many points.

**Tips for taking MATCHING exams**

1.  Carefully read directions. Usually a choice may be used only once, but some exams allow for a choice to be used more than once.

2.  Before beginning to match, review all the information in the two columns (the terms and the descriptions). Then begin working from the column or side which contains the most writing (the descriptions). It takes less time to read a description and then look through the terms column to find the correct term than to start with the term and then read all the descriptions.

3. First, match up the terms of which you are sure. It is important to avoid making an error early in a matching exam because if you do, it is likely to lead to several more mistakes.

4. When you are unsure, eliminate choices which you know are not correct to improve your chances of choosing the correct one from the remaining alternatives. Realize that matching exams are harder than multiple choice and true-false to guess correctly.

5. Review and check your work to make sure all questions have been matched, and that you have put the response in the correct place.

6. Look for grammar clues. Processes, people, and inanimate objects often need to be matched to descriptions from a set of descriptions. It is usually easy to sort these descriptions into the three categories (processes, people, objects), thus cutting down the choices for each term.

**Tips for taking ESSAY exams**

1. Carefully read the directions. Identify how many questions you are required to answer. In many cases, you may choose which questions to answer rather than being required to answer them all. Also, note any length limitations or instructions to write on only one side of a page or every other line.

2. Know how many points each question is worth. This helps you to budget your time and gives you some indication about the appropriate length of your answer. Obviously, you should spend more time and write more for a 40-point question than a 20-point question. Budget your time according to the point value and wear a watch.

3. Read the entire question looking for and underlining key words on the test page that will help you in constructing your answer. In other words, be sure you are answering the right question, or answering it in the manner which the instructor wants or requires. Knowing the key task word in an essay question helps you to focus, avoid misinterpretation, and improve your answers and test scores. A list of some frequently used terms is presented in Table 6.10. You should become familiar with these terms and their meanings.

4. Plan your answer before you write. The key task word should set the direction for how you construct your answer. Construct a brief outline (in a couple of minutes) and include any notes or ideas which come to you as you first read the question. Should you not have time to finish writing a response, there is the possibility of getting some credit for having an outline with accurate and correct information. Validate this with your instructor before taking the exam.

5. Write focused, organized answers. Avoid writing sentences just to fill space. Use your outline to present the most important, pertinent facts and information. Your answer should begin with a topic sentence. One technique to help you get started and stay focused is to begin your answer by restating the question in the form of a statement. Next write the main points and sentences to support your main points. Offer a conclusion or summary of your main points at the end. Write legibly as neatness may influence the grading.

6. Allow time to proof-read what you have written for spelling and grammatical errors.

Table 6.10

| Key Task Words for Essay Exams | |
|---|---|
| analyze | Divide something into separate parts to better understand the whole and see how the parts work together. |
| compare | Tell how two or more things are similar or alike. |
| contrast | Tell how two or more things are different. |
| define | Give the meaning or definition to a word or phrase - not an example. |
| describe | Provide details, characteristics, and qualities about a subject. |
| discuss or explain | Examine in a broad, detailed way using evidence, supporting points, reasons, and examples; may involve telling why or how something came to be. |
| evaluate | Present the strengths and weaknesses of a topic and then give your opinion or make a judgment. |
| illustrate | Give examples which relate ideas to actual experience. |
| justify | Show evidence or give proof to support or back up a point, decision, or conclusion. |
| outline | Describe and present the main ideas or points in a logical order. |
| relate | Show the connection or relationship between things - how each depends on the other. |
| summarize | Give a brief review of the main points along with any conclusions, omitting unnecessary details. |
| trace | Describe the order of events as they occurred, a narrative of sorts. |

# Performance Levels for Listening

### Level 5        Quality Listeners

1. Are self-motivated in every context, regardless of benefit, and focus on maximizing others' messages.

2. Will vary the sequencing of classifying and comprehending to specific contexts; expand word meaning to increase the effectiveness of both the sender and listener.

3. Navigate easily in the language of the sender, leveraging each key word, and selecting the most important details.

4. Prepare by obtaining the appropriate knowledge for a given sender and use this knowledge to effectively compare and contrast their new information with this knowledge.

5. Correctly interpret the politics, emotions, and values of the sender and clearly frame the context for the message.

### Level 4        Effective Listeners

1. Seek long-term benefit for themselves and others; can recall accurately and give meaning to meet each other's purposes.

2. Understand the meaning of the message by effectively classifying the information into their existing framework, processing the language being used and thinking critically about implied relationships.

3. Comprehend language keys and phrases, and carefully select important specifics to build a story.

4. Have continual interest in expanding horizons, seek background knowledge in preparation, and know how to evaluate, compare, and contrast new information into their background.

5. Understand the context of the sender and his/her values and signals, so that they can place meaning to nonverbals.

### Level 3        Maintenance Listeners

1. Will listen when it is to their immediate benefit; they can obtain most of what is being conveyed.

2. Know what they want to collect; discard what they don't want; fit in what they do want, comprehending a portion of the message relevant to the listener's goals.

3. Understand the importance of key words and will collect specifics for building a strong information base.

4. Will find short-cuts to obtain the minimal information necessary to make some sense of the message.

5. Have some understanding of the sender's values and catch the essential signals made by the sender.

**Level 2    Survival listeners**

1. Will listen when critical needs are identified so they can apply it to their immediate needs.

2. Selectively choose information that is relevant for immediate critical use; they can fit information within the current defined structure and bring meaning to what is relevant to the current context.

3. Will focus on only the most prominent words of the sender and collect the most obvious details presented.

4. Operate with a surface knowledge and see only blatant similarities and contrasts.

5. Only explore the motivation of the sender when it directly impacts critical areas or matches personal values.


**Level 1 Novice (clueless) listeners**

1. Only listen when directed; find anything beyond momentary concentration difficult.

2. Have little structure to classify incoming information; find comprehension extremely difficult; must have the sender slow down the process of communicating and repeat much of the message.

3. Are unfamiliar with the sender's language and have difficulty distinguishing any specific details from context.

4. Have little background knowledge and make little, if any, connection between the message and prior knowledge.

5. Have little background understanding of where the sender is coming from and miss most signals.

# Discussion Questions

## Preparing for Tests and Exams

1. In general, when should you begin to prepare for an exam?

2. As you begin preparing for an exam, what information should you try to obtain?

3. What are four study techniques that work well for you (or which ones do you plan to use in the future)? Why do you find them useful?

4. How does knowing the type of exam you will be taking help you to study?

5. In what ways would you expect your knowledge of course content to be different in order to do well on a true-false exam as compared to an essay exam?

6. Why are managing time and having a plan important to effective exam preparation?

7. What are the advantages to being part of a study group when preparing for an exam? What makes a study group effective?

8. What are the differences and similarities in preparing for exams in different disciplines (e.g., preparing for an exam in a math course as compared to an exam in a literature course)?

*Task:* When preparing for your next exam, keep notes and a calendar regarding what you did. Afterwards, assess your performance indicating strengths, areas for improvement (with how to make improvements for the next exam) and insights you gained.

## Test-taking Strategies

1. Why should you answer the easy questions first and then come back to the harder questions later?

2. What three items of general test-taking advice do you feel are most important and why?

3. What can you do to be more effective the next time you take each of the following types of exams: multiple choice, true-false, matching, and essay?

4. What is the best test-taking advice you can offer a friend who is about to take an essay exam?

5. Why is it important to look for key words in both the questions and the choices? Cite an example for two different types of exams.

6. Why is time management important to doing well on exams?

7. How well do exam scores *really* reflect what a person has learned in a course? How are exams effective? What are limitations of exams?

*Task:* Predict your score on exams immediately after taking them. See if you can make your predictions more accurate over time. Keep a journal with assessments of your performance noting strengths, areas for improvement, and insights.

# Chapter 7

# Reading Skills

> Reading is to the mind what exercise is to the body.
> — *Sir Richard Steele, Irish-born, British essayist and dramatist, 1672–1729*

## Connection between Reading and Writing Processes

The next two chapters are devoted to two key processes that are an integral part of your college experience—reading and writing. In fact, these two processes are closely linked. Reading is crucial to strong writing and writing is crucial to effective reading. This cyclical reading/writing process is a key to successful academic performance.

While the connection between good reading and writing skills and success in college is quite obvious, it is important to realize that the ability to apply and use these two processes significantly influences your performance in other areas, especially when it comes to communicating. In fact, most all the methodologies presented in this book draw upon or require proficiency with reading and writing in some way. For example, good reading and writing skills are essential for creating definitions (of missions, problems, or purposes), collecting information, developing plans, and making assessments.

You learn to write well by reading other people's writing and assessing what works and what does not work for them. Also, you can think of most academic writing as participation in an on-going conversation with published sources on a particular topic. Thus, most of the academic writing you will be asked to do, will be in response to material you have read. When you have an assignment that asks you to write in response to a reading assignment, the *reading process* might also be the prewriting stage of the *writing process*.

Your reading process will vary depending on your task. Each of the following involves using a different approach to reading:

- reading a novel for a literature course,

- reading a novel on the beach for entertainment,

- reading an article as a source for a research paper,

- reading the newspaper at the breakfast table, and

- reading a textbook for a course.

# Improving Your Reading Skills

How strong are your reading skills? Since many students believe they are already good readers, a better question to ask is, would you like to improve your reading skills, regardless of your current reading ability?

While being able to read faster may improve your reading performance, building speed is not the main concern of this chapter. More important is that you are able to comprehend, retain, and apply what you read. For many students, the bottom line is that they would benefit greatly from simply retaining more of what they read.

Improving your effectiveness as a reader requires that you read *actively*. This means your eyes are not simply passing over words on a page but that you are *thinking* while processing the information you read. In order to get the most benefit from your study and reading time, you must be *critically engaged* without distractions. This applies to any reading where comprehension is important such as reading a textbook, your own notes, research sources, or laboratory data.

Language development skills are the foundation from which a person's reading process can be improved. Table 7.1 lists the skills from the *Classification of Learning Skills* that are associated with language development. The table includes general skills (e.g., building vocabulary) as well as specific skills (e.g., defining).

Table 7.1

| Language Development Skills | | | | |
|---|---|---|---|---|
| **Building vocabulary** | **Decoding communication** | **Understanding syntax** | **Identifying semantics** | **Identifying context** |
| defining | pattern recognition | word recognition | recognizing meaning | identifying cultural background |
| practice and usage | assigning meaning | proper use of grammar | recognizing connotations | identifying historical background |
| using contextual cues | recognizing symbols | proper use of sentence structure | using rhetoric | |

As proficiency with language development skills increases, so will a person's reading skills. Specifically, reading skills improve by:

- *building vocabulary*, being able to define and apply words;

- *decoding communication*, putting meaning to words and symbols (so that you understand and not just recognize);

- *understanding syntax*, properly using and grouping words in sentences;

- *identifying semantics*, recognizing the meaning of speech forms and grouping of words; and

- *identifying context*, understanding that words have different meanings in different contexts.

# Reading Methodology

The Reading Methodology presented in this chapter is a valuable tool that you can use to improve reading comprehension. In addition, there are some general guidelines that you can adapt to various reading situations. If you are to see improvement in your reading, you should be prepared to practice using the Reading Methodology often enough to get proficient with it. Don't let the fact that reading can sometimes be an unpleasant chore stop you from benefiting from this tool.

The Reading Methodology is a general methodology for reading. Realize that not every step is required for all reading contexts. Trying to use all the steps in the methodology in *all* contexts can lead to frustration and discourage you from using the methodology.

Initially focus on using the Reading Methodology in academic reading situations where it is an especially useful and appropriate guide to follow.

Table 7.2

| **Reading Methodology** | |
|---|---|
| 1.  Establish purpose. | Determine why you are reading the material. |
| 2.  Set objectives and criteria. | Determine what you want or need to get from the reading. |
| 3.  Estimate the time involved. | Browse the reading to determine the level of difficulty and how long it will take you to do the reading. |
| 4.  Read critically. | Carefully read and ask questions which involve: <br><br> – understanding vocabulary by keeping a dictionary nearby to look up unfamiliar words. Write down the definitions so you can refer back to them. <br><br> – determining the author's purpose, intended audience, and the genre or type of writing as you read. <br><br> – writing by taking notes and highlighting important passages, annotating in the margins and marking difficult passages. <br><br> – asking questions and forming opinions by jotting down questions you have, as well as the opinions you form as you read. |
| 5.  Assess and reread. | Assess your progress. Reread to clarify questions and ensure that objectives are met. |
| 6.  Synthesize information. | Integrate new information with your existing knowledge base. |

Table 7.3

| Reading Methodology — A Simple Example | | |
|---|---|---|
| **Scenario:** You subscribe to the daily newspaper. You pick up the morning newspaper and want to read the paper during breakfast. | | |
| 1. | Establish purpose. | Gain information about local, national, and world events. |
| 2. | Set objectives & criteria. | Read one article completely. |
| 3. | Estimate time. | You only have fifteen minutes for breakfast. Skim the main section of the paper to select which articles are of most interest to you. |
| 4. | Read critically. | Begin reading an article on health care legislation.<br><br>• Look up unfamiliar words as you read.<br><br>• Is the author's purpose to provide information, or is it to argue for or against proposed laws? How does this influence the presentation of the material?<br><br>• As you read, formulate questions regarding your own health coverage, and write these down. |
| 5. | Assess and reread. | Glance back over the article to reacquaint yourself with some of the facts. |
| 6. | Synthesize information. | You plan to read more about your own health care coverage and decide to discuss some points from another article with a friend. |

# Discussion of the Steps in the Reading Methodology

**Establish Purpose**

Before you begin reading, identify why you are reading, what you want to get out of the material, and how thoroughly you need to understand it. Determine if you are reading for a general idea or for details. The purpose will vary depending on the context, whether you are reading for a test, to complete an assignment, or for pleasure. By carefully defining your purpose, you can set your reading strategy to accomplish this purpose. For example, if you are reading for details, your reading speed will be slower than if reading for just a general idea or for pleasure. However, if you are reading only to get some idea of the main points, then skimming alone may be sufficient.

## Set Objectives and Criteria

Based on the purpose, set objectives and criteria which specify your expected outcome of the reading, i.e., what you want to accomplish. How the Reading Methodology is used will depend a great deal on the specific purpose and objectives. For example, if you are reading for leisure, your only objective may be to enjoy the reading. In this case, many of the steps of the methodology are not applicable. On the other hand, if you are studying for an exam, the purpose and use of the methodology are very different. All the steps of the methodology become important in this situation.

## Estimate Time

Consider the total amount of time you have available for the reading and compare it to the estimated time to complete the reading. Skim the reading to estimate the difficulty of the material and your familiarity with the material. Be sure to consider the level of difficulty as you budget your time. Remember, when reading for academic (rather than leisure) purposes, you will usually need to read through the text more than once. Make sure you schedule adequate time to allow you to do this.

## Read Critically

Mark the parts of the reading that are difficult, complex, or confusing. After reading through the material, refer back to the areas you've marked. Spend additional time working to build comprehension. The following will help you to read more critically.

*Build your vocabulary.*

Identify terminology in the reading that is unfamiliar to you. Write down these words and obtain the definitions. In effect, build your own glossary. You may also want to write notes and definitions to "key" words in the margins of your outline, your notes, and if allowed, in the reading itself.

*Get the big picture about what you are reading.*

As best you can, as you read, try to determine the author's purpose, intended audience, and the type of writing style. These factors influence what is being said and how it is being said. Different kinds of writing (e.g., a novel, play, poem, personal essay, lab report, newspaper article, or scholarly article) have different requirements that determine the form in which the material is presented. Similarly, the intended audience will determine the level of difficulty of the reading and how formal or informal the writing is. Take note of the author's purpose in writing, point of view or attitude toward the subject matter, and expertise.

> Nothing is worth reading that does not require an alert mind.
> —*Charles Dudley Warner, American editor and author 1829–1900*

*Write to help process what you read.*

Writing is a good way to process what you have read and to make it a lasting part of what you know (rather than something you forget right after a test or quiz). There are a variety of possibilities appropriate in different contexts. For example,

- take notes in a notebook,

- annotate the text by writing comments and notes in the margin of the text itself,

- summarize by condensing and recording the subject matter, without including your own questions and opinions, and

- write a response in a reading journal; summarize what you read but include your own thoughts, questions, and opinions.

Summarize and read your responses. This works well when you are reading sources for a research project. It is also helpful for courses based on class discussions of reading assignments. In these cases, you will have to represent what your source said as well as offer your own commentary on the source.

Summarize, annotate and take notes when reading textbook material that you will be tested on later. In these situations your personal opinion is usually less relevant than showing that you know the material. Many of you will find using a combination of these options will work best for you. There is more information about note-taking in Chapter Six.

*Ask questions and form opinions as you read.*

Ask and jot down questions you would like answered about the material. This increases your concentration and keeps you actively engaged in the reading. Critically engaged reading may mean that at times you are willing to disagree with or challenge the author. Write down these opinions too.

## Assess and Reread

Assess what you have read. Make modifications to your notes as needed. Summarize what you have gained from the reading. Determine if there are errors, inconsistencies, and pieces of information which are still unclear or missing. Reread what is needed to enhance understanding, clarify and answer questions that remain unanswered, and make sure that objectives for the reading are met.

## Synthesize Information

Make connections between what you are reading and other materials you have read. Also, make connections with other courses you have taken or are currently taking as well as connections with personal experience in other contexts in your life (e.g., at work or at home). Ask yourself, what questions does the reading raise for you that will require further reading and learning to answer? And how can I best make use of what I read?

No entertainment is so cheap as reading, nor any pleasure so lasting.
—*Lady Mary Wortley Montagu, English writer and poet 1689–1762*

# Example of the Reading Process

**Scenario:** Your political science instructor assigns two articles to read about the Vietnam War.

1. The purpose is to learn the basic history of the United States during the Vietnam War era and to understand why the war was controversial.

2. The objectives you establish are:

   - to read both articles completely, and

   - to retain most of what you read so you can participate intelligently in class discussion.

   The criteria you set for your performance are:

   - how your instructor and classmates respond to your comments in class the next day, and

   - your performance on a quiz covering the reading given at the beginning of class.

3. You skim the articles and estimate it will take you an hour to read each one. The reading level of each is somewhat difficult. You decide to read one this morning and the other later tonight.

4. As you read the articles, you highlight important points, put brackets around difficult passages, underline unfamiliar terms, and write your questions and comments in the margins. For each article, you look up unfamiliar vocabulary in a dictionary. You write the definitions in the margins near the word in question.

   You realize as you are reading that purpose, audience and type of writing are important factors in this reading. The essays are from the same book but are written by different authors. The book is a collection of essays written by different experts on the Vietnam War who have very different opinions. Both essays offer historical information, and each subtly argues a different position on the war. The audience is a general, educated audience. In addition to your notes in the margins, you write a brief summary of each article in a notebook. You also note specific points where the authors disagree with one another.

5. After reviewing definitions for new vocabulary, you reread difficult passages. When you have finished reading the second article, you go back to review an opposing argument offered by the first article.

6. After completing both articles, you find yourself agreeing with one author more than the other. Following the summaries of the articles you entered in your notebook, you write down the opinion you are forming in response to the reading and briefly explain why you feel as you do. A week later, you decide to watch a documentary on the Vietnam War on television to gain another perspective.

# Textual Analysis –
# Applying the Reading Process in the Humanities

Textual analysis is a reading practice employed by the humanities disciplines that includes academic approaches to literature, film and art. It is one application of the reading process that can be applied to a variety of cultural products which includes but is not limited to written work. Textual analysis differs from other reading tasks, such as reading literature for entertainment or reading a textbook, in that the *emphasis is on how a given text makes meaning*.

For example, when you analyze a literary text such as a novel, you pay special attention to the novel as a work of writing. However, when you read a chapter in your chemistry textbook, your primary purpose is to process the information presented and incorporate it into your own knowledge base. You probably pay very little attention to the chapter as an example of writing. Similarly, when you read a novel for entertainment, you may focus on digesting the story, but you may not concentrate on why the story appeals to you, or how the writing evokes a particular emotional response from its readers.

## Defining Terms

Before going further, let's take a moment to define what is meant by the following textual analysis terms.

| | |
|---|---|
| **Text** | an object to be interpreted through analysis; such as a literary text, a film, a work of art, or any cultural artifact. |
| **Medium** | the material or technique employed to create something. |
| **Analysis** | the process of critically engaging material to understand how it makes meaning. |
| **Genre** | designating a type of book, film, etc. which is distinguished by subject, theme, or style such as science fiction, mystery, etc. |
| **Narrative** | a story, which can be based on actual events, as in a biography which is a narrative of a person's life; or it can be fictional, which means the story does not claim to relate to actual events. |

## Applying Textual Analysis

The purpose here is to give you some basic tools of analysis so that you can approach any text and begin to read, interpret and understand that text. Then intellectual curiosity will lead you in any variety of directions.

## Identify your purpose as a reader

Your purpose or job as a reader is to make sense of the text. There are many approaches to textual analysis which define the reader's purpose slightly differently, but all require the reader to pay attention to details.

Making sense of a text might mean:

- interpreting the explicit message or content of the text,

- uncovering the taken-for-granted assumptions or hidden agendas that subtly inform the explicit message,

- bringing historical information to bear on the text,

- considering how the text engages social issues, and

- understanding the text as an example of a particular genre or type of text and paying close attention to how the formal conventions of the genre work in this instance.

These various approaches require different kinds of knowledge bases that the reader brings to the text. Depending on your purpose, which may be defined in part by a specific class assignment, you may have to do some research or secondary reading. In some cases, the knowledge base might be acquired during the class.

## Determine the main objective of the analysis

The objective of textual analysis is to develop an "interpretation" (also called a reading) of the text in question. Performance criteria reflect how well you can defend that interpretation with evidence relating to what you read. This evidence might include historical information and will usually include references to the text, such as quotations and paraphrases of key passages that support your reading.

## Utilize your time

Make sure you allow adequate time to complete the reading. With shorter, more difficult texts, you should plan to read the material more than once. For longer texts such as novels, you will probably not have time for more than one reading. In these cases, you should be sure to mark passages, annotate (take notes in the margins), and take good notes. This allows you to go back to key passages without needing to read through the entire novel again. For visual texts such as films, it is a good idea to get access to a video so that you can review key scenes. In the case of an art exhibit, you may need to plan more than one visit.

## Build your vocabulary

Reading literary texts is a good place to expand your vocabulary. Keep a dictionary nearby and look up unfamiliar words. Write down the definitions so you can refer back to them. In cases where it is not a written text (such as film, painting, or sculpture) try to become familiar with the basic conventions of the medium.

> The man who doesn't read good books has no advantage over the man who can't read them.
> —*Mark Twain, American journalist and novelist 1835–1910*

**Determine the scope of the reading**

What kind of text you are approaching will influence the clues you look for when analyzing it. At the most basic level, in a visual medium such as painting you will look for visual clues. While in a written medium you will look for language clues. In film or the performance of a play, consider the interaction of dialogue and visual clues.

Audience and purpose are also key factors in understanding any text. A text attempts to have some effect on an audience. Try to determine who the text addresses and who it may exclude. Also, determine how the text is trying to influence the audience. Is it to protest an injustice; memorialize or personalize history; provoke laughter or anger; create a shared sense of community; or, experiment with language and the formal characteristics of a genre of writing or artistic medium?

**Things to write down**

Take notes, highlight important passages, annotate in the margins, and mark difficult passages. In the case of literary forms where there are many characters, keeping a list with a brief description of each can be helpful. Also, summarizing and writing a response in a reading journal are good ways to help you remember and understand what you have read.

**Formulate questions and opinions**

You should actively question and form opinions as you read, rather than waiting until you are finished to do so. Key questions to ask as you read include:

- Who does this text address as its audience, who does it exclude, and how do you know?

- What picture of the world does this text present, and what pictures of the world does it exclude?

- When was the text written and why?

- How is this text relevant to the course in which it is assigned?

- What is most interesting about this text?

- If there are characters, try to understand their complexities, what motivates them, how they interact. Does the text elicit an emotional response, and if so, what is it and how is this response accomplished?

- How is this text relevant to current events, other texts you have encountered, material you have learned in other courses, your personal experiences?

**Assess and reread**

Assess your reading process and ask what assumptions influenced your reading. Reread to clarify questions. Assess the opinions you have formed and the responses to questions you have posed so that you can synthesize these into a developed interpretation.

**Synthesize information**

Synthesize your opinions, questions, and responses to the text to develop an interpretation (*a statement of what the text does or says*). Synthesize what you have learned from paying attention to the details to come up with a statement of the big picture (*in relation to the text in question*) and a justification (*a defense or proof*) of the accuracy of this statement. Also, determine what questions the reading raises (or leaves unanswered) which will require further reading and study.

## Example of Textual Analysis

**Scenario:** you must read and be prepared to discuss Frederick Douglas's *Narrative of the Life of Frederick Douglas* (1845) for an American Literature course.

Your *purpose* is to make sense of the text and to acquire a sense of its relevance to United States history and literature.

The *objectives* you establish are to:

- read the entire text,
- develop an interpretation as you read, and
- mark key passages in the text which support that interpretation.

The *criteria* for performance you set are:

- how well your comments are received by your instructor and classmates during the class discussion , and
- your performance on a final exam essay developing and supporting your interpretation of the text.

You *estimate the time* for reading, based on the size of the text, to be six hours. You will take two-hour sessions on three days to complete the reading.

As you read you look for new *vocabulary*. You encounter the word "abolition." You look it up and see that its use in the text refers to the nineteenth century movement to outlaw slavery in the United States.

You determine the *type of writing* to be an autobiography, which means it relates the story of the writer's life. The *purpose* of the text is to explain the injustices of slavery as experienced by the author. The *audience* is all U.S. citizens who can read, but especially those in the nineteenth century who had not yet decided to support abolition.

You *write* as you read. This includes highlighting important passages and writing your responses to the text in a reading journal. You *formulate questions and opinions*. You decide the text attempts to provoke horror and disgust at the practices of slavery in its readers. You also find the last section on religion somewhat confusing and decide to ask your instructor about it in class. You decide the text is important as an historical document of the nineteenth century, as well as an example of writing by an African American at a time when many African Americans did not have access to education.

You examine how your own assumptions informed your reading of the text. You *assess* how your previous knowledge of slavery and more generally, nineteenth century American culture informed your reading of the text. You assess what new knowledge about slavery or nineteenth-century American culture you acquired from the text. You also *reread* the passages you highlighted to prepare you for the synthesis stage of the Reading Methodology.

When *synthesizing information*, you decide that the text is an argument against slavery made by relating the story of a former slave's life. The writing is eloquent and educated, which works to counter the racist argument in favor of slavery that claimed slaves were ignorant and uncivilized and therefore could not be free participants in American society.

## SQ3R Reading Method

SQ3R is a well-known system for reading developed by psychologist Francis Robinson in 1941 as a tool for training World War II army recruits. SQ3R stands for **S**urvey, **Q**uestion, **R**ead, **R**ecite, and **R**eview.

### Survey

Before you begin reading, glance over the material. Focus on the title, subtitles, and headings to see the main points that will be developed. Also note any pictures, charts and graphs. Read the summary or last paragraph. This step should not take more than a couple of minutes (depending on the length of the reading) and should identify three to six "core" ideas. This orientation step should help you to organize the ideas as you read them later.

## Question

Turn the headings you read into questions (and then read to find the answers). The process of asking and writing down questions stimulates interest and increases comprehension. Draw upon and integrate prior knowledge as you read. If reading a textbook, anticipate possible test questions.

## Read

Read the material looking for answers to the questions you posed in the previous step. Actively read and search. Be aggressive rather than plodding along. Try to create meaning as you read.

## Recite

After reading and searching for answers to your questions, recite or record your answers. Use your own words rather than copying what you have read. Try to synthesize information. If necessary, refer back to the reading to gain clarity and understanding. Jot down cue phrases as you read to help jog your memory.

Continue the process of questioning, reading, and reciting as you work your way through the entire reading.

## Review

After completing the reading, review your notes and reinforce the main points. Reinforce the big picture and the relationships between the main points and major subpoints. Identify areas you need to spend more time with. You can test your memory by covering up your notes and trying to recall the main points.

**http://www.pcrest.com**

# Web Information about Improving Reading Skills

For more information about improving reading skills and the SQ3R method, go to Chapter Seven of the *Foundations of Learning* web site.

The Center for Academic Enrichment and Excellence at Virginia Tech University has a page titled *Techniques for Improving Reading Skills* which discusses skimming, scanning, and comprehension. There is also a link to the Academic Skills Center at Western Michigan University that describes reading a textbook using the SQ3R method.

# Writing Skills

> Our admiration of fine writing will always be in proportion to its real difficulty and apparent ease.
> — *Charles Caleb Colton, English poet, 1630–1687*

## Thoughts about Writing

Have you ever felt frustrated when doing a writing assignment? The words just don't flow and you struggle to get your thoughts on paper or on the computer screen. Or, you find it difficult to get started on a paper as thoughts of "how am I ever going to write ten pages?" fill your head.

Many of us, at one time or another have felt this way. It's quite natural considering that writing is not a trivial process and there is no quick, easy way to learn it. In fact, for some people, writing can be quite emotional. Frustration can build when the initial putting ideas down on paper does not come easily and the result is not a polished product. Also, with most forms of writing, you put yourself in a position to be evaluated and open to potential criticism from others.

Should you feel frustrated at times, don't let it affect the belief that you can be a skilled writer. The good news is, regardless of current ability, we can all improve our writing skills.

It definitely is to everyone's benefit to work to develop his or her writing skills. Good writing skills not only contribute to success in college, but are also an asset for most any professional career. On the other hand, poor writing skills can put you at a serious disadvantage. A few years ago, the University of Maryland polled 3,000 of its graduates. Nearly all respondents, including professors, lawyers, engineers, and police officers, reported spending at least 20% of their workweek writing; one in four reported spending at least 70% of their time writing.

The process of writing involves the interaction between reading, thinking critically, putting ideas down on paper, drafting those ideas into an appropriate form, and revising. Did you realize that writing in itself promotes learning? Studies have shown that students who write about what they are learning, learn the material more thoroughly and remember it better and longer. Just simply writing about a topic can stimulate critical thinking.

# Formal and Informal Writing

If you wish to be a writer, write.
— *Epictetus, Greek philosopher 50–130 A.D.*

**Formal writing** is writing that is meant to be read by someone other than the writer. Papers, reports, essays, articles, and books are examples of formal writing. Usually, formal writing is *evaluated* in some way. For example, instructors evaluate essay exams and term papers to determine the grade a student should receive. An admissions counselor at a college evaluates letters of application to help determine if an applicant is accepted or not. Job application letters are evaluated by hiring committees to determine if an applicant is granted an interview. Published writings in journals, newspapers, and books are evaluated by an editorial board before being accepted for publication. The writing methodology presented later in this chapter is useful for any *formal* writing task.

**Informal writing** is writing that is done for personal use and is not necessarily read or evaluated by others. Examples of informal writing include keeping a diary or a journal, taking lecture notes, taking notes on reading material, writing to brainstorm ideas, and writing entries into a *learning assessment journal.* In most cases, you do not need to use the Writing Methodology for informal writing. However, these types of informal writing can contribute to the development of formal writing skills.

# The Writing Process

Sometimes writing is viewed as simply the act of putting a pen to paper (or hands to the keyboard) and letting the thoughts flow. While this may be true for some types of informal writing, instant writing and "one-shot" drafts just don't work when it comes to formal writing.

**Did you know?**

Cradled by the Euphrates and Tigris Rivers in what is today Iraq, the Sumerians of Mesopatamia established the earliest known society in which people could read and write around 3000 B.C.

Writing is a process with multiple steps or stages. Even professional writers must prepare, plan, write, then rewrite, and produce multiple drafts before achieving a finished product. In fact, most published writing has been revised extensively and is not the author's first effort. Therefore, if professionals don't expect to get it right the first time, neither should you.

When you look at writing as a process, your main concern should not be the final product you produce but what you *think* and *do* to create the final product. For if you correctly apply a quality process, then the end result (of that process) will be of high quality.

That's where methodologies serve a valuable purpose in helping people learn to improve their use of processes. In this case, the Writing Methodology is a quality model that you can use to practice and improve your writing process.

# Writing Methodology

Consider the Writing Methodology as a valuable tool or guide that you can use to produce quality work when it comes to *formal writing*. The Writing Methodology simplifies the writing process by breaking it down into a series of manageable steps or stages. As you will see, there are various activities that a writer can use at each step depending on the particular writing task at hand.

While it is important to thoroughly follow the Writing Methodology and not skip steps, it is misleading to think that the steps in the methodology always occur in the same order. Realize that the steps overlap and can occur in a different order or even simultaneously.

Finally, the Writing Methodology is meant to enhance your writing. So while using the methodology, don't put any restrictions on your creativity and individual writing style!

Table 8.1

| | Writing Methodology | |
|---|---|---|
| 1. | Prepare for writing. | Read, write, research, brainstorm, and participate in classroom activities to form ideas for a writing topic. |
| 2. | Identify topic, purpose, and audience. | Decide what you will write about, why you are writing and who your writing addresses. |
| 3. | Perform exploratory writing. | Write to expand and develop your ideas without worrying about grammar, style or organization. |
| 4. | Compose a thesis statement. | Narrow your topic and write a statement that summarizes the ideas you want to discuss. |
| 5. | Devise a plan. | Organize your ideas by outlining. |
| 6. | Create a draft. | Craft sentences and paragraphs to develop your exploratory writing so it fits your plan. |
| 7. | Assess the draft. | Read your first draft and decide where it is strong and where it needs improvement. |
| 8. | Revise. | Reorganize paragraphs, clarify ideas, rephrase sentences. |
| 9. | Proofread. | Check spelling, grammar, and typos. Have someone else proofread, time permitting. |
| 10. | Produce a final copy. | Produce the final copy. |

# Using the Writing Methodology

Writing is a cyclical process, rather than one that follows each step in order. This means that the process you follow will vary with each specific writing task, and you may move back and forth between steps several times. For example:

- You might compose a thesis statement at the same time you identify a topic and the purpose (doing Step 4 at the same time as Step 2).

- In the case of an essay exam, you usually don't have time to revise extensively. So while you may not use Step 8, you should still develop a thesis statement, do some exploratory writing, and sketch a brief outline to organize your thoughts before composing your response.

- In the case of a term paper or other longer writing assignments, it is a good idea to assess and revise (Steps 7 & 8) several times before proofreading and producing a final copy (Steps 9 & 10) of your writing.

As you become more comfortable with the writing process, you will learn to adapt it for your writing needs in a variety of courses as well as non-academic contexts.

Table 8.2

| Writing Methodology — A Simple Example | |
|---|---|
| **Scenario**: You are writing a cover letter for a job application. | |
| 1. Prewriting | Read the classified advertisements. Gather information about the company. Think about specific qualifications and decide that the job is a good match for your abilities. |
| 2. Topic, Purpose, Audience | The topic in this case is a job application, the purpose for writing is to get an interview, and the audience is the person screening applications and making hiring decisions. |
| 3. Exploratory writing | List qualifications and reasons why the job is attractive. |
| 4. Thesis statement | In a letter of application the thesis statement might be your first sentence which summarizes why you are applying for the job or summarizes your qualifications. |
| 5. Planning | Decide how the letter should sound (e.g., impersonal and very formal or try to reflect something of your personality). Decide what order you should present your qualifications as well as the reasons the job is attractive. Use your list from Step 3. |
| 6. Draft creation | Arrange, rephrase items from your list. Supplement with more prose, explaining items from list. |
| 7. Draft assessment | Reread what you have written, decide what is strong and what needs improvement. |
| 8. Draft revision | Rephrase, cut, and rearrange. Repeat Steps 7 and 8. (reassess) Have a friend read the letter and give you feedback. Revise again based on your friend's feedback. |
| 9. & 10. Proofreading & Final copy production | Carefully proofread and produce the final copy. |

# Discussion of the Writing Methodology

In order to save time, many students limit their formal writing process to composing a thesis statement, planning, and drafting just one draft. However, all the steps of the methodology are important. Prewriting and exploratory writing are helpful for developing interesting and intellectually challenging ideas. An awareness of purpose and audience is essential to making sure that you state your ideas in an appropriate manner for the context in which you are writing. Finally, assessment, revision, and proofreading are crucial to improving the quality of both what you say and how you say it in your writing.

## Prepare for writing or prewriting

Examine the context in which you are doing the writing. In other words, why are you writing? Most writing is done in response to something. For example, a job application letter is written in response to a classified ad. Most academic writing is in response to the content of a specific course; thus classroom assignments and discussions should help to generate topic ideas for papers.

Prewriting involves formulating ideas. Examples of prewriting activities include reading, gathering data and researching, brainstorming, writing to generate ideas, involvement in classroom discussions, doing assignments, and listening to a lecture. For example, the Reading Methodology discussed in Chapter Seven could be the prewriting stage for an assignment that includes reading and writing.

> What is written without effort is in general read without pleasure.
> — *Samuel Johnson, English writer, literary arbitrator, and lexicographer (writer of a dictionary) 1709–1784*

## Identify topic, purpose and audience

This step of the methodology involves determining what you want to write about, why you are writing, and who you are addressing in your writing. In some cases, this will be Step 1 and prewriting will be Step 2. In other cases, you may discover a topic, purpose, and audience through prewriting activities.

Your purpose for writing and your audience will determine how formal or informal, personal or impersonal your writing should sound as well as what the most appropriate form of writing will be. In many cases of academic writing, the form is determined by the type of assignment; whether it be a lab report, reading response paper, personal essay, or essay analyzing a literary text.

For example, a personal essay that requires you to express yourself on a current events issue might sound personal and a bit informal, reflecting your values and opinions. On the other hand, a lab report or term paper might be more impersonal and formal, and probably has a specific format your instructor would like you to follow.

**Perform exploratory writing**

At this stage of the methodology, expand and develop your ideas. This might involve rethinking assumptions and preconceptions, forming a position or taking sides on a controversial issue, and considering the complexities of a topic.

In exploratory writing, the point is to get all of your ideas on paper without worrying about style, organization, type of writing, grammar, and spelling. If you stop writing to correct mistakes, you might lose your train of thought. Similarly, if you are worried that your sentences do not sound sophisticated enough, you might not get anything written at all. At this stage, the act of writing often helps you to formulate and clarify your thinking.

Quite often exploratory writing will include returning to the sources you read and other resources from the prewriting stage. As you are exploring your ideas at this stage, you might find that you need to do more research and reading to better explain what you are trying to say in your writing. Exploratory writing can be structured around critical thinking questions, or it can be unstructured. Sometimes beginning with a blank sheet of paper or a blank computer screen and just following your train of thought is a great way to explore your ideas.

**Compose a thesis statement**

A thesis statement narrows a general topic and introduces the specific aspects of the topic you want to discuss. It reflects your purpose for writing and summarizes the main idea that the rest of your writing will develop. In contrast to exploratory writing where the purpose is to expand your ideas as much as possible, a thesis statement should be concise and specific. It may take several revisions to get your thesis statement right.

**Devise a plan**

At this point, you want to organize your ideas. An outline is a good way to do this. You should decide which of the sources you read will be important to cite and discuss in your writing. You may find that not everything you read about your topic is relevant to what you want to discuss in your writing. The planning stage is also a good time to identify a time schedule for completion, standards for assessing quality, a listing of possible resources to help with the writing, a determination of the availability of resources, and information about the audience. The plan you create can be modified as you proceed through the writing process.

## Create a draft

Drafting involves rereading what you have already written and keeping what you like, deleting what you do not like, and developing your ideas with expanded discussions. It also involves crafting sentences and paragraphs, cutting and pasting to move around paragraphs, citing sources with quotation and paraphrases, adding examples to illustrate ideas, and developing transitions to clarify the relationships among ideas and between paragraphs.

When you are drafting, you alter your exploratory writing to fit the plan you have developed.

In college courses, the most common format that papers follow contains an introduction, followed by a body of paragraphs, and then a conclusion.

An effective **introduction** catches the reader's interest, presents the thesis, and summarizes the main points that support the thesis. Except for very long papers, most introductions can be kept to a single paragraph.

The paragraphs which form the **body** of the paper should follow your outline and logically develop your thesis. Each paragraph should contain a topic sentence that presents the main theme for that paragraph. The remainder of a paragraph should support the topic sentence with examples, facts, details, data, descriptions, and narratives. Define terms and adapt the text with the audience in mind.

A **conclusion** should refer to the thesis statement in some way and bring the paper to a logical end. A conclusion may include a summary of the main points, an answer to a question posed in the introduction, a solution to a problem, or a reflection about the issues raised in the paper. There should not be any new ideas or irrelevant information included in the conclusion.

## Assess the draft

Have your peers and your instructor read the draft you've written and offer feedback. Ask for strengths and areas for improvement regarding *what you've written* (including your ideas and the content of your writing) and on *how well you've said it* (including style, organization, grammar). As you gain more experience, you will learn to self-assess your work with greater quality. Revision, which is the next step, happens in response to assessment feedback.

## Revise

Revise your writing in response to the strengths and areas of improvement identified in the previous step (i.e., using the assessment and self-assessment feedback you receive). Revising includes rewriting and rephrasing, reorganizing sentences or paragraphs, cutting and pasting, clarifying thinking, expanding and refining ideas.

> The beautiful part of writing is that you don't have to get it right the first time, unlike, say a surgeon. You can always do it better, find the exact word, the apt phrase, the leaping simile.
> — *Robert Cormier, Massachusetts newspaper reporter and writer*

> No passion in the world is equal to the passion to alter someone else's draft.
> — *H.G. Wells, English writer 1866–1946*

### Proofread

This essential step sometimes gets overlooked. Check spelling, grammar, and look for typos. Although word processing programs can be helpful at this stage, don't rely on the computer alone to find all of your mistakes. For example, if you misspell a word as another word that the computer recognizes, it won't catch your mistake. Also, vocabulary that is specific to certain subject matter sometimes will not be recognized by the computer. Keep a dictionary handy and double-check your work.

### Produce a final copy

Your final copy should be as error-free as possible and reflect all of your revisions and hard work. Most college courses require papers to be double-spaced, in a standard type size, on white 8½ x 11 inch paper, with one-inch margins all around. Be sure to check your syllabus to see if your instructor has specific requirements.

## Writing Resource on the Web

**http://www.pcrest.com**

The National Writing Centers Association (NWCA) has one of the most comprehensive sites about writing on the Web. The NWCA can be accessed from the *Foundations of Learning* web site. *Note: additional writing resources are presented at the end of this chapter.*

The NWCA page is a comprehensive and up-to-date listing of writing centers. This site alphabetically lists online writing centers by educational institution. You can also find resources offered by on-line writing centers, such as handouts or electronic tutoring, listed by category. The home page has links to the following areas:

- writing center resources,
- writing centers online,
- resources for writers,
- tutor stories,
- e-mail discussion groups, and
- electronic and print journals.

# Example – Writing an Argumentative Essay

**Scenario:** Your instructor assigns a reading about censorship and the Internet, and asks you to write an essay that states and supports your position on this issue.

1.  *Prewriting* involves reading the assigned essay. Take notes that record important facts, as well as notes that record your opinions and responses to the arguments made by the reading.

2.  The instructor facilitates a class discussion of critical thinking questions in response to the reading (otherwise you could have informally written your responses to critical thinking questions on the reading on your own). Your responses to the critical thinking questions help you to identify the position you will argue, *purpose* for writing and *audience*.

3.  The *exploratory writing* on the topic involves developing your ideas and opinions along with justifications and supporting facts. Consider opposing arguments and your responses to them.

4.  Compose a *thesis statement* which states your position.

5.  *Plan* your essay. Decide what kind of data is necessary to support your ideas. Do you need to do research, or is all the necessary information presented in the reading assignment? Reread the assignment if necessary. Organize quotations from sources and your own ideas with an outline. Anticipate how much time it will take to complete the remaining steps, and schedule enough time for assessment and revision.

6.  Create a *draft*. Rearrange exploratory writing to follow the plan. Develop exploratory writing to form an introduction, body and conclusion. Compose complete sentences and paragraphs. Include examples and quotations from sources. Add transitions between paragraphs to establish relationships among ideas.

7.  Make an appointment at your school's Writing Center for a tutor to read and *assess* your first draft.

8.  *Revise* in response to the tutor's feedback.
    *   Read your second draft and *assess* its strengths and areas for improvement.
    *   Clarify, rephrase, rewrite, cut, expand/explain, refine.

9.  *Proofread* your third draft.

10. Correct any mistakes you found while proofreading. Produce a *final copy* to submit to your instructor.

# Writing College Papers

Writing papers is a process that involves aspects of idea generation, planning, drafting, revising, and assessing. While good writing skills are highly marketable, many students dread the thought of writing essays, reports, and term papers. Being able to write your ideas and information in a clear, effective, and convincing manner not only helps you with your grades but also enhances your learning skills and increases your career choices and job opportunities.

The Writing Methodology provides an excellent guide for writing a paper. Below are some additional tips to use along with the Writing Methodology.

## Tips for Writing a Quality Paper

### Plan

Identify important dates such as the due dates for outlines, drafts, and the final paper. List the tasks associated with completing the paper, and note target dates for each. Refer to your schedule frequently doing your best to stick to the plan and avoid a last minute rush and panic.

### Generate topic ideas

Brainstorming is one way to generate ideas (see Chapter Six for more information). In situations where you are not familiar with the topic and brainstorming is difficult, you can generate ideas by listing questions about the topic. In certain cases, you may need to do some initial research to gain a better understanding of the general topic before trying to come up with a specific topic. Finally, your instructor may be able to help with possible topic ideas.

### Scope your paper

Your final topic should not be so broad that your paper is full of general discussion lacking depth and insight. A narrower topic allows for information to be presented more clearly. The required length of your paper will also influence how broad or narrow your focus is. If entire books have been written on a subject, then it probably is too broad of a topic for a three or four-page paper. On the other hand, writing a ten-page paper on an extremely narrow topic may be just as inappropriate.

### Develop a thesis statement

A thesis statement presents the main theme in one specific sentence. Use the thesis statement:

- to help you organize information,
- to plan and shape ideas before you write,
- to keep from wandering astray during your writing, and
- as a benchmark for assessing how well you did what you set out to do.

You may find that you need to modify your thesis statement as you learn more about the topic.

> Words are, of course, the most powerful drug used by mankind.
> — *Rudyard Kipling, English author and winner of the Nobel prize for literature 1865–1936*

## Outline

An outline shows the direction your paper is taking, analogous to a road map. An outline lets you determine whether your material supports the thesis statement and whether the material is presented in the proper order. When outlining, (1) make sure all parts are included (thesis, main heading, subheadings), (2) use an appropriate method of outlining, (3) check that the items in the outline are logical, specific, and in the proper order, and (4) realize that you can be flexible with the outline — it is not a fixed or rigid structure.

## Gather information

Draw upon your information processing skills (see Chapter 6) to utilize resources found in places such as the library and the Internet. It is a good idea to cite references and jot down ideas as you come across them, on 3 x 5 cards or in a file on the computer.

## Create a draft

Realize that a good paper almost always requires some revision and rewriting, and that the first product you create will be a draft. In some cases, you may need to revise your draft several times. The main idea with a draft is to get the writing process started. Let the ideas flow. The editing will come later.

> How do I know what I think until I see what I say?
> — *E.M. Forster, British writer and novelist 1879–1970*

The most common format that papers follow contains an introduction followed by body paragraphs and then a conclusion. However, this may not always be the order in which the paper is written. For those who have a hard time writing an introduction, it may be better to start with the body and come back to the introduction later.

### Introduction

Except for longer papers, most introductions should be kept to a single paragraph. An introduction may include a quotation, pertinent facts or statistics, an interesting statement or question, a brief story or incident, or perhaps even a definition of an important word.

### Body

The paragraphs and sections which form the body of the paper should follow your outline and logically develop your thesis. The remainder of each paragraph should convincingly support the topic sentence with examples, facts, data, specific details, descriptions, and narratives. Keep in mind the audience for the paper as you write. Be sure to define terms and adapt general statements to the reader's needs.

### Conclusion

A conclusion should restate or refer to the thesis statement and bring the paper to a logical end. You should not introduce new ideas or irrelevant information in the conclusion. A conclusion may include a summary of main points, an answer to a question raised in the introduction, a dramatic statement or quotation, the solution to a problem, or a reflection about the issues raised in the paper.

**Assess the draft**

Since most of us initially are not accurate judges of our own writing, it is a good idea to have someone else read and honestly edit the writing that we do.

**Perform a final assessment**

An important step that many students neglect involves taking time to do a final assessment. In many cases, the additional editing and revisions that you incorporate can increase the grade you receive.

**Know the evaluation criteria**

You should know what criteria your instructor will be using to evaluate your paper. If you don't know, ask your instructor. Throughout the creation of your paper, you should be assessing your paper against the given criteria. At the same time, you should perform an ongoing assessment of the quality of the paper and your performance in creating it. Compare and assess your performance to previous papers where you performed well.

**Utilize feedback**

Welcome feedback from others, and look to continuously improve. Refer to comments instructors have made on previous papers in addition to your own comments and assessments of previous work. Identify the strengths, areas for improvements, and insights of both the paper itself, and the process you followed to write the paper. This will help you to get a better grade on the current paper, and strengthen your ability to perform effectively on future papers you write.

## Quoting and Citing Other People's Work

Many aspects of learning involve developing the ideas, concepts, and work of other writers, researchers, and scholars. Consider the following pointers or tips when writing papers or creating other work to ensure that you credit ideas to their rightful origins.

- A citation is needed when using another person's specific ideas, phrases, or words.

- Be careful when you change the words of others. Words added or changed within a quotation should be enclosed within square brackets [ ]. Making too many changes can be awkward and change the original meaning. If you have to make more than a couple of adjustments, think about paraphrasing or at least reducing the length of the direct quotation.

- Double-check the accuracy of any quotation you use, and any citation you make. Identify the author, title, volume and page number.

*Note*: Different disciplines have different rules for the syntax of a citation. In any class where you are turning in a paper, make sure you know what the required syntax or structure of the citation is.

- It is unethical to quote in such a way that changes the context of the passage quoted. For example, an **improper** use of the original quote *"I found the play so bad that my urge to leave after the first act was compelling"* would be to say *"One critic said that he found the play...compelling."*

- Whenever possible, refer to the original, primary sources you find in secondary sources.

- When not sure, document your source in detail.

For more information about citations, refer to the writing-related web sites mentioned in this chapter.

## The Impact of E-mail on Writing and Thinking

The emergence of e-mail as a common form of communication has placed new demands on peoples' writing skills and certain cognitive skills. Cognitively, the way in which you communicate has an effect on the way you think. When you communicate verbally, you do so in a more spontaneous manner. In a conversation, you don't have time to think through everything you say and sometimes your thoughts are less focused and more directed at responding to the other person.

Writing allows you to think about what you will say before it is communicated on paper or on a computer screen. Also, when writing, you have time to be able to check the logic of your arguments or statements, unlike in a conversation. In essence, when you commit your thoughts to the process of the written word, language takes on a different meaning. Writing stimulates different portions of the brain and enhances the critical thinking process. When you write, you become a more focused thinker. This is why using e-mail for classroom journals or assignments can help you to become both a better writer and a better learner.

## Additional Writing Resources on the Web

Chapter Eight of the *Foundations of Learning* web site provides links to many helpful writing resources. The Winthrop University site has a tour or guide to some of the better Writing Center resources available on the Web.

http://www.pcrest.com

Capital Community Technical College has a very comprehensive site which includes 75 computer-graded quizzes, numerous handouts on writing and style (from basic to advanced), an "Ask Grammar" feature, and a section called Principles of Composition, containing sample essays for the various traditional modes of composition.

The University of Illinois Writer's Workshop also has an annotated list of the best web sites for writers which includes:

English?
Who needs that?
I'm never going
to England.
—Homer Simpson,
The Simpsons

- resources for teachers of writing and writing across the curriculum,
- Internet sources for a friendly critique of your writing,
- hypertext writing guides and collections of self-help documents on the writing process,
- resources for business and technical writers, and
- a section for students and teachers of English as a second language.

The following writing reference sources are also available on-line:

- Webster's Dictionary,
- Roget's Thesaurus,
- OneLook Dictionaries (use this site to search 55 scientific, technical, or medical indexed dictionaries), and
- Strunk and White's Elements of Style.

# Utilizing Tools and Technology

> I do not fear computers. I fear the lack of them.
> —*Isaac Asimov, Russian-born, U.S. biochemist
> and science-fiction writer 1920–1992*

## The Impact and Significance of Computer Technology

Nothing epitomizes modern life better than the computer. Consider how computers have infiltrated most every aspect of our society and then try to imagine a world without computers. It would be far different from the one in which we live today.

Just think if computers just suddenly disappeared. There would be no telecommunications without computerized switching centers to play traffic cop to millions of calls and keep the lines of communication untangled. Stock markets would close. Financial records at banks would disappear and transactions would be severely limited—no ATM's at your convenience. Modern medical care would not be possible. There would be no television or radio. Gas pumps wouldn't function but what would it matter since your new car would not operate anyway.

Are you beginning to get a sense of the dramatic impact of computer technology? From the perspective of preparing for a career, understand that the computer has long been a common tool and resource in the business world and that in most fields, those seeking employment without certain basic computer skills are putting themselves at a serious disadvantage.

Realize that today's computers do much more than simply compute. As a result, we are seeing the creation of a new electronic world with a fundamentally different kind of economy impacting the way we live and do business.

Each year a growing percentage of business transactions are conducted over the Internet. For consumers, "e-commerce" or "e-business" offers convenience, greater choices, and potential cost savings. For many businesses, it is a matter of determining how to utilize e-commerce or risk losing future revenue.

In terms of higher education, technology has made it possible for students to take courses without ever being on a college campus. Distance learning is a growing segment of higher education which is redefining "the college classroom." Students no longer need to be in the same place, at the same time for a class to function. Also, colleges are offering an increasing number of on-line courses, and more individual faculty are incorporating the use of the World Wide Web, specific course web pages, and e-mail into the design of their courses. In fact, colleges now offer courses and programs dealing with the subject of e-commerce.

## Computers as Tools

...man is still the most extraordinary computer of all. —*John F. Kennedy, 35th President 1917-1963*

Despite all the advancements in computer technology, a computer will never do the learning for you. That will always be your responsibility! Simply put, computers don't replace learning, they enhance it. Computers are *tools* that you should use in order to be a more productive and effective learner. Computers can be used as productivity tools, communication tools, and learning tools.

Various types of software allow you to use the computer to be more productive with certain tasks. The most common **productivity tools** are word processors, spreadsheets, databases, presentation software, and desktop publishing. Note that there are other software productivity tools that have been developed and continue to be developed. The above-mentioned are just the most common.

Using various types of links, the computer allows you to communicate quickly and easily with others around the world. E-mail, chat rooms, and video conferencing are examples of how the computer can be used as a **communication tool**.

With a computer (and Internet access) you can gain access to vast amounts of information and specially designed curricula that allow you to increase your knowledge base and learning skills. The World Wide Web, "on-line" courses, tutorials, and informational CD's are examples of how the computer can be used as a **learning tool**—to learn about most any topic.

## The Internet

Wow! They've got the Internet on computers now! — *Homer Simpson, The Simpsons*

The Internet is a massive worldwide network of computers that are linked together in a way that information can be shared. This inter-connection of networks is where the "Internet" literally gets its name. The Internet in itself is comprised of thousands of networks connected by a common "Internet Protocol" or IP that allows information to be routed efficiently from one computer network to another. It is not so important to know exactly how the Internet works as it is to realize that it is a method to move information around a network of computers.

Originally created by the Pentagon and the Department of Defense as a means to facilitate communication with its contractors, the Internet has grown beyond all expectations. Millions of people from more than fifty countries access the Internet every day. The ability to access the Internet requires a link from your computer to an Internet Service Provider (ISP). As a college student, you usually have access to the Internet through the computer network at your school.

The Internet is the physical structure (computers and cables) through which information travels. The information traveling across the Internet comes in a variety of forms. Examples include the World Wide Web (WWW), e-mail and listservs, file transfer protocol (FTP), Usenet newsgroups, and Telnet.

## The World Wide Web

The World Wide Web or WWW is different from the Internet. Think of the Internet as a car engine (that's hidden under the hood) and the World Wide Web as the body of the car (the thing you actually see and use). The Internet serves as the means or power to move the information while the World Wide Web refers to the visible interface of information itself.

The World Wide Web began in 1989 as a project by a team of high-energy physics researchers in Europe working with the CERN laboratory in Geneva, Switzerland. The goal of the project was to develop a useful means of communication so that ideas and research could be effectively transported between researchers in different countries.

The result was a software language called HTML or HyperText Markup Language. The main difference between hypertext and regular text is that hypertext contains connections embedded within it that link the text to other documents or text. In other words, hypertext makes it possible to click on a word, phrase, or even a picture and be moved to a new location containing linked or related information. As you can imagine, hyperlinks make it possible to create a complex "web" of connections.

While the Web uses hypertext, the documents on the web are by no means limited to simply text. Web documents may contain any combination of text, pictures and images, sounds, and movies.

## Finding Your Way Around the Web

Browser software is needed in order for you to navigate, "surf," or browse (as you might in a store) sites on the Web. A *browser* allows you to view web pages created in HTML, access files, read Usenet newsgroups, or telnet to remote sites. There are text-only, full-screen browsers such as Lynx™. However, the most common browsers are graphical browsers such as Netscape™ or Explorer™. Graphical browsers allow for pictures and sound to be accessed as well as text.

Each Web page has an electronic version of an address and zip code on the Internet called a Uniform Resource Locator or *URL*. By typing the correct URL, Web browsers take you directly to the page of your choice. Internet addresses for the Web usually appear in the following general format:

*http://www.websitename.ext*

After *www* (which refers to World Wide Web), the name of the web site is given along with a three-letter extension set apart by a dot (the period symbol is pronounced "dot"). The three-letter extension or suffix helps to identify what type of organization is hosting the web site.

Common extensions are as follows:

| | |
|---|---|
| .com | commercial or business |
| .edu | educational |
| .gov | government |
| .mil | military |
| .net | networks |
| .org | non-commercial organization |

A **home page** is the starting point to a document or larger collection of information. Home pages typically provide a brief description of the information provided along with different links from which a person can go down a particular path or specific area of interest. Some Internet Service Providers have home pages that provide general information with links in a well-organized and convenient manner. You will find home pages and accompanying documents for corporations and businesses, schools, newspapers, cities, virtually any type of organization, and even individuals.

Home pages can be created by anyone with access to the Internet and software for creating web pages (software packages exist that create HTML code without you having to know how to program in HTML).

**Links** are specially highlighted text that allow you to move to a completely different site on the Web, move to another Web page at the current site, or move to a different location within the current page. Typically, these linking words appear in a different color and are underlined. Sometimes a link will change to another color after you "click" it, indicating that you have visited that link.

If you want to frequently return to a particular Web site, you can use **bookmarks** to save or mark locations. With bookmarks, you can quickly and easily find your way back to a site or page of your choosing.

## Search Engines

If you don't know a specific URL or know where to find information, searching devices called "search engines" make it easier to find what you're looking for and allow you to navigate your way around the Web. There are more than a hundred search engines for use on the Web, including some very specialized ones. A few of the more common general search engine services include: Yahoo, Infoseek, Excite, Lycos, and Alta Vista to name just a few.

Search engines require you to type in words or phrases into a search box when beginning a search. Search engines work in different ways. Some search titles of documents, others search the documents themselves, and still others search indices or directories. Because of these differences, search engines will yield very different results to searches when using the exact same word or phrase. To get a more complete listing of Web resources, it's best to search using several different search engines as well as search engines of search engines (such as AskJeeves). Your search results are also greatly affected by exactly what you type into a search box. That leads us to the next topic of keyword searching.

...computer hardware progress is so fast. No other technology since civilization began has seen six orders of magnitude in performance-price gain in 30 years.
—*Fred Brooks Jr.,author and essayist about computers and software*

# Keyword Searching

What is a keyword search and how do you do one? If someone said to you, how many different words can you come up with for the word "bicycle," how many words could you brainstorm?

When doing a keyword search, try to use the words that will find the best information you want. In this case, examples of words that might depict a bicycle or bicycling include ten-speed, two-wheeler, tricycle, recumbent bike, tandem, Schwinn™, Trek™, racing bike, trail bike, mountain bike, etc.

A search engine provides a listing of related web pages and web sites based on the words or phrases that you give it to work with. However, by changing the context of the keyword search, you will see that search engines find different information although the general category may be the same.

Looking at the proliferation of personal web pages on the net, it looks like very soon everyone on earth will have 15 Megabytes of fame.
—*M.G. Siriam*

# Category or Subject Searching

Often it is easier and more thorough to find information searching within a general category or subject area. The home page of search engines gives you the option of going to various subject areas (such as health, entertainment, travel, computers, science, etc.) to do specialized searches or readily provide you with more detailed categories and/or links to related web sites. For example, let's say you would like to read reviews for several newly released movies. Rather than typing in the name of each movie, you could click on the "entertainment" link from the home page of a search engine and then click on "movies or film" from which you could then choose from a list of links for reviews and reviewers of movies.

In summary, be aware that in certain situations, using category or subject searching will be quicker and result in a larger list of potentially useful web sites. Also note that the home pages of search engines have links to useful tools such as yellow page directories, maps, people searchers, stock quotes, and weather reports.

# E-mail

E-mail allows people with computers, mail delivery software, and appropriate hardware to link to the Internet (or to an internal network within an organization) a means to quickly and easily communicate electronically. Similar to written correspondence, e-mail can be used in all different contexts including personal use, business and professional use, and for collaboration and research. Unlike written correspondence, e-mail communication  can take place between two people half way around the world in a matter of minutes and is available for use any time of day. Also, files and images can be attached and sent along with a message.

There are a couple of important reasons for using e-mail, one is cognitive and the other is practical.

Cognitively, people think differently depending on the way they communicate. Verbal communication is much more spontaneous than written communication. In a conversation, you don't have time to think through everything you say. As a result, sometimes your thoughts are less focused and more directed at responding to the other person.

Writing allows a person to think about what he or she will say before it is communicated on paper or the computer screen. Writing also makes it easier to check the logic of arguments or statements, unlike in a conversation. In essence, when you commit your thoughts to the process of the written word, language takes on a different meaning. Writing stimulates different portions of the brain and enhances the process of critical thinking. When you write, you become a more focused thinker. For this reason, you will find that some instructors will require you to use e-mail in conjunction with classroom journals or assignments. E-mail also provides instructors an opportunity to get their students writing on a regular basis.

From a practical aspect, e-mail is now such a common means of communication that if you aren't familiar with e-mail, you will need to learn how to use it soon. You will not only need to use e-mail in your future work but also during your time in college.

Actually there are several reasons why it's important to learn to use e-mail. First, e-mail allows students, instructors, and counselors another avenue to communicate other than the telephone or through one-on-one meetings. Obviously, many would prefer speaking with instructors and counselors in person, but this is not always possible. E-mail gives students an opportunity to ask instructors questions about a class or inform them of any particular problems. On the other hand, instructors can appraise students individually or as a class about any significant changes in the class, and they can directly send students important information. E-mail also provides an easy way of filing correspondence by saving messages that are both received and sent.

There are a wide variety of e-mail programs available for use on campus networks. After checking with your campus computer support service, read the Help documents, user's guide, or other information available on what it takes to create and "log into" an e-mail account. After logging into the system, explore the different windows, fields, and pull-down menus.

## E-mail Addresses

The following is a general format for e-mail addresses: name@server.ext

The address consists of four main components:

1. a name for the user,
2. the @ symbol (pronounced "at") which separates the user name from the location,
3. the location of the server computer, and
4. a three-letter extension or suffix, set apart by a period (or dot).

The three-letter extension in the location name helps to identify the kind of organization operating the server. Examples of organizational extensions include: *com*, *net*, and *org*.

Some locations use a two-letter geographical extension. Examples include: .jp (Japan), .uk (United Kingdom), .nl (Netherlands), .ca (Canada) and .au (Australia).

In some cases, the name of the location might require several subparts to identify the server. If so, each part is separated by a dot. For example, the address, name@aserver.bserver.com, contains one additional part (or subdomain) in the location name.

## Using E-mail

While the interface differs among the various e-mail software packages, there are certain common components. E-mail messages consist of two main sections, the header and the body.

Within the header lines, the sender of a message supplies the following:

**To:** The place where you put to whom the e-mail is being sent to (you can send an e-mail to more than one person). It is important that you use the exact address because if just one character is not correct, the e-mail will not be delivered. There is no margin for error.

Note: you have the option of sending a copy of the message to other individuals using the header **CC:** or to groups of people (using a listserv).

**Subject:** identifies to the person(s) receiving the e-mail the general subject matter of message

E-mail software automatically identifies the address of the **sender** and the **date** and **time** as part of the e-mail message being sent.

---

### Listservs

A listserv is a mailing list program designed to copy and distribute electronic mail to everyone subscribing to a particular mailing list. Any e-mail letter sent to the list's address is copied and mass-mailed to the e-mail box of every person subscribed to the list.

---

You create the body of the e-mail message using the word processing tools that are part of the e-mail software package. This usually includes full editing capabilities, formatting options, and spell-checking.

The purpose of your e-mail may include sending an attachment or file. In this case, click on the "attachment" icon from the tool bar. You must then specify or locate the file or files to be sent. Realize that large files (particularly those with pictures and graphics) can take a long time to send and receive (especially with slower modems).

To open an e-mail attachment, click on the attachment icon (often a paper clip) and then click on the file(s) that are displayed. The files will open provided you have the compatible software (compatible with the attached file). Note: it is important that you open attachments only from trustworthy sources as this can be a means for viruses to be spread.

Use the pull-down menus, tool bars, and help system of your e-mail software to explore and learn more about it's features and capabilities; such as customizing your window, organizing your mail folders, creating an address book, assigning priority to messages, sending secure messages, and subscribing to a newsgroup.

## Other Ways of Accessing and Sharing Information on the Internet

### Usenet Newsgroups

Newsgroups are set up by people who want to share information on common interests. A Usenet group can be considered an international cyber meeting place. When sending an e-mail to a Usenet group, only those who are part of the group and reading the discussion that day or week will receive the message.

### File Transfer Protocol (FTP)

FTP is a computer protocol that allows you to hook up to a remote computer and transfer files across the Internet. With FTP you can copy files from another computer to your computer and visa versa. You must know the Internet address of the remote computer in order to establish a FTP connection.

### Telnet

Allows your computer to hook up to a remote computer and run a program on the other computer. With Telnet it is possible to access large research databases, search remote libraries, or use resources not available on one's own computing system.

### Push systems

Push systems let a user passively receive information rather than actively search for it. As the receiver of the information, you choose from a menu of sources and specify what information you want to receive. An example of a push system is a screen saver that downloads and displays information such as news, weather, or sports to the user's system during periods of inactivity.

Any sufficiently advanced technology is indistinguishable from magic.
—*Arthur C. Clarke, Technology and the Future*

# Evaluating the Quality of Internet Information

With so many people now turning to the Internet and the WWW as a primary source of information, it is important that sources be evaluated, just as print resources are evaluated. The unregulated nature of the Internet and its information make it necessary to scrutinize and check sources when using and relying on this information. This is true not only for your work at school but also for other aspects of your life where you might use information from the Internet.

While the Internet contains a vast amount of information and resources which are beneficial to users, some resources may not pass the test of need and worth. It is important to realize that in some cases, Internet resources may be poorly maintained, contain inaccurate information, and may only be available on an intermittent basis, i.e. here one day, gone the next. Internet sources should be evaluated on the basis of quality, credibility, and accessibility.

The following criteria and questions serve as guidelines for evaluating sources of information. However, realize that a source does not have to meet all these criteria to be acceptable.

> Technology makes it possible for people to gain control over everything, except over technology.
> —*John Tudor*

## Useful

- Is the material at this site organized in a manner that is easy to use?
- Are user help files available?
- Is the organization of information easy for the user to grasp?
- Is the information easy to get to? Does it take less than three "clicks" to access?
- Is the information divided into logical parts?
- Are the links arranged in an orderly manner?
- Is the content of the information comprehensive and unique?
- Does the search follow a standard format familiar to Internet patrons?

## Accurate, Credible, and Unbiased

- Does the resource cover the subject area in a comprehensive manner?
- Do the information headings accurately describe the contents?
- Is the source credible?
- Where was the information obtained? What references are given?
- What are the credentials or institutional affiliation of the person responsible for the material?
- Is this resource produced as part of the mission of a national or international organization?
- Is it produced by an academic institution, or a reputable commercial enterprise?

### Current

- Is the site current?
- Is the site updated on a regular basis?
- Is ongoing maintenance demonstrated?
- How recent is the information?
- Is the Internet version of the resource more current than the printed version?

### Reliable

- Is the resource generally available?
- Is the site available on a consistent basis?
- Is the response time fast?
- Are address changes infrequent and announced?
- Is the information unavailable to patrons elsewhere?

## Information on the Web about Evaluating Internet Resources

**http://www.pcrest.com**

For more information about evaluating Internet resources, go to Chapter Nine of the *Foundations of Learning* web site. Several library directors have identified criteria, created checklists, and provided examples to illustrate concepts.

## Methodology for Learning a New Tool

As was mentioned earlier in the chapter, computers are tools which can be used to increase or enhance productivity, communication, and learning. The specific applications used on the computer in each of these areas can also be considered a tool.

While in college and throughout your life, you will continually be learning to use new software packages and applications as well as learning procedures for handling and working with hardware (equipment). The Methodology for Learning a New Tool is a resource you can use to help you in these situations.

While similar to the Learning Process Methodology, the following thirteen-step methodology can help you learn to use any new tool or tool package in a systematic way.

Table 9.1

| | Methodology for Learning a New Tool | |
|---|---|---|
| 1. | Why | Why learn this tool and what will it do for you? |
| 2. | Overview | Learn the main features of the tool. |
| 3. | Prerequisites | What do you need to know before you start? |
| 4. | Learning objectives | What specifically do you need to learn about this tool? |
| 5. | Performance criteria | How will you tell if you have met your objectives? |
| 6. | Information sources | What sources of help and information are available? |
| 7. | Plan | Make a plan of the essential tasks to be learned. |
| 8. | Model | Refer to tutorials, on-line help, experts, etc. |
| 9. | Try it out | Explore the essential tasks. |
| 10. | Think | Answer critical thinking questions that are posed. |
| 11. | Practice | Do additional exercises to enhance your knowledge. |
| 12. | Self-assessment | Did you meet your criteria? Identify strengths and areas to improve. |
| 13. | Additional study | Expand your knowledge of this tool and transfer to other tools. |

## Discussion of the Methodology

**Why**

Why do you want to learn to use this tool? There will often be two parts of this question to address. The first is "why do you need it?" and the second is "what will it do for you?" Your own need for it may be imposed by an employer, or because you have a particular short-term goal in mind. In addition, it is worth asking what else it might be good for, beyond the immediate task.

**Overview**

To orient yourself, it is useful to obtain an overview of the tool from the vendor's point of view. This could include a sales brochure listing the main features and/or a user's manual. Also, someone who knows the tool could provide you with an overview.

**Prerequisites**

Is there any specialized knowledge you should have before you begin? For example, in the case of using a power tool (a table saw, router, etc.), a basic familiarity with standard power tool safety procedures is necessary.

### Learning objectives

Synthesize the information from the first three steps into a small number of clear, measurable goals. It is a good idea to make a fairly short list of the *most essential* specific tasks that will help you gain a sufficient mastery for your purposes. For example, "the top ten things to know about…".

### Performance criteria

For each of the objectives in the previous step, you should now be able to state clearly how you will measure your success in reaching your objectives.

### Information sources

Survey all available sources of help about the tool or package. This includes manuals, help systems, experts (such as your teacher or other users), third-party books (available at your library or at bookstores), librarians, the Internet, etc.

### Plan

Devise a plan to help you meet your objectives.

### Model

Observe others using the tool; watch videos or interactive teaching systems about the tool; imagine all steps of using the tool.

### Try it out

By now you have a well-designed plan of attack. To learn any tool, you should be willing to try experiments and to explore. Your plan should be viewed as a set of suggestions, and you should be quick to make up new experiments as questions arise and as you gain familiarity with the tool.

### Think

Answer the questions that help you to know how well you understand the tool. Generate your own questions as you work through the previous steps of the methodology. In cases where the instructor has prepared a structured activity for you, the questions, called "critical thinking questions" will already be provided.

### Practice

Follow-up exercises (your own or the book's) can help you to cement the skills you have obtained from your first explorations.

### Self-assessment

Study the learning objectives and criteria again, and determine how well you have met those criteria.

### Additional study

Now that you know the essentials, you can apply the same techniques to learning more advanced features of this tool, or to learning other tool packages.

A lot of people find technology terrifying because they think it forces them into a box, when, in fact, what happens is that technology overwhelms us with choice.
—*Paul Saffo, Institute for the Future (1999)*

# Learning A New Tool — A Simple Example

**Learning a New Tool Scenario**

With the proceeds from his first job, Harry has just bought his first car, which he plans to learn how to maintain all by himself. His grandfather owned and tinkered with several cars when he was much younger, and he has advised Harry on just what tools to buy for maintaining his shiny new machine. Accordingly, Harry runs out and buys a spark plug wrench, an ignition point file, an ignition timing light, and a tool for setting the gap on the ignition points, as well as various wrenches and socket sets. Harry comes home with his new tools and a large credit card bill, and asks his grandfather how to use the ignition timing light. Grandfather is enormously embarrassed when they discover, upon looking under the hood, that Harry's car does not have ignition points at all. It has a modern computer-controlled ignition system instead. This renders the ignition timing light and several of the other tools useless, even though Grandpa is an expert at using each of them. They both come to the realization that cars have changed a lot since Grandpa's day, and the tools that were useful then are no longer of much use in a modern car.

Harry ruefully decides he had better be a little better organized about his tools. He realizes that he needs to understand the purpose of a tool before he can learn how to use it, or even decide whether or not to buy it. He then seeks out the chief mechanic at the local auto repair shop, who suggests that Harry start by buying a tire pressure gauge (yes, modern cars do still use air in their tires), and learn how to use it. "That's easy" says Harry. "You just stick it on the thing that sticks out of the tire..."

"You mean the valve stem."

"Yeah, the valve stem, and see what it says."

"Does it make any difference when you check the tire pressure?" asks the mechanic.

Harry spends fifteen minutes more with the mechanic, learning more about checking tire pressure than he ever thought possible. He then begins to appreciate the value of using a methodology for learning a new tool.

# Web Pages Related to Computers and Internet

Refer to Chapter Nine of the *Foundations of Learning* web site for additional information related to computers and the Internet.

**http://www.pcrest.com**

Example links include:

- a site with an on-line encyclopedia that provides articles and information about the technologies, legislation, corporations, and people that have shaped current technology and the Information Age; including the history and development of computers, personal computers, and software.

- the impact of computers on health; including general ergonomics, ergonomic concerns, exposure to VDT emanations, eyestrain, and carpal tunnel syndrome.

- information about the Internet for a "Computers in Our Society" course at Mesa State College.

- an article about etiquette on the Internet.

# Personal Development

> If education is always to be conceived along the same antiquated lines of a mere transmission of knowledge, there is little to be hoped from it in the bettering of man's future. For what is the use of transmitting knowledge if the individual's total development lags behind? —*Maria Montessori, Italian physician and educator, 1870-1952*

## Aspects of Personal Development Covered in this Chapter

Personal development refers to the process where you seek to grow, improve, expand, and advance as a person. Fully applying this process involves making a conscious and deliberate effort to grow in all aspects of your life. This includes growth in the following areas:

- mentally and intellectually,  *(cognitive domain)*
- socially,  *(social domain)*
- physically (including health), and  *(psychomotor domain)*
- emotionally and spiritually.  *(affective domain)*

Concepts and processes associated with your mental and intellectual development (*cognitive domain*) are specifically addressed in Chapter Six (Information Processing) and Chapter Twelve (Problem Solving). In Chapter Eleven, the social domain (including communication and teamwork processes) is discussed. This chapter focuses on personal development from the perspective of the skills and processes associated with the affective and psychomotor domains. Primarily, the concepts introduced (in Chapter Ten) involve a person's physical and emotional well-being. The Personal Development Methodology, a general methodology that can be applied to different aspects of your life, is also introduced.

## Belief and Desire Must Come First

Before you begin to experience the growth you desire, you must first *believe* in your potential for growth and improvement. You must acknowledge that you are not "stuck" where you are and that you are not limited or constrained by your current level of ability in any area.

You must also possess the *desire* to improve, which will motivate you to take action and ultimately "make it happen." Mentors and friends can assist in this process but ultimately, you and only you, are responsible for your growth and personal development.

# Self-grower — A Quality Model for Personal Development

Everyone thinks about changing the world, but no one thinks about changing himself.
—Leo Tolstoy, Russian novelist 1828-1910

Recall from Chapter Five that *self-growers* represent the highest level of performance for learning. Self-growers not only exemplify excellent learner performance but also provide a good model for performing the process of personal development. With strong learning and self-assessment skills, self-growers have the greatest capability to develop their skills and improve future performance. More can be learned about self-growers by (1) looking at a profile (of a self-grower), and (2) focusing on a key tool used by self-growers, the Personal Development Methodology.

## Profile of a Self-grower

*A self-grower...*

- has a high degree of self-confidence and emotional maturity.

- has a strong desire to grow and develop in all aspects of his or her life.

- uses information effectively for specific needs and processes information in an efficient manner to limit "information overload."

- has developed emotionally so that he/she is willing to take risks to put himself or herself in challenging environments which require an increased performance level.

- creates his/her own challenges, but also responds to external challenges that are personally critical or important to society.

- seeks to improve his/her own performance with every experience.

- takes control of his/her own destiny—there are no bounds.

- serves as a mentor to others.

- thinks critically in different contexts so as to be efficient while producing quality results from the processes utilized.

- self-assesses and self-mentors to facilitate his/her own growth.

- is a strong problem solver who understands and recognizes relevant problems and can properly define them; he or she can also clarify issues and identify critical assumptions associated with problems.

Continual improvement is an unending journey.
— Lloyd Dobens & Clare Crawford-Mason, Thinking About Quality

# Personal Development Methodology

We all make decisions regarding what we do and how we choose to spend our time. However, few people utilize a methodology to assist with their personal development. The Personal Development Methodology, presented below, serves as a framework to help you focus more clearly on your personal growth. By using the Personal Development Methodology you can gain a greater sense of self-confidence and self-esteem as well as a greater appreciation for who you are as a person.

The Personal Development Methodology begins with self-assessment. This involves determining likes, dislikes, and looking at personal values. Based on this self-assessment, each individual proceeds through the methodology in his or her own unique way. The concept of a mentor is introduced in step four of the methodology. A mentor is similar to a coach or teacher; a person who works with you during the process and offers assessment and encouragement as needed.

> There was that law of life, so cruel and so just, that one must grow or else pay more for remaining the same.
> —*Norman Mailer, The Deer Park*

Table 10.1

| | Personal Development Methodology | |
|---|---|---|
| 1. | Pre-assess likes and dislikes. | Identify your interests and preferences. |
| 2. | Establish values. | Decide what is important to you. |
| 3. | Determine objectives. | Set goals with criteria. |
| 4. | Select a mentor. | Designate a person to assess the quality of your performance. |
| 5. | Develop a plan. | Create a plan which includes defined activities and time allocation. |
| 6. | Collect data. | Monitor progress toward objectives. |
| 7. | Adjust the plan. | Evaluate criteria during activities, measuring progress, and making adjustments accordingly. |
| 8. | Reflect on growth. | Regularly assess efforts and acknowledge growth and progress. |
| 9. | Reward achievement. | Motivate yourself for future successes. |

Table 10.2

| **Personal Development Methodology — A Simple Example** | |
|---|---|
| **Scenario**: Jason would like to take up a recreational activity during the summer. He isn't sure what he would like to do. He would like to narrow his choices and make a decision. | |
| 1. Preassess likes and dislikes. | Jason likes interacting with others, the sunshine, and competitive games. He dislikes activities associated with water, and recreational activities that have undefined endings and are played alone. |
| 2. Establish values. | It is important for Jason to get exercise and meet other people. |
| 3. Determine objectives. | Jason wants to find an activity or sport where he can improve each week during the summer, measured by number of points (games) won against a specific competitor. |
| 4. Select a mentor. | Matt, Jason's older brother agrees to help and provide feedback with respect to the objectives Jason has set for himself. |
| 5. Develop a plan. | Jason makes a list of possible activities. He chooses the top three possibilities taking into consideration likes, dislikes, and values. He makes a list of possible people who might like to join him. |
| 6. Perform the plan and collect data. | The list includes golf, volleyball, and tennis. Jason finds many interested people in golf and tennis but not enough interested people to play volleyball. |
| 7. Adjust the plan. | The cost of golf equipment and fees leads Jason to choose the cheaper of the remaining activities. Jason decides on tennis. |
| 8. Reflect on growth. | All the players are better than Jason at the beginning of the summer. Each week, he improves the number of games won against his neighbor. By the end of the summer he occasionally wins a set. |
| 9. Reward achievement. | Jason joins a health club with indoor tennis courts so he can continue to play during the winter months. |

## Discussion of the Personal Development Methodology

### Pre-assess Likes and Dislikes

A key to personal development is knowing your preferences. Create a self-assessment report which looks at a variety of areas related to you and your interests. Examples include your learning style, educational interests, career preferences and skills, recreational interests, and social concerns. Research and write a comprehensive personal assessment. This will help to clarify who you are and define your vision and goals for the future.

### Establish Values

Your life experiences have helped to shape and define your personal value system which impacts and influences the daily decisions you make. Values also affect how you interact with the feelings, concerns, or problems related to other individuals and events in a variety of contexts. Knowing and understanding your value system helps you to choose activities, experiences, and goals which are more likely to be positive and rewarding. Exploring values is also critical to understanding ethical issues and how they relate to your personal value system and to a societal value system.

To change and to improve are two different things.
— *German Proverb*

| Table 10.3 | Affective Domain — Value Development Skills | |
|---|---|---|
| | **Valuing Self** | **Valuing Others** |
| | building self-esteem | respecting |
| | attending to personal needs | being nonjudgmental |
| | identifying personal values | empathizing |
| | establishing an ethical code | caring |
| | committing to self | sharing |
| | trusting self | forming shared values |
| | creating a vision | committing to others |
| | maintaining a sense of wonder | desiring to serve others |
| | following convictions | appreciating diversity |
| | desiring self expression | practicing family values |

## Determine Goals and Objectives

Having specific, meaningful goals (with measurable and/or observable criteria) plays a significant role in the personal development process. Goals and objectives serve in a positive way to channel your efforts into actions and activities that will get you to where you want to be in the future. You should allocate time to regularly review your progress toward meeting your goals as well as to review the processes used to achieve them. Goals should be self-chosen and realistic with action statements written in a positive manner.

## Select a Mentor

Identify and select a person who has an interest in helping with your personal development. A mentor is like a personal guide, teacher, tutor, or counselor who is positive, supportive, and gives you constructive feedback. A mentor can help motivate you and keep you moving forward toward meeting your goals and objectives. A mentor also assesses the quality of your plan, the processes you use (to meet your objectives), and the ongoing progress you make.

*Responsible mentoring…*

- is a structured, one-to-one relationship or partnership that focuses on the needs of the mentored participant (mentee).

- fosters caring and supportive relationships.

- encourages individuals to develop to their fullest potential.

- helps an individual to develop his or her own vision for the future.

- is a strategy to develop active community/campus partnerships.

Source: National Mentoring Working Group, convened by United Way of America and One to One, The National Mentoring Partnership, 1991.

Mentoring is a process of developing an interdependent relationship between a mentor and a "mentee" for the expressed purpose of helping the mentee learn the skills and behaviors necessary to accomplish the mentee's goals (which the mentor has no stake in).

You can find more information about mentoring in Chapter Ten of the *Foundations of Learning* web site.

http://www.pcrest.com

### Develop a Plan

Develop a comprehensive action plan. As part of the plan, include activities that will help you achieve your stated objectives. Identify and list the people and resources you think can assist and facilitate your growth. Also, consider potential negative or blocking forces which could impede your progress, and how you might deal with each of them. Include a time schedule. Take into account the availability and cost of resources.

### Perform Plan and Collect Data

Put your plan into action and gather data in a timely manner and on a regular basis. Monitor planned versus actual results. Assess your plan to determine what is working well and what is not. Document your progress toward the identified objectives and criteria. Your mentor should be involved as you implement the plan. He or she should help collect data and regularly assess your performance, identifying strengths and areas to improve.

### Adjust the Plan

Based on the data collected in the previous step of the methodology, adjust and modify the plan accordingly. Change tactics, if necessary, but do not change or alter your overall objectives. Adjustments may include revising the planned activities, the performance criteria, or the way in which progress is measured. Continue to apply what is working well.

### Reflect on Growth

Throughout the entire personal development process, be sure to record, reflect, and document your positive thoughts, your accomplishments, and the personal growth you notice. This serves as a motivator in addition to building self-esteem and self-confidence. Assessing and recognizing incremental growth improves your chances for maintaining and repeating successful behaviors in the future.

### Reward Achievement

When you reach an objective, celebrate your achievement with those who appreciate and care about what you have accomplished. Acknowledge what you have achieved and treat yourself to something you enjoy.

To teach a man how he may learn to grow independently, and for himself, is perhaps the greatest service that one man can do another.

—*Benjamin Jowett ,English scholar 1817-1893*

## Health and Physical Well-Being

The main factors that affect your health and physical well-being and impact your performance as a student are nutrition, fitness, stress, and sleep. Within the *Classification of Learning Skills* (found in the Appendix), notice that these specific skills are identified within the Wellness process from the Psychomotor Domain.

Table 10.4

| Psychomotor Domain — Wellness Skills | |
|---|---|
| **Maintenance** | **Renewal** |
| eating a healthy diet | managing stress |
| exercising | recreating |
| sleeping | relaxing |
| maintaining hygiene | |

## Nutrition

Eating a nutritious diet is an important part of maintaining good health. However, for many students, nutrition is a topic that is often neglected or misunderstood.

The Center for Nutrition Policy and Promotion has a web site that you are encouraged to look at. This site provides information about dietary guidelines, nutrition insights, a food guide pyramid, an eating healthy index, information about the nutrient content of different foods, links to other nutrition-related sites, and more. The staff at the Center is composed of expert nutritionists, nutrition scientists, and economists who provide nutrition guidance based on sound research and analysis.

## Fitness

One of the most effective ways to promote good health is through exercise and maintaining a level of fitness. Exercise provides benefits to both your physical and mental health. As a student you should take advantage of the facilities and programs your college has to offer. Involve a friend or fellow student to add to your enjoyment.

The links from Chapter Ten of the *Foundations of Learning* web site provide a great deal of information about health and fitness. <u>However, before you start any exercise program you should consult a physician.</u>

## Stress

Stress is a physical and psychological reaction that occurs as a result of being in situations that cause some degree of anxiety or tension. Stress is an unavoidable part of life. Stress is not a pressure exerted from the outside. Exams, an illness, the break-up of a relationship are examples of some *causes* for stress. Your *response* to those situations is what constitutes the stress.

Some stress can be natural, perhaps even exciting — giving you energy to meet a challenge or opportunity. However, problems occur when stress becomes excessive. It can become destructive and can turn into distress. Too much stress on your mind and body can make you feel miserable, worried, sad and ill. The amount of stress each person can handle differs for each of us in different situations. For more information about stress and how to handle or best cope with it, visit a campus counselor and/or read more from the links provided in Chapter Ten of the *Foundations of Learning* web site.

## Sleep

Regular sleep habits help you to perform at your best. A lack of sleep can cause poor concentration or attention. For information about sleep, sleep research, and sleeping disorders, refer to the links provided in Chapter Ten of the *Foundations of Learning* web site.

**http://www.pcrest.com**

## Health and Wellness-Related Information on the Web

Chapter Ten of the *Foundations of Learning* web site has numerous links to sites on the World Wide Web pertaining to topics related to health and wellness issues.

### Nutrition and Fitness

The Center for Nutrition Policy and Promotion is a government site with a great deal of useful information. The site has dietary guidelines, an index for healthy eating, recipes, tips, a variety of nutrition-related articles, and links to other nutrition sites.

There are links to both commercial and noncommercial sites dealing with fitness and nutrition. These sites deal with topics such as getting and staying active, weight management, various types of fitness and sports equipment, maintaining a healthy lifestyle, book reviews, getting advice from professionals, and information about specific sports and activities. One site provides links to more than 40 professional associations related to fitness (e.g., American Academy of Health and Fitness Professionals, American College of Sports Medicine, American Council on Exercise, American Running and Fitness Association, National Endurance Sports Trainers Association, etc.).

## Stress and Sleep

The American Institute of Stress is a non-profit organization that has a web site which serves as a clearinghouse for information on stress-related subjects. Other links provide information about the medical basis for stress, causes for stress, results of stress, recognizing stress, ways to handle, relieve, and overcome stress, and job-related stress.

There are links to several sites which provide information regarding all aspects of sleep. Information at these sites includes the physiology of sleep, sleep disorders, clinical sleep medicine, sleep research, federal and state information, sleep-related education, business-related groups, and a question and answer forum.

## Public Health and Disease

The federal government has three helpful web sites with information regarding public health and disease:

- Office of Disease Prevention and Health Promotion

- The Office of Public Health and Science (OPHS)

- U.S. Public Health Service's Office on Women's Health

## Alcohol and Substance Abuse

There is a great deal of information about alcohol and substance abuse to be found on the web. Among the links provided are:

- The National Center on Addiction and Substance Abuse at Columbia University

- The Alcohol and Drug Education Project of Hobart & William Smith Colleges

- The National Clearinghouse for Alcohol and Drug Information

These sites provide a broad collection of information and research designed to inform readers about alcohol, drugs, and problems of abuse. The Columbia University site looks at the economic and social costs of substance abuse and its impact on our lives, and assesses what works in prevention, treatment, and law enforcement.

# Emotional Well Being

Take a moment to look at the emotional management skills shown below. These skills are from the Affective Domain within the *Classification of Learning Skills*.

Table 10.5

| Affective Domain — Emotional Development Skills | | |
|---|---|---|
| **Emotional Management** | | |
| responding to success | coping | decision making |
| responding to failure | grieving | being confident |
| responding to humor | managing frustration | being patient |
| managing dissonance | managing worry | being assertive |
| asking for help | maintaining balance | being nurturing |
| recognizing emotions | taking risks | being courageous |
| expressing emotions appropriately | using intuition | being competitive |

At various times throughout your life, you will be in situations that require you to use each of the above-mentioned skills for emotional management. Realize that by improving your performance with any *one* skill, you are making a contribution to your overall emotional well-being. Imagine the growth that occurs when you focus on improving *several* skills. A few of the skills important to you as a student are discussed in more detail.

**Responding to failure**

How a person responds to an *unsuccessful* outcome and his or her subsequent actions is an especially important skill. Those who are strong with this skill display emotional maturity and balance. They are able to reduce the impact of the failure realizing that a failure is only a temporary outcome and does not diminish current strengths. This is in contrast to those who wallow in self-pity and make excuses after a failure.

When an unsuccessful event happens, a person who is strong at responding to failure:

- puts the event/failure in proper perspective,

- self-assesses and determines what can be improved and identifies how to make the improvement (realizing that overcoming the failure will require some extra effort), and

- continues to recognize and believe in his or her personal strengths.

> We're supposed to be perfect our first day on the job and then show constant improvement.
> —*Ed Vargo, major league baseball umpire*

## Responding to success

How a person responds to a *successful* outcome and his or her subsequent actions is a skill. Those who are strong with this skill are humble about their accomplishments and have learned to build upon their successes. This is in contrast to those who behave in a cocky manner and live in the glory of past accomplishments.

When a successful event happens, a person who is strong at responding to success:

- is future-oriented rather than living in the past,

- looks for areas to improve (in the future),

- enjoys the journey on the road to a success and does not dwell strictly on the outcome, and

- maintains emotional balance; he or she doesn't get too high and puts the accomplishment in the proper perspective.

## Managing frustration

Typically, frustration occurs when the degree of challenge in a learning situation is too great compared to the available skills and resources. Those who are strong at managing frustration are able to keep their emotions in check without getting to the point of anger or complete disengagement. They believe that frustration, at the right levels, can be positive and lead to productive outcomes as well as building emotional skills. This is in contrast to individuals who when they get frustrated, let initial frustrations quickly get out of control and the result is unproductive behavior.

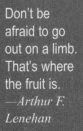

When a person who is strong at managing frustration gets frustrated, he or she:

- does not let frustration decrease his or her level of performance,

- uses frustration as a motivating tool,

- does not let his or her frustrations affect others and their performance, and

- uses a variety of techniques to release or neutralize the frustrations.

## Taking risks

Risk-taking involves taking on new challenges that have uncertain outcomes. Success is not guaranteed and the possibilities for failure are real. Those who are strong risk-takers are willing to move outside of their comfort zones in various contexts (mind, body, relationships, etc.) focusing on the upside potential rather than the downside. They are willing to accept short-term failure to obtain long-term success. This is in contrast to individuals who do not venture outside their comfort zones and need the security of certain positive outcomes before taking on new challenges, thus limiting their opportunities for personal growth.

> Don't be afraid to go out on a limb. That's where the fruit is.
> —*Arthur F. Lenehan*

Typically, strong risk-takers:

- focus on the potential benefits rather than costs or downside,
- are strong at responding to both successes and failures,
- are strong emotionally; not letting fear be an immobilizing emotion,
- are able to make great intuitive leaps, and
- view risks within realistic contexts.

## Coping

It is a rare person who does not experience some form of emotional turmoil at some point in their life. Emotional and mental difficulties may simply be due to ineffective coping skills. The result can be a feeling of walking about in a state of confusion, or doubting one's ability to deal with situations and surroundings. Developing good coping skills forms the foundation for emotional stability, and empowers individuals to feel good about how they think and feel as they deal with life's situations.

Table 10.6 breaks the "coping process" into ten stages that represent various aspects of the coping process. Each stage is equally important although not all stages are necessary for every (coping) situation.

Table 10.6

| **Stages of the Coping Process** | |
| --- | --- |
| Awareness | Look about (inside or outside oneself) and ascertain what exactly happened. |
| Understanding | Describe what happened, how it happened, and why it happened. |
| Rationalization | Constructively place what happened into a context that works for you. |
| Acceptance | Acknowledge what is factual. Recognize what has happened and accept that you can't change it. Rid yourself of all the "what-ifs," thus accepting the situation to be true. |
| Change | Accept, feel comfortable with, and welcome change or something new. |
| Inner Strength | Believe in yourself, knowing what you feel and think can be validated. |
| A Sense of Control | Know that ultimately you are in control of your future. You, and no one else but you, makes the choices and decisions that guide your way. |
| Positive Attitude | View the world positively rather than negatively. Focus on the good rather than the bad side of situations. |
| Caring | Possess the basic belief of the good in humankind. Have faith in your environment, systems, society, people and share this faith with others. |
| Selective Focus | Understand that we as humans have enormous potential to comprehend and internalize our external world. As a coping mechanism, we select and focus on specific areas and aspects (of our lives) which we are best equipped to deal with emotionally. Based on our value systems, we subconsciously determine (and prioritize) what we are best able to cope with. |

# An Ethical Model to Live By

Contributed by Dr. James J. Seymour, Saint Augustine's College, Raleigh, NC

According to author David L. Bender, the prevailing attitude on our American society's ethical climate is very negative indeed.

> Newspapers daily record the crimes and unethical escapades of Americans from every part of the country. From the latest serial murderer with a new record body count to a white collar criminal who managed to bleed a bank or company and its investors dry of a previously unheard of amount, in addition to the millions of ethical and criminal offenses in between, the reading public has probably decided that these are indeed the worst of times. From the halls of government to the streets of every small town, Americans may wonder what happened to traditional values like honesty, integrity, accountability, and concern for others. (Bender, 1993)

> In a society that seems to have lost its ethical rudder, citizens will find it more difficult to steer their individual ships straight. In America, the problem is compounded by cultural diversity. Although pluralism brings the strength of many talents to the melting pot, it also presents the difficult choice of whose ethical system individuals should adopt. In a more monolithic or homogeneous society, the choice is made for you. You simply do what the majority does. Peer pressure forces you to accept and follow the dominant ethical standard of the society. In contemporary America, the dominant ethical standard has become blurred. We are each the captain of our own ship, adrift in a sea of confusing choices. We must chart our own course with little or no help from our culture or family. (Bender, 1993)

Students in particular are faced with a host of ethical situations and many seem terribly ill prepared to make wise moral decisions, leading sometimes to horrendous consequences. Observe these *headlines of horror* and ask yourself two questions; "what has gone wrong?" and "what can we do about it?"

> June 1997: A New Jersey teenager gave birth to her baby in the bathroom stall at her high school prom. She dropped the baby in the trash, then returned to the dance floor, where she asked the band to play her favorite song, "The Unforgiven." (The Washington Post, June 10, 1997)

> October 1997: A 16 year old boy in Pearl, Mississippi, allegedly murdered his mother, then went to school and shot nine students, killing two, including his former girlfriend. (CNN October 2, 1997)

> December 1997: A young boy opened fire on a prayer meeting at Heath High School in West Paducah, Kentucky, killing three and wounding five of his classmates. (The Washington Post, October 22, 1997)

> March 1998: In Dallas, Texas, four teenagers claiming to be vampires went on a drug-crazed destruction spree, vandalizing dozens of cars and homes, spray-painting racial slurs and burning down the office and fellowship hall of Bethany Lutheran Church. (Associated Press, March 6, 1998)

> April 1998: In Yonkers, New York, a 15 year old girl, upset that her teacher called her parents about her poor academic performance, attacked the pregnant instructor with a hammer. The teacher suffered multiple skull fractures. (Associated Press, April 8, 1998)

April 1999: "Massacre Kills up to 25"... Suicide mission terrorizes a Colorado high school. Two young men, both Juniors at Columbine High School in Littleton Colorado, outside of Denver, responded to their rage and humiliation at being made fun of by the high school athletes and went on a rampage that ultimately left 13 people dead, including themselves, by self inflicted wounds. The boys were a part of a group of students who considered themselves outcasts among their peers and called themselves the Trenchcoat Mafia. (Raleigh News and Observer, April 21, 1999)

A suggested model for making ethical choices, called *The Four C's*, is presented next. An important premise of this model is that it is possible to have a clear understanding of how to think through implications, and then make moral choices that can greatly assist an individual to *steer a straight course* through the stormy seas of this life. In some cases, these choices make it possible to steer away from the dangerous reefs that lure us to almost certain destruction. This is not to minimize the power of free choice. However, freedom is accompanied by awesome responsibility and it is important to be as equipped as possible to make wise choices.

No one can avoid making decisions on ethical issues. Even routine, everyday choices often involve judgments about good and bad, right and wrong. The more one's choices affect other people, the more urgent the moral problem becomes. (Crook, 1995) Let us examine one potential model to live by.

## The Four C's

The Four C's model is a simple tool that is easy to remember. If remembered and applied, this tool can help a person make wise choices and decisions in college and throughout the rest of his or her life.

The first "C" refers to **Circumstances**, those things that are going on around us. This refers to the *objective realities* around you at this moment. What are *the facts* of your life at the time that you are preparing to make a moral decision. Are you being encouraged to lie, get high, have sex, cheat on a test, hand in someone else's assignment with your name on it? Are you failing a course and do you think that cheating is the only way you can pass? Do you have the opportunity to steal something from work and not get caught, and is this all right because they pay you such a low wage? Your finances are insufficient, but because your best friend is a cashier at the local grocery store you can buy a large quantity of groceries but she only rings up a part of the actual bill. Is this really stealing, or just a wonderful opportunity that you would be foolish to pass up? What are your circumstances?

The second "C" speaks of one's **Context**. The focus here is on what is happening within you. What are you thinking, fearing, feeling, or concerned about? This is a *subjective experience*. Are you afraid that you won't pass your courses and your family will be angry? Are you afraid of being rejected by your friends, not having a boyfriend or girlfriend, or being called a coward if you don't get involved in what others are doing, even if you have been instilled with values that say *this is wrong*?

> **Ethics** is a systematic, critical study concerned with the evaluation of human conduct. It is concerned with helping people answer the question, "What is the good or right thing for me to do?"

The third "C" is about your **Choices** that inevitably follow your circumstances and personal context. We all have to make choices every day. What clothes to wear in the morning, what to eat for breakfast etc. Not all choices are moral or ethical choices.

The combination of your circumstances, what is going on around you, and your context, what is going on within you, will largely influence your choices. However, those choices that deal with your behavior and how it will effect ourselves or other people, or deal with the issues of what is right or wrong, are ethical choices you must consider very carefully because they bring you to the fourth "C."

The fourth "C" brings us to the **Consequences**. The final result of your choices based on the circumstances you face and the way in which you respond to them, brings about either positive or negative consequences. Be sure of one unchangeable truth, *all moral choices will have consequences*. An act of kindness, or bravery, or generosity will have some kind of a consequence either in your life or in the life of the person you reach out to. By the same token, an act of selfishness, deception, or violence will also lead to some form of consequence for you or other people. Some religions refer to this as the *law of sowing and reaping.*

> We don't see things as they are. We see them as we are.
> —*Anais Nin, French-born, U.S. writer and diarist 1903–1977*

## Applying the Model to Real Life

### The tragic love story of two college freshman

In November of 1996, two college students met in a motel room in the state of Delaware. Brian and Amy had been a couple since high school. They were both Caucasian and came from fairly wealthy middle class families in the state of New Jersey. After becoming sexually intimate, Amy became pregnant. They were both afraid to tell their parents. On a chilly November day the time for the baby to be born arrived, and Brian assisted Amy in giving birth to their son. Within moments he killed the baby, put it in a trash bag, and threw it into the dumpster behind the motel. They then got into their separate cars and drove back to their dormitory rooms, one in Pennsylvania, and one in Delaware. They had seemingly solved their "problem."

The hopes of this traumatic event fading from memory quickly became impossible as Amy began to hemorrhage and had to be taken to the emergency room of a local hospital. The doctor immediately realized she had recently given birth, but wondered where was the baby? It didn't take long for the police to get involved and for the whole tragic story to unfold. The young college couple was arrested, and charged with first-degree murder. How could the love story of two college freshman, full of hopes and dreams for a wonderful future take such a tragic and irreversible turn? Perhaps we can gain some insight by applying the 4 C's.

Bender, D.L. (1993). How Do Others Make Moral Decisions?
California: Greenhaven Press Inc.

Cook, R.H. (1995, 1990). An Introduction to Christian Ethics (Second Edition)
New Jersey: Prentice Hall Publishers.

## Discussion Questions

1. What were the *circumstances*, the objective facts that you have learned by reading this story?

2. What do you think might have been some of the areas of emotional turmoil Brian and Amy were dealing with during the nine months that they were aware of her pregnancy? This refers to their subjective reality, that which we have labeled *context*.

3. What are some of the things *you* would be dealing with emotionally if you were in Brian's situation? What would you be concerned with if you were in Amy's situation as a pregnant college freshman?

4. What are four other *choices* that Brian and Amy could have made to address their situation?

5. Apart from the imminent *consequence* of having to go to prison for their crime, what other consequences do you envision that Brian and Amy now face in their lives? How would you recommend they learn to cope with these consequences?

**Homework**

Choose a newspaper or magazine article that deals with an ethical situation. Apply the 4 C'S Model to the article or story. Examine the story by asking the discussion questions listed above.

<table>
<tr><td>

**Chapter 11**

</td><td>

# Relating and Working with Others

</td></tr>
</table>

> Only a life lived for others is a life worth while.
> —*Albert Einstein, German-born U.S. physicist , 1879-1955*

## The Importance of Skills in the Social Domain

Communication is a process by which information is exchanged between individuals (a source and an audience) using a common system of words, symbols, signs, or behaviors.

Think for a moment about how much of your everyday life is filled with communication and interactions with people. Whether talking, e-mailing, making facial expressions, using body language, waving, or drawing a map, these are all forms of communicating.

Now try to imagine what it would be like to endure a lengthy period of time in solitary confinement. From that perspective, you can begin to realize and appreciate just how much relating and communicating with others gives meaning and adds richness to life. Man truly is a "social creature."

Interactions with others are not only significant on a personal level but are very important at the professional level too. Employers highly value and seek out people with strong communication and teamwork skills. In many cases, it's these skills that are essential for acquiring, keeping, and being promoted within a job. In fact, a 1991 report issued by the U.S. Secretary of Labor entitled *What Work Requires of Schools* highlighted the importance of communication and interpersonal skills. The report outlined the skills necessary for success in the workplace that young people should develop while in school (see page 30).

A great number of the skills required to relate and work with others are from the *social domain* in the *Classification of Learning Skills*. The three processes from the social domain (communication, teamwork, and management) will be the main focus of this chapter. The topics of appreciating diversity and service learning are also addressed in this chapter as they pertain directly to relating and working with others.

# Teamwork

Teamwork is defined as the joint action by a group of people in which individual interests become secondary to the achievement of group goals, unity and efficiency (Webster). In other words, teamwork involves a group of people actively cooperating in an organized manner to achieve a goal. The benefits of teamwork are numerous. When an effective teamwork process is employed, more can be accomplished with greater quality outcomes. Many interpersonal skills are developed as a result of teamwork. Also, individuals within a team benefit by:

- teaching others new skills,

- learning to negotiate,

- exercising leadership,

- working with diversity, and

- being part of a team effort with individual accountability.

The skills associated with teamwork are presented in the table below.

Table 11.1

| Teamwork Skills | | |
| --- | --- | --- |
| **Team Building** | **Peforming in a Team** | **Team Maintenance** |
| defining team roles | following | negotiating |
| commitment to a group | collaborating | supporting |
| team goal setting | cooperating | compromising |
| planning | performing within a role | resolving conflict |
| | group decision making | politicking |
| | | attending to group needs |

Note that teamwork skills can be separated into three areas, (1) skills used when the team is first formed and being developed, (2) skills related to doing a job or performing within the team, and (3) skills to maintain the team when there's conflict or difficulty.

The process of teamwork is fast becoming commonplace throughout organizations in all areas of society, including business and industry, health care, public service, government, and education. Since most of you will more than likely be in team situations in your careers, it is to your advantage to develop proficiency with a wide range of skills from Table 11.1.

# Profile of a Good Team Player

Below are some characteristics and traits that are associated with people who have good teamwork skills and are good team players.

Table 11.2

| Profile of a Good Team Player | |
|---|---|
| **A good team player...** | |
| Affective Issues | • respects the opinions and values of others.<br>• allows team members the freedom to fulfill their assigned tasks and provides assistance when needed.<br>• takes pride in the team and its members. |
| General Behaviors | • accepts full responsibility for her/his role, actions, and outcomes.<br>• is willing and eager to perform tasks that advance the team's performance.<br>• matches individual strengths with particular tasks.<br>• adapts to changing situations and team dynamics.<br>• makes positive contributions toward solving group problems. |
| Assessment and Feedback | • helps others improve their skills.<br>• continually assesses the progress of the team against the mission statement.<br>• challenges the team to increase the efficiency and quality of the processes they use.<br>• reflects on experiences and provides insights for improvements or future changes. |
| Social Issues | • seeks opportunities for collaboration and teamwork.<br>• is punctual and prepared for meetings.<br>• does not force his or her ideas onto others in decision-making situations. |

# Teamwork Methodology

An effective teamwork process involves a great deal more than putting people together in a group with a task to work on. The Teamwork Methodology outlines a general process by which teams can be formed and function effectively. Note that the effectiveness of the process is enhanced by having a mission or common vision, using team roles, having a plan, and assessing the performance of the team as a whole as well as the performance of individuals within the team.

**Table 11.3**

| | **Teamwork Methodology** | |
|---|---|---|
| 1. | Define the mission. | Establish a common vision and goals for the team. |
| 2. | Recruit members. | Assemble the individuals to meet the needs of the team. |
| 3. | Collect resources. | Identify and collect resources available to the team. |
| 4. | Build the team. | Assign members to appropriate roles. |
| 5. | Create and implement a plan. | Schedule the resources for identified tasks and perform the plan. |
| 6. | Assess performance. | Assess the performance of the team against the plan. |
| 7. | Modify the plan. | Make periodic adjustments and improvements to the plan. |
| 8. | Provide closure. | Provide a final point or end to the team. Celebrate accomplishments. |

**Table 11.4**

| | **Teamwork Methodology — A Simple Example** | |
|---|---|---|
| **Scenario:** A suggestion has been made by a few people in your residence hall to have a Halloween Party. As the suggestion has been shared with others, there is common agreement about having such a party. The people in your residence hall must now work as a team to make it happen. The Team Captain leads the following process. | | |
| 1. | Define team mission. | Plan and implement a fun and safe party. |
| 2. | Recruit members. | Create and post fliers asking for volunteers. Also, the Team Captain asks for volunteers as he/she meets people in the residence hall. |
| 3. | Collect resources. | Determine what money is available for the party from the Residence Hall director and determine what space or location is available for the party. |
| 4. | Build the team. | Have a meeting of the volunteers to find out what task each person would like to do. Assign roles. Determine tasks based on each volunteer's interests and strengths. |
| 5. | Create and implement a plan. | Assign refreshments, decorations, and publicity to volunteer groups. Create a time line for each task and a system to report progress to the Team Captain. |
| 6. | Assess performance. | Have each group of volunteers implement the assigned tasks and report when completed or when more help is needed. Check with each group periodically and make sure tasks are being accomplished and completed in a timely manner. |
| 7. | Modify the plan. | As the time nears for the party, the group assigned to refreshments is overwhelmed. The Team Captain asks the group assigned to publicity to help out. |
| 8. | Provide closure. | After the party, meet, review and write down notes for next year's volunteers. The left-over food and beverages are split among the team of volunteers. |

# Discussion of the Teamwork Methodology

## Define Mission

The first step to building a team involves identifying and defining the purpose and objectives for the team. The mission influences who is recruited for the team, what resources the team needs, and the main tasks team members need to perform. Teams are formed for various purposes. In some cases, teams are formed to accomplish a specific goal, while other teams keep the same structure but the people may change.

## Recruit Members

Identify and recruit people who believe in, and are committed to, the stated mission. These individuals should define their goals and objectives, share reasons for involvement, and indicate how they can add value to the team.

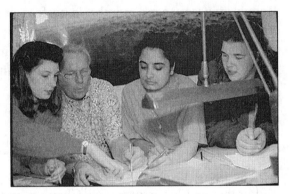

## Collect Resources

The mission statement of the team influences what resources are required and necessary to meet the team's goals and objectives. Identify what resources are available to the team and then determine what additional resources need to be obtained. Examples of a team's resources include the team members and their skills, money and financial assets, information, computers, physical equipment and facilities, time, and team members' individual resources they are willing to contribute for use by the team.

## Build the Team

It is important that team building occurs at this point and continues throughout the process. An important component of team building is the creation of shared ownership of goals and objectives. Team members must believe that the team's goals are worthwhile and obtainable.

The creation of team roles, with job descriptions, enhances accountability, performance, and unity while helping to facilitate team goals. Depending on the purpose and length of the team's mission, roles should be periodically rotated among team members so that everyone can gain experience, and improve skills in different areas.

### Create and Implement Plan

Develop a plan for achieving the team's goals and objectives. The process of creating the plan need not be democratic. However, it is important that all members accept responsibility for their role in performing the plan. Successful completion of the plan depends on "buy-in" or acceptance by all team members. Implement the plan with team members performing according to their roles. The Team Captain is responsible for the overall performance of the team.

### Assess Performance

Regularly assess each member's performance according to the criteria set for each role. Also assess the team's progress as it performs the plan, and works toward meeting goals and objectives. By assessing during the early stages of the plan (as well as on a regular basis), you can determine what is working and what needs to be changed.

### Modify Plan

Update the plan of action based on the assessment or as dictated by the situation and/or the team's performance. Changes and modifications can be made for both the short term and long term. In addition to modifying the plan, options for change include shifting roles within the team, adding new team members, obtaining additional resources, and changing the goals and objectives.

### Provide Closure

All team members should know when the plan is completed or the objectives have been met. Both individual and team accomplishments should be acknowledged and celebrated.

## Communication Skills

Recall that the communication process involves transmitting information between a source and an audience; something we all do regularly as part of our everyday lives. Yet for as much as we communicate, poor skills and ineffective use of the communication process contribute significantly to the problems that occur in relationships —working, personal, or otherwise.

In other words, it's wrong to assume that just because we communicate so regularly, we have all developed into skilled communicators. Growth of skills using a process, such as communication, is minimal without critical thought, a good model or a methodology to follow, and assessment.

Friendship improves happiness, and abates misery, by doubling our joys, and dividing our grief.
— *Joseph Addison, English essayist and poet 1672-1719*

The table below lists the specific skills that are associated with the communication process.

Table 11.5

| Communication Skills | | | |
|---|---|---|---|
| **Creating the Message** | **Presenting the Message** | **Receiving the Message** | **Effective Use of Form** |
| articulating an idea | selecting the appropriate time | attending | conversing |
| defining the purpose | selecting the appropriate place | rephrasing | debating |
| defining outcomes | using appropriate verbal elements | checking perception | informing |
| choosing the medium | using appropriate nonverbal elements | reading body language | persuading |
| generating credibility | using graphics effectively | retaining | public speaking |
| structuring the message | | feeding back | writing with technical detail |

Communication skills can be separated into four areas.

The first two areas, creating and sending the message, are skill sets from the perspective of the sender of a message or information. The first set of specific skills deals with putting together the message and takes into account the purpose and intended outcomes. The second set of skills pertains to how the message is presented.

The third area lists skills from the perspective of the receiver of a message; skills that help to better understand the message.

The last area identifies different forms of oral and written communication, each having a different intent or purpose.

## Web Pages Related to Various Forms of Communication

Chapter Eleven of the *Foundations of Learning* web site has links to information about various forms of communication including debating and body language.

http://www.pcrest.com

# Communication Methodology

The Communication Methodology breaks down the process of communication into a series of steps and provides a useful framework for improving your performance.

This methodology is especially useful in more structured or formal communication situations. You do not necessarily need to use the Communication Methodology with every form of communication. For example, during a friendly or informal conversation, several steps are done instantaneously without thinking. However, whenever there is a breakdown in communication, even with informal situations, walking through the steps of the Communication Methodology can help to identify and remedy the problem.

As a reminder, the benefits from simply reading a methodology are minimal compared to the benefits gained when a methodology is practiced many times with assessment (or self-assessment) feedback.

Table 11.6

| ◁))) | Communication Methodology | |
|---|---|---|
| 1. | Identify the audience. | Define the characteristics of your audience. |
| 2. | Select a topic(s). | Define the topic or topics, the purpose, and scope of your communication. |
| 3. | Set objectives and criteria. | Set objectives to measure the outcomes and effect of your communication. |
| 4. | Gather information. | Find resources and gather information for your communication. |
| 5. | Select a medium. | Decide what you will use to deliver your communication. |
| 6. | Develop the structure of the message. | Create your message and determine how it will be best communicated. |
| 7. | Test and revise the communication. | Practice, test, and revise the communication. |
| 8. | Deliver the communication. | Send the communication. |
| 9. | Assess message and process. | Assess the received message and the communication process. |

Table 11.7

| Communication Methodology — A Simple Example | |
|---|---|
| **Scenario:** A friend of yours is a fifth grade teacher at the local elementary school. She asks if you could give a 10-minute talk to her 5th grade class on the Bill of Rights. You agree. | |
| 1. Identify audience. | Class of 20 fifth-graders (10 and 11-year olds). |
| 2. Select topic. | The Bill of Rights. You want the class to understand why it exists and its importance for ratification of the Constitution. |
| 3. Set objectives and criteria. | Objective: that the students will understand why the Bill of Rights is important and how it affects them. Criterion: the students' performance on a written test. |
| 4. Gather information. | Look at the fifth grade social studies textbook and an encyclopedia. |
| 5. Select a medium. | You choose an oral presentation with the chalkboard. |
| 6. Develop the structure of the message. | The three main points chosen are (1) the need to balance the role of the Federal government with an individual's rights, (2) how the Bill of Rights helped to do this, and (3) its relevancy today. |
| 7. Test and revise communication. | Practice the presentation for timing and content. |
| 8. Deliver communication. | Give the talk to the class of students. |
| 9. Assess message and process. | Write test questions to evaluate students' understanding. Reflect and assess your performance looking for strengths and areas for improvement. |

## Discussion of the Communication Methodology

**Identify Audience**

Identify various characteristics of the audience which are relevant to your communication. Examples of audience characteristics you might identify include predicted size, general knowledge level about the content, perceived attitudes about the content, the setting or location for the communication, and demographic information (age, gender, cultural background, etc.). The more you know about the individual or group with whom you are communicating, the more effectively you can craft your message.

**Select Topic**

Before going any further in the process, it is important to identify your intent or purpose of your communication, i.e., what and why are you communicating to this particular audience? Answering these questions helps you narrow the focus of your message. Use the information about the audience from the first step to help define the scope of your communication. Other factors such as the environment in which the communication will occur and the length of time allowed for the communication are important issues which influence the remaining steps of the methodology.

### Set Objectives and Criteria

Use the previous steps (identify topic, purpose, and scope of your communication) to help establish the objectives for your communication. Your objectives should also include specific criteria used to assess the message and the effectiveness of the communication.

### Gather Information

Prepare to construct your message by gathering information relevant to the topic. Begin with identifying what you already know and then determine what information you still must obtain. Use the Information Processing Methodology to increase your knowledge of the subject area and enhance understanding of the language used to communicate effectively.

### Select Medium

Decide what form (oral, written, or some other) the message will take and how you will communicate your message. Determine what medium (or media) is (are) most effective and appropriate to use based on the audience, objectives, scope of the communication, and resources available. Remember it is not only what you communicate but how you communicate that determines the effectiveness of the message. For example, using an overhead transparency with regular sized type is not a good medium if the people in the audience are seated too far away to read what's on the screen.

### Develop Structure of Message

Develop the message you will communicate taking into account all the previous steps of the methodology (the purpose, the audience, the media, etc.). Generate a logical sequence of topics or concepts that provides a framework for you to deliver your message and for the audience to understand it. You should also consider the amount of audience interaction you want in your presentation.

### Test and Revise Communication

Test your communication before you deliver the final version. Obtain feedback and assessment from others who are in a position to help you. For example, deliver a practice speech before presenting to your audience or have your instructor review a draft of your paper before submitting the final copy. Based on the feedback you receive, revise the message and/or the means in which the message is communicated accordingly.

**Deliver Communication**

Send or deliver your communication. If the situation allows, observe the audience's reactions to your message. If necessary and appropriate, modify the communication to make it more effective.

**Assess Message and Process**

It is important to assess the message, the means of communication, and the entire communication process in order to improve future performance. Follow the Assessment Methodology using criteria established in Step 3 of the methodology. Identify strengths and areas for improvement and look for ways to improve your use of this process.

# Preparing a Presentation

Preparing for an oral presentation involves first knowing what the requirements and constraints are before you start writing what you are going to say. When you make presentations to others, the end result is likely to be of high quality if you adequately prepare and practice rather than just "winging it." Good preparation improves your confidence, reduces any anxiety you might have prior to the presentation, and leads to a better outcome, that being a more professional presentation.

The criteria for an effective oral presentation vary depending on the context and the circumstances. However, there are a few general questions you should always consider when preparing an oral presentation or speech. The following questions serve as a good checklist.

**Initial Preparation**

1. What is the purpose of the presentation? Is it to inform or educate, convince or persuade, stimulate to action, or entertain?

2. Who is the intended audience? Here are some questions to ask to get to know your audience.

    - How many people will be there?

    - What are the background, gender, age, careers and interests?

    - What do they already know about your topic?

    - How much more will they want to know?

    - What's in it for them?

    - Will there be other speakers?

    - How much time have you been given for your speech, including time for questions and answers?

3. What is the room like? Do a room analysis. Go to see the room before the presentation if possible.

- How large is the room?
- How does sound carry? Will you need a microphone?
- Will it be possible to use PowerPoint slides, videos or overheads?
- Will there be a podium?
- Where will you be seated before you're introduced?

4. What physical format do you want for your speech notes?

- Note cards are preferable to writing the entire speech.
- Use large letters to make it easier to read.
- Double or triple space between lines.
- Number the cards, rather than stapling them together.
- Don't break up a thought from one card to the next.

### Components of a Presentation

1. Does the *introduction* gain attention, contain a good opening statement, define the problem or purpose?

2. Does the *body* contain sufficient background information, place information in a logical sequence, and explain any methods used and results obtained? Have you made appropriate use of statistics, stories, or examples?

3. Does the *closing* contain conclusions, recommendations, and/or a strong ending statement?

4. Be prepared for questions. Think about possible questions and prepare answers, especially those possible questions that you are most anxious about. Keep your answers short and to the point.

### Visual Aids

1. Are visual aids visible to all? Are they bright, clear, large enough and well-labeled?

2. Do the visual aids illustrate key points?

3. Are they well-placed within the presentation (timing)?

4. Is there a good explanation of the figures?

### Practice

Rehearse your delivery. Do this in front of a mirror, friends, or into a video camera or tape recorder. Visualize the audience being in front of you.

# Delivering a Presentation

Being able to communicate effectively in the form of a presentation or speech is a highly valued skill, especially in the workplace. Your current presentation skills can be improved with practice, good preparation, self-assessment and assessment from others.

After researching, creating necessary visual aids, and writing the outline and presentation, you are now ready to practice and test the delivery. Practice not only builds your confidence but also helps you to make better use of your allotted time, and enhances the quality of your communication. The following are some general guidelines and tips to keep in mind when making your presentation.

> To speak, and to speak well, are two different things.
> — *Benjamin Jonson, English Elizabethan dramatist 1573-1637*

## Voice and Delivery

1. When using notes, do not allow them to interfere with the speech.

2. Project your voice loud enough for all to hear. Observe closely to make sure that all audience members (especially those at the edges of the room) can hear you.

3. Enunciate your words clearly. Make sure you know how to pronounce difficult words and practice beforehand if necessary.

4. Speak with interest and enthusiasm. Avoid speaking in a monotone fashion.

5. Pace your delivery. Change the rate and avoid the extremes of being too slow or fast. Use occasional pauses.

6. Be aware of using filler words (e.g., "um," "uh," "you know," and "er") and repetitious phrases.

7. Remember to focus on the audience as a whole.

8. Pause a few times to gather your thoughts and then proceed.

9. Act poised and in control.

10. Forget about yourself and focus on the speech.

**Appearance and Body Movement**

1. Keep good posture. Stand tall and straight in a position where the audience can see you.

2. Maintain eye contact with audience members. Focus on those who give you positive feedback in the audience but also be sure to move your gaze around the room during the presentation.

3. Use audience eye contact as a tool to gauge attention and reaction.

4. Use minimal gestures. Be aware of flailing, fidgeting, pointing, or mannerisms that can distract the audience. Between gestures, rest hands at your sides or lightly on the lectern.

5. Use facial expressions to enhance the delivery. Avoid extremes such as smiling or scowling excessively.

# Diversity

While in college, you are in a unique environment that affords you many opportunities to grow and develop your skills in all domains – cognitive, social, affective, and psychomotor. Adding to the richness of your college experience is the diversity that fellow students and faculty bring to your campus. You are encouraged to make the most of this opportunity to learn about others and to practice the skill of appreciating diversity.

In simple terms, appreciating diversity means to value others who may be different in some way. First, let's look closely at the skills associated with valuing others and then look for contexts to apply these skills.

Table 11.8

| **Valuing Others** |
| --- |
| respecting |
| being nonjudgmental |
| empathizing |
| caring |
| sharing |
| forming shared values |
| committing to others |
| desiring to serve others |

Appreciating diversity does not mean that you must agree with other people's values, behaviors, or actions. However, it does mean that you treat others with the degree of respect that every person deserves. The more you practice the skills in Table 11.8, the greater the rapport, respect, and common ground you will find when working with others.

In what contexts does appreciating diversity apply? The answer is most any context where there might be differences between you and someone else. Examples include differences in race, religion, ethnicity or culture, gender, disability, age, sexual orientation, geographical background, interests, and profession or occupation.

Another example of diversity was presented in Chapter Two. Recall the discussion about ways of being and the diversity between behaviors in different disciplines. Differences in personality types can be viewed as another form of diversity.

Behaviors that are dangerous and counter productive to appreciating diversity include being judgmental, believing stereotypes, rationalizing, and permitting feelings of superiority.

What can you do to avoid these behaviors? Honestly evaluate your beliefs. Try to catch yourself prejudging. Listen and learn from others. Be sensitive and think before speaking. Focus on the things you have in common rather than the differences. Allow for opportunities to explain or clear up any misinterpretations.

## Service Learning

Service learning is a way of learning that combines academic study, community service, and reflective thinking. It's a chance for students to learn from real-world experiences as well as from classes, and to put their knowledge and skills to use in service to others.

Similar to volunteering, service learning programs involve students in organized community service that addresses local needs. In addition, students analyze and reflect about their experiences from different perspectives including:

- personal growth,

- application of academic knowledge (relating the meaning of service to course materials),

- developing a sense of civic responsibility, and

- commitment to the community.

Service learning is an application of John Dewey's (American philosopher, educator, social critic, and political activist, 1859-1952) theory that the interaction of knowledge and skills with experience is key to learning.

There are three basic components to effective service learning. The first is **proper preparation** that includes setting goals or objectives for skills to be learned, and plans for how to best provide the service. Second is **performing the service**. The third component is **reflection and analysis** of the experience. This could take the form of journals, discussions, and written papers.

Students do have a say in the nature of their involvement in a program as well as a role in decision-making. However, the specific type of service a student is involved in should relate in some way to his or her academic studies.

Service learning works in all different contexts; in large and small schools, in rural and urban settings, and in all types of disciplines or areas of study.

Examples of service learning include:

- math students tutoring third-graders in arithmetic.
- English students assisting in an adult literacy program.
- sociology students educating their peers on HIV/AIDS prevention.
- nursing students providing home health care to the elderly or disabled.
- chemistry students educating middle school students on proper disposal of household hazardous waste.
- criminal justice students walking downtown streets in a community policing program.
- accounting students helping senior citizens with their tax returns.

The benefits of being involved in service learning programs are numerous. For students, service learning is an opportunity to:

- enhance personal growth and self-image,
- enrich and apply classroom knowledge,
- investigate and explore careers or majors,
- develop both learning skills and occupational skills,
- open doors to new job opportunities (job links),
- develop a greater sense of citizenship and social responsibility,
- foster a concern for social problems, and
- enhance a commitment to public/human service, realizing that one person can make a positive difference in the life of another.

## Information about Service Learning on the Web

For more information about service learning, go to Chapter Eleven of the *Foundations of Learning* web site.

**http://www.pcrest.com**

# Management

The field of management is broad and encompassing with numerous contexts in which principles are studied and applied. Books have been written on different management styles and philosophies. Colleges offer courses which relate to management in a variety of areas including health management, operations management, computer management, information management systems, facilities management, marketing management, and management science.

The focus of this section however, is on the process of management and not on the study of management as a whole. The management process, which is the effective and efficient use of resources to achieve a desired purpose or goal, is not limited to professional managers or those who carry the title of manager. To some extent everyone is a manager, having control over things such as time, stress level, and money, and can therefore benefit from the skillful use of this process.

Improving your proficiency with the management process helps you develop skills that allow you to better manage yourself, resources you have access to, and other people. The result is that you can accomplish more in school and other areas of your life, and gain greater confidence in what you can accomplish and do in the future. The table below lists the skills associated with management.

Table 11.9

| Management Skills | | | | |
|---|---|---|---|---|
| **Leadership** | **Managing Resources** | **Managing Systems** | **Managing Organizations** | |
| leading | utilizing resources effectively | designing | motivating | marketing |
| mentoring | utilizing resources efficiently | implementing | facilitating change | hiring |
| performing by example | utilizing resources within a budget | modifying | building concensus | firing |
| accepting challenge | | networking | evaluating performance | promoting |
| | | | creating a productive environment | delegating authority |

## Management Methodology

Most of the time, the management process takes place in a changing environment that requires you to be flexible in using the Management Methodology. You should look at the methodology as a framework that is applicable in all contexts, but requires adjustment and flexibility depending on the situation. Notice too that the management process draws upon the skills from many of the processes previously introduced in this book.

Table 11.10

| Management Methodology | |
|---|---|
| 1. Define the scope and goals. | Define the scope of the process or activity to assist in setting goals. |
| 2. Create ownership. | Create individual and/or shared ownership of the process. |
| 3. Assess resources. | Gather information to assess the quantity and quality of available resources. |
| 4. Develop a plan. | Develop a plan to allocate the given resources to accomplish the objectives. |
| 5. Create an assessment plan. | Create an assessment system to control the performance of the process. |
| 6. Implement the plan. | Direct and implement the plan. |
| 7. Continue assessment. | Monitor and continuously assess the process. |

## Discussion of the Management Methodology

### Define Scope and Goals

Scope is defined as the range or extent of an action or activity. In the context of this methodology, you should evaluate the extent of the proposed activity or undertaking, gathering relevant information in the process. This allows you to better define goals, criteria, and desired outcomes, which should be done once the scope has been defined. If you are managing others, it is important that you and your team have a clear definition about what you will be doing and why.

### Create Ownership

Enthusiasm for and belief in the established goals and criteria is necessary for a successful outcome. When you are managing a team, you must create a sense of unity, ownership, and shared responsibility by effectively communicating and building interest, excitement, and motivation for achieving the common goal. Without a sense of ownership, you (and your team) are less likely to accept the goals and work hard to achieve them. The Teamwork Methodology is a useful resource for this step of the methodology.

Table 11.11

| Management Methodology — A Simple Example | |
|---|---|
| **Scenario:** You have just opened a checking account at a local bank. You now begin the process of "managing" the account and the resources in it. | |
| 1. Define scope and goals. | This will be a monthly task for the rest of your life. Your goal is to maintain the account accurately. The criterion: to the penny. |
| 2. Create ownership. | It is your money of which you have ownership and interest. If you know how much money you have, you can better plan your expenditures. |
| 3. Assess resources. | Resources include money in the account, the statements provided by the bank, a record of written checks, canceled checks, a calculator. |
| 4. Develop a plan. | After writing each check or using an ATM, subtract the amount from the running balance. After making a deposit, add the amount to the running balance. When a bank statement comes, add the accrued interest and subtract the bank fees. |
| 5. Create an assessment plan. | When you know your balance and the bank's balance agree to the penny, you know you have met the criterion. |
| 6. Implement the plan. | You balance your checkbook for each of three consecutive months. |
| 7. Continue assessing. | After managing your checkbook for a few months, you find that the checks that have not cleared cause you the most problems when balancing. With practice you are able to figure out how to overcome this problem. |

## Assess Resources

Before developing a plan of action, you should first assess the available resources you can use to achieve the goal. This includes identifying what resources are available, as well as the quantity and quality of each of those resources. Examples of the most common resources include time, money, and people. Aspects of the Information Processing Methodology (found in Chapter Six) can help you with this step of the methodology.

## Develop Plan

This step integrates the first and third steps of the Management Methodology to form a plan which meets the goals and objectives. The goals you set and your evaluation of available resources are key elements in developing a plan of action. Since the plan is a guide for future action, you should identify potential pitfalls, possible contingencies, and modifications to the plan to overcome such pitfalls should they occur. In general, the plan should seek to achieve team cohesiveness while at the same time facilitating individual participation and growth.

### Create Assessment Plan

Both improvement of the process as a whole and improvement of individual performance require frequent and regular assessment. You should put into place a system to gather information during an activity or process. This information then becomes the basis for making assessments which include suggestions for improvement and insights about growth. The team role of the Reflector (who assesses the team's performance) and the SII Method of assessment (found in Chapter Thirteen) are examples of tools that can be used as part of an assessment system. The Assessment Methodology (found in Chapter Thirteen) should be referred to as a resource for this step of the methodology.

### Implement Plan

After the plan and the assessment system are created, you (the manager) are now responsible for putting the plan into action and continually directing the course of action. Depending on the particular activity or process, you may need to draw upon a variety of skills such as time management, task delegation, conflict resolution, and problem solving to name a few.

### Continue Assessment

Once the plan has been implemented, assessment should occur continuously. Regular feedback to team members assures that the final goals will be reached. As a manager, you should monitor the assessment system (put into place during Step 5 of the methodology) making adjustments if necessary.

# Chapter 12

# Problem Solving Skills

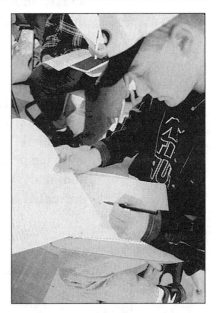

> The best way to escape from
> a problem is to solve it.
> —*Alan Saporta*

## Problems and Problem Solving

A problem is a question, matter, situation, issue, or person that is perplexing, thought provoking, or difficult to deal with. While we all face and deal with problems of varying scope, magnitude, and complexity on a daily basis, some of us are better problem solvers than others. Why is this so?

Several factors influence how effectively people are able to solve problems. First, there is the issue of motivation on the part of the problem solver. You will be much more motivated to put forth effort and perform if the problem to be solved is *relevant* and if you are in a situation that you find interesting or important. In other words, the key question asked by the problem solver is, *how important is it to me that the problem gets solved*? If you don't care about the problem itself, you tend to have little motivation to put forth your best effort.

Another issue that effects the quality of the problem solving process is the complexity and scope of the problem compared to the *knowledge base* of the problem solver. For example, if you were taking an algebra course, regardless of your level of motivation, you would have a great deal of difficulty solving a calculus problem. Also, if you have some familiarity and experience with a problem, that can be a definite advantage over someone who is completely new to the situation. However, this may not always be the case if you did not learn from your first experience.

A person's *self-confidence* at problem solving is an important factor that influences the quality of problem solving. Confidence is gained through past successes which come from the skillful use of a process that can be applied to any problem (situation). This is where a methodology comes in.

Those who are good problem solvers follow and *apply a methodology* to every problem. Whether it's done consciously or not, the approach (or process) to solving the problem is consistent.

Using a methodology is especially important for solving real-world problems. Real-world problems do not come with all the necessary information neatly packaged or with an example problem to follow or with a "right" answer to look up in the back of a book. In fact, there may be many possible solutions. Also, the appropriateness of the solutions will vary dramatically if an important issue is overlooked or a wrong assumption is made.

The best problem solvers tend to have very strong critical thinking skills. There is a connection or linkage between these two processes. Table 12.1 presents the general skill areas and specific skills associated with critical thinking. All the general skill areas contribute to being a strong problem solver. These include applying prior knowledge, modeling the current situation, reasoning, synthesizing and analyzing, and creativity. The skills associated with problem solving are presented in Table 12.3.

Table 12.1

| Critical Thinking Skills | | | |
|---|---|---|---|
| **Applying Knowledge** | **Modeling** | **Reasoning** | **Synthesizing** |
| transferring | visualizing | evaluating | combining |
| generalizing | abstracting | using induction | summarizing |
| contextualizing | exemplifying | identifying consequences | recognizing contradictions |
| using metaphors | building analogies | logical thinking | making connections |
| | simplifying | inferring | integrating prior knowledge |
| | | | defining rules |
| | | | designing systems |

| Analyzing | | Creativity | |
|---|---|---|---|
| interpreting | using deduction | being open minded | lateral thinking |
| identifying similarities | parallel processing | inquiring/questioning | divergent thinking |
| identifying differences | making assumptions | challenging | making assumptions |
| identifying learning needs | evaluating appropriateness | questioning assumptions | ignoring assumptions |
| identifying function | deconstructing | | |
| identifying rules | determining the quality of data | | |

# Profile of a Good Problem Solver

The table below describes the characteristics and traits associated with good problem solvers.

Table 12.2

| Profile of a Good Problem Solver | |
|---|---|
| A good problem solver... | |
| Affective Issues | • enters into problem solving situations with confidence in his/her abilities. |
| | • is able to effectively manage frustration so he/she is able to take on more challenging problems. |
| | • enjoys the problem solving process as much as obtaining a solution. |
| | • enjoys participating in activities that produce opportunities to solve intellectual problems. |
| Strong and Varied Skill Set | • is able to appropriately identify and define the current problems confronting a process, system, person, or group. |
| | • logically identifies key issues by utilizing previous problem solutions or outside expertise. |
| | • selects relevant available information and determines what additional critical information is worthwhile to obtain. |
| | • partitions a problem into a clear set of manageable sub-problem types which have been previously solved. |
| | • learns from past experience and effectively applies prior knowledge. |
| | • effectively integrates sub-solutions into a cohesive solution. |
| | • documents every problem solution so that others are able to use both the solution and the documentation. |
| Quality Solutions | • improves the quality of problem solutions through the selection and use of analytical modeling tools. |
| | • produces multiple problem solutions to test and give depth and richness to the problem solution. |
| | • makes sure that every solution is tested for both reliability and robustness. |
| Technology | • seeks out, learns, and uses technological tools to improve both the problem solving process and the presentation of problem solutions. |
| | • adapts to changing technological environments by identifying, analyzing, or discovering what needs to change. |
| Assessment and Feedback | • assesses and validates the problem solution to make sure that every underlying assumption has been identified, tested, and documented. |
| | • desires assessment of his/her problem solving process and uses the feedback to strengthen his/her problem solving skills. |

## Problem Solving Skills

The table below presents a listing of the general skill areas and specific skills associated with problem solving.

Table 12.3

| Problem Solving Skills | | | |
|---|---|---|---|
| **Setting up the Problem** | **Structuring the Problem** | **Solving the Problem** | **Assessing Problem Solution(s)** |
| identifying the problem | partitioning | reusing problem solutions | understanding context |
| defining the problem | sequencing | integrating solutions | validating |
| identifying key issues | defining knowns | applying prior knowledge | ensuring solution robustness |
| identifying assumptions | defining unknowns | | documenting |
| | | | generalizing problem solution(s) |

## Defining Terms Related to Problem Solving

**Assumption**    Supposition (of something) to be a fact, whether proven or not.

**Generalization**    In the context of the Problem Solving Methodology, the process of making a solution usable in a range of situations or circumstances.

**Integration**    The process of putting parts together into a whole.

**Key Issues**    In the context of the Problem Solving Methodology, important points, matters, or questions to be considered about the problem situation.

**Problem**    A question, matter, situation, issue, or person that is perplexing, thought provoking, or difficult to deal with.

**Sub-problem**    One part of a problem resulting from subdividing.

**Validation**    In the context of the Problem Solving Methodology, the process of testing assumptions and solutions to assess that they are correct, relevant, and cogent.

Problems cannot be solved at the same level of awareness that created them.
— *Albert Einstein, German-born, U.S. physicist 1879-1955*

# Problem Solving Methodology

The process of problem solving is the focus of this chapter and the Problem Solving Methodology is an important tool you can use to improve your use of this process in all contexts.

While problems that are easier may not require you to use every step, you are strongly encouraged to get into the habit of thinking through the entire methodology with every problem, regardless of whether or not you use every step. This strengthens your capabilities with the methodology, making it easier to solve the complex problems you encounter.

Table 12.4

| | Problem Solving Methodology |
|---|---|
| 1. Define the problem. | Identify and clearly state the problem. |
| 2. Identify key issues. | Determine important issues associated with the problem. |
| 3. Collect data and information. | Collect and assess available information relevant to the problem; determine what information is missing. |
| 4. Identify assumptions. | Clarify what assumptions are being made concerning the problem. |
| 5. Break the problem apart. | Separate the problem into smaller sub-problems. |
| 6. Model sub-problems. | Generate solutions for each sub-problem. |
| 7. Integrate solutions. | Integrate the solutions from sub-problems into the main problem. |
| 8. Test and validate. | Validate the solution; assess the quality of the solution. |
| 9. Generalize the solution. | Determine how to generalize the problem solution for use in other situations. |
| 10. Communicate the solution. | Present the solution in oral and/or written form along with documentation of the process. |

Table 12.5

| Problem Solving Methodology — A Simple Example |
|---|

**Scenario:** You have completed your first semester at college and are returning home for the Christmas holidays. Since you will be home for five or six weeks, you want to get a short-term job to keep you busy and earn spending money for when you return to school.

| 1. | Define the problem. | Finding and choosing a job during the Christmas break. |
|---|---|---|
| 2. | Identify key issues. | Must be a short-term job, maximum money, and within commuting distance from home. |
| 3. | Collect and assess information. | Obtain a list of temporary agencies from the phone book, names of stores in nearby malls, and the "jobs" section from a local newspaper. |
| 4. | Identify assumptions. | Retail businesses need short-term, full-time employees in December, and employers reward initiative. |
| 5. | Break apart the problem. | Determine who is hiring for the most money, the most hours per week, and how many weeks the employment will last. |
| 6. | Model sub-problems. | Amount of money = number of hours/week times hourly wage times the number of weeks worked. |
| 7. | Integrate solutions. | The temporary agency can get you work for 5 weeks at 40 hours/week for $7/hour, a possible total of $1,400. That is if they are satisfied with your work evaluations. If they are not satisfied with your work evaluations, you may get no other job offers from the agency. You have found two jobs on your own. The best paying job is for $10/hour for 15 hours/week for 3 weeks, a possible total of $450. The other job is for 6 weeks at 40 hours/week at $5.50/hour, a possible total of $1,320. You choose the job offered by the temporary agency. |
| 8. | Test and validate. | You call possible employers to verify your information. |
| 9. | Generalize the solution. | You generalize that the temporary agency is a good solution because you can use the agency to seek summer employment also. |
| 10. | Communicate the solution. | You write a letter to the agency accepting a job offer. You explain the process used to make your decision to your parents. |

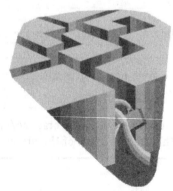

# Discussion of the Problem Solving Methodology

## Define the Problem

The first step in the problem solving process is to correctly identify and clearly define the problem. The ability to assess situations and interpret information properly contributes to correct problem definitions. It is important to define the problem clearly and correctly so that time and effort are not expended in an activity that leads to a solution of the wrong problem. Sometimes it is helpful to get the opinion of others who may perceive and see problem situations differently than you. Their input may improve your original problem statement.

## Identify Key Issues

By asking critical questions, you can identify and clarify important issues (surrounding the problem) which should be considered as you work through the problem solving process. Diagrams associated with the problem situation can also help to identify key issues. When key issues are identified, it often leads to stronger and more comprehensive (problem) solutions. Sometimes, the key issues may cause you to reformulate the problem definition.

## Collect and Assess Information

Once you have defined the problem and understand what the key issues are, you have a better idea as to what information is most relevant and necessary to solve the problem. Assess the quality of the information you collect based on criteria such as accuracy, reliability, appropriateness, and accessibility. Strong information processing and assessment skills produce better quality information resources that contribute to clearer insights and more creative solutions.

## Identify Assumptions

Before proceeding any further in the methodology, you should identify and write down the assumptions you are making concerning the problem situation. Be sure to test the validity of the assumptions you make. The problem definition, the scope of the issues raised, and the quantity and quality of the information you collect all influence the assumptions you make. For example, if you have less available information, you may have to make more assumptions. In some cases, you want to make (valid) assumptions to help simplify the process of solving the problem. Finally, realize that when you change, alter, or make additional assumptions, it can lead to completely new and different solutions. If the assumption is false, it can lead to wrong or poor quality solutions.

### Break Problem Apart

In general, the problem solving process is made more effective and efficient by dividing the problem into manageable, logical pieces (sub-problems) dealt with one at a time. Subdividing or breaking apart the problem makes it easier to begin developing and formulating possible solutions. With complex problems, breaking apart the problem is a necessity.

### Model Sub-problems

Once the problem has been broken apart, you must generate possible solutions to the sub-problems. Building models that replicate the principles and relationships at work in a given problem can be a great help with the sub-problems. Examples of models include diagrams, equations, graphs, tables, and computer programs. Models should make use of available and appropriate resources, including the information and assumptions from Steps 3 and 4, and your own knowledge, experiences, and creativity. Realize that many times, there is not just one right answer. Therefore, you should generate several possible solutions which you can later evaluate.

### Integrate Solutions

The solutions to the sub-problems generated in the previous step must be put together, in many cases, with modifications. This involves evaluating possible solutions and determining how the parts will best work as a whole. The result is often a set of larger models which serve as possible solutions or means to a solution for the defined problem. The next step of the methodology requires you to examine and assess these solutions.

### Test and Validate

Since the outcome of the previous step in the methodology typically results in more than one solution, criteria need to be established to assess these solutions. Testing and validating involves using these criteria to determine how well each solution measures up. The strength of the assumptions should also be tested because the choice and ranking of solutions may vary based on the assumptions made.

### Generalize the Solution

A solution to a problem becomes much more valuable and useful when it can be generalized and applied to many different situations rather than being limited to one unique situation. By making modifications and adaptations to the solution, you can make it such that the solution will work for other people as well as for yourself. You can save yourself a great deal of time and effort in the future by using (previously solved) generalized problem solutions in applicable situations.

**Communicate the Solution**

In many situations, you must communicate your solution(s) and the processes used to arrive at the solution(s) to an audience. It is important that solutions to problems be effectively and persuasively communicated. Otherwise, the value of the solution and all the work associated with it are diminished or even dismissed. You want your oral and/or written communication to include the significance of the problem, the fact that assumptions have been made and tested, that you have examined possible solutions, and the rationale for your final recommendations and conclusions.

## Problem Solving Example — The Rent Problem

**Scenario**: Three students are going to share a two-bedroom apartment for the school year. The rent is $700 per month, and the size of the apartment is 1,720 square feet. The students need to figure out an equitable way to choose rooms and then assign rent for each person.

> No problem can withstand the assault of sustained thinking.
> —*Voltaire, French philosopher 1694-1778*

**Problem statement**

Determine who gets which bedroom and how much each person should pay toward the total rent of $700.

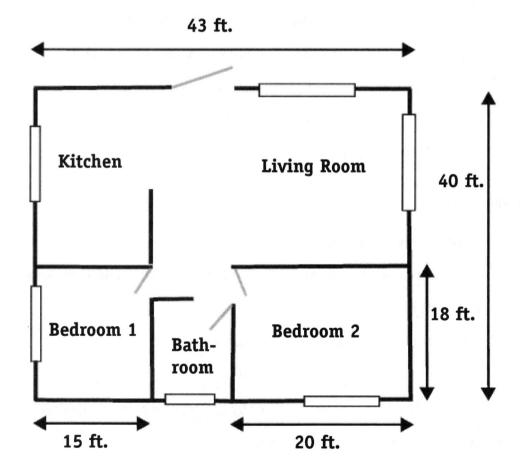

## Key Issues

The following are issues that should be considered:

- Does each student need or want his or her own room?
- Can another room be converted to a bedroom?
- Are some rooms better (worth more) than others?
- What characteristics should be used to place a value on each room?
- What is the value of a private room?
- What is the value of the common area (the non-bedroom space)?
- Is it a mixed gender group of students?
- How much rent can each student afford?
- Do two people want to share a room?
- How should the order for choosing rooms be decided?

## Information

Summarize the information that is known.

- The two bedrooms are 270 square feet and 360 square feet.
- The total area of the apartment is 1,720 square feet (40 ft × 43 ft).
- Total house area = common area + large bedroom + small bedroom
- $1,720 \text{ ft}^2 = 1,090 \text{ ft}^2 + 360 \text{ ft}^2 + 270 \text{ ft}^2$
- The monthly rent is $700.

## Assumptions

- Every square foot of space has the same value.
- Students have an equal share and financial responsibility for the common area.
- A private room is worth $50 more per month.
- Only two rooms can be used as bedrooms.
- Two students will share the larger bedroom.
- Room assignments will be made first by choice, then by a random drawing.
- Any two students could share a room.

Too often we give answers to remember rather than problems to solve.
—Roger Lewin, Science author and writer

## Sub-problems

1. What is the cost of each room per month?
2. How should rooms be chosen?

## Model

Model of the cost of each room using the stated information and assumptions:

The one student with a private room will pay $50/month premium for that room. This leaves $650 per month in rent to be paid for the remaining area of the house by all three students.

Since every one of the 1,720 square feet of the house has equal value, the cost per square foot will be $650 divided by 1,720 square feet = $.3779 per square foot (this figure can be used to calculate the financial worth of the square footage of each bedroom as well as the common area).

Each person will be responsible for one third of the cost of the common area. The two people who share the larger bedroom will each be responsible for half of the cost of this bedroom. The person who has the private room will be responsible for the value of the entire bedroom and pay a $50 premium for the privacy.

## Model for Choosing

Students choose the room they want in writing. A person who chooses a room that is not chosen by the other students gets that room. When there is competition for the same room, a random drawing selects the student who will get the room. Those students not assigned will choose again and go through the steps until all the room positions are assigned.

## Integration

Calculate the cost of each bedroom plus the common area.

*Small bedroom with an area of 270 ft²*
cost/month = 270 ft² × .3779 dollars per ft² = **$102.03**

*Large bedroom with an area of 360 ft²*
cost/month = 360 ft² × .3779 dollars per ft² = $136.04

cost/month per student for the large bedroom = $136.04 divided by 2 = **$68.02**

*Common area = total house area minus total bedroom area*
common area = 1,720 ft² – 270 ft² – 360 ft² = 1090 ft²

*Cost of the common area = common area times cost per square foot*
cost/month = 1090 ft² × .3779 dollars per ft² = $411.92

cost/month per student for the common area = $411.92 divided by 3 = **$137.31**

That which we persist in doing becomes easier, not that the task itself has become easier, but that our ability to perform it has improved.
—*Unknown*

*Monthly cost per room*

The two persons sharing the larger bedroom each pay the following amount each month:

$137.31 (common area) + $68.02 (share of the large bedroom) = **$205.33**

The person with the small bedroom pays the following amount each month:

$137.31 (common area) + $102.03 (small bedroom) + $50.00 (private room) = **$289.34**

All three students choose the single room. A random drawing is held and a name is drawn. This person takes the small bedroom leaving the two other students to share the larger bedroom.

### Validation

Does the sum of the rents equal $700?

$205.33 + $205.33 + $289.34 = $700
(*yes, the sum of the individual rents are validated*)

Are the rents equitable? The person with the small bedroom feels that the private room is not worth the extra cost of nearly $100 per month. All three feel that they would have lowered the premium if they had considered that the person in the private room would be paying a premium for privacy AND for the additional cost for more space. However, since both students in the large bedroom would gladly pay the extra money for the private room, the person in the small bedroom decides not to give up the room even under the current cost arrangements. All agree to keep things as they are.

Were the assumptions valid? All three students agree that the assumptions were valid. However, they were surprised at how long the process took.

### Generalization

All three students realize that they could generalize this method for any number of students and any number of rooms. After subtracting the monthly "privacy premiums" from the rent, the cost per area can be figured. Then the cost per bedroom and the cost for the common area can be calculated. The cost of the common area is evenly divided by the number of tenants (unless agreed upon otherwise). The cost of each bedroom is evenly divided by the number of roommates.

### Communication

The students share the generalized solution and its effectiveness with their friends.

# Solving Word Problems

Mathematical story or word problems require you to take real-life situations and find solutions by translating the given information into equations with unknowns. Since very few problems in life are clear cut with simple steps and easily defined numbers, knowing how to set up and solve (word) problems is very beneficial.

Although you may be anxious when you see a word problem, once you understand the process for analyzing, setting up, and solving word problems, your confidence will grow and you will find that they are not as difficult as you once thought.

Table 12.6

---

**Methodology for Solving Word Problems**

1. Read and define the problem.

2. Identify the given information.

3. Decide what information is relevant.

4. Decide what is (are) the key unknown value(s).

5. Model the problem. Begin with an equation containing the most important unknown value (from Step 4). Then write additional equations for any unknown variables. Continue writing equations until the number of unknowns equals the number of equations.

6. Evaluate the model (solve the equations from Step 5).

7. Validate the solution.

---

## Web Pages Related to Problem Solving

Chapter Twelve of the *Foundations of Learning* web site has links to more information about problem solving including commonly used problem solving strategies and problem-based learning.

**http://www.pcrest.com**

# Chapter 13

# Assessment and Evaluation Skills

> To change and to improve are two different things.
> — *German Proverb*

## Familiarity with Evaluation and Assessment

For most of you, evaluation is a far more common process than assessment. As a student you are accustomed to being evaluated. In fact, you *expect* to receive a grade when you take a quiz or exam, or turn in a paper, lab report, or some other academic work product. Many of you were evaluated when you went through the college admissions process. Admission officers evaluated you on factors that included class rank in high school and scores on the SAT or ACT exam.

Evaluations in the workplace are common also. Employees expect to receive periodic evaluations from managers and supervisors. In fact, despite being a bit nerve-racking at times, many people want to be evaluated in order to receive a reward for good performance. As a worker who has been doing an excellent job, you want to be evaluated so you can receive a raise or a bonus. As a student who has done an excellent job of preparing, you want to take the exam to show what you know and earn a high grade or score.

Assessment on the other hand is a process that most people are less familiar with but is just as important. In fact, if you are interested in improving the quality of your work or your performance, the assessment process is essential. While evaluation is used to judge the quality of a product or performance against a stated standard, the main purpose of assessment is to provide feedback that helps a person to improve the quality of a product or performance.

We have all received some form of assessment in the past. What makes assessment more difficult to distinguish is that for most people their past assessment experiences have been much less formal than the structured evaluation they have gone through. The assessment may have come from a parent, teacher, coach, or friend who offered feedback, pointing out things that you were doing well and offering advice on how to improve the next time. You may not have known it at the time but you were receiving an informal and unstructured assessment.

# Why Improve Your Assessment Skills?

Both evaluation and assessment are important. However, if assessment is not used along with evaluation, then a great deal of potential benefit (in the form of feedback to improve) is lost. Without assessment, it is possible, and quite likely, that a process that is repeated over and over will result in little or no change to the quality of the performance or outcome.

Good students typically have developed strong assessment (and self-assessment) skills so that upon receiving an evaluation they can figure out how to improve the next time. Students without these skills, however, know how well they did, but not *how* to change to improve, or *why* the level of performance was at the level it was.

In this chapter, you will learn more about assessment so that you can perform a quality assessment in a structured manner; including establishing guidelines for what is to be assessed, knowing how the information is to be collected and how the feedback is to be reported. You will also learn about the differences between assessment and self-assessment, and between evaluation and assessment.

# Defining Important Terms

Before going any further, let's define what we mean when using certain terms in this chapter. Note that the definitions below are the author's definitions. They apply in the context of this book. Uses of these words in other contexts may vary to some extent. The four main processes for this chapter are:

| | |
|---|---|
| **Assessment** | giving feedback that documents progress (*strengths*) and provides ways to improve future performance (*areas for improvement*). The feedback is given after measuring the quality of a performance, a work product, or a learning skill. |
| **Evaluation** | using measurements to make a judgment (about the quality of a performance, work product, or learning skill) against a standard. |
| **Measurement** | collecting data and information about the quality of a performance, work product, or use of a skill using a measuring system. |
| **Self-assessment** | the process of assessing yourself, whether it is your performance, work product, or use of a specific skill. |

The names for the people involved in the above processes are:

| | |
|---|---|
| **Assessee** | the person whose performance, work product, or learning skill is being assessed with regard to specific criteria he or she has set for the assessor. |
| **Assessor** | the person who performs the assessment process on behalf of the assessee. |

**Evaluatee**   the person whose performance or work product is measured against a set of standards established outside of the person's control.

**Evaluator**   the person who renders or reports a judgement (conclusion) concerning the performance or work product of an evaluatee against a set of prescribed standards; the evaluator may or may not be in a position to reward or punish the evaluatee.

The following are important components in the design of an assessment:

**Criterion**   a focus area of quality; a characteristic or standard by which something (product) or someone (performance) can be measured.

**Factor**   a characteristic of a criterion that can be measured using a single scale.

**Scale**   a standard against which measurements are made.

## Measurement, Evaluation and Assessment

Consider the following scenario to help you distinguish between measurement, evaluation, and assessment. Assume you took a 20-question multiple choice exam. You receive your exam back and see that you answered 17 out of the 20 questions correctly. Your instructor has marked the letter grade "B" next to your score of 85%.

By determining the score of 85%, your instructor needed to come to a decision, or **measurement** of whether each individual answer was right or wrong. After determining which answers were correct, your overall performance on the exam was graded or **evaluated** against a set standard or grading scale used by your instructor. In other words, the instructor used the results of the measurement to make an evaluation (give you a grade) of your performance on the exam.

*Note:* some evaluations are scored against a standard that is set in advance such as in the example in the preceding paragraphs. Some are scored against a standard that is statistically created from all results. An example of this would be "curved grades," where the grade ranges are determined only after the measurements of all the students have been made.

However, simply receiving a score of 85% and a letter grade of "B" does not help you understand *why* you knew the answers to 17 of the questions or *why* you got the answers correct! Nor would it help you know how to study to get more answers correct the next time. This is where assessment comes in. By **assessing** your performance on the exam, strengths would be identified along with areas for improvement. When discussing areas for improvement, suggestions for *how* to improve future performance would be included.

Suppose when grading your exam, the instructor wrote comments such as, "you listened well in class" next to a correct answer, or "read the long-worded questions more carefully, slow down the next time" next to a wrong answer. These would be examples of receiving feedback to help improve future performance. Actually, in this case, the instructor is both assessing *and* evaluating your work.

Let's summarize our discussion up to this point.

**Measurements** are data, information, decisions, observations, or opinions that are collected or obtained during a performance. Measurements represent the information that is used to make both assessments and evaluations.

For example, a manager could be asked to both assess and evaluate an employee. The manager would need to first make some measurements by collecting information about the employee (first-hand observations, review work-product, etc.). Then the manager could give assessment feedback by providing strengths and areas for improvement. An evaluation could be made about whether to give a bonus based on whether the employee's performance meets or exceeds certain pre-established criteria.

**Evaluation** uses a measurement for the purpose of categorizing or judging. Examples include a boxer who is weighed prior to a fight to make sure he is within the proper weight class, or a person who wants to be an airline pilot who has his or her eyesight evaluated to determine eligibility into a pilot program.

**Assessment** is quite different from evaluation, although measurement is a necessary component of assessment as it is with evaluation. Assessment is not carried out solely to categorize or to judge, but rather to improve the quality of a performance. For example, a doctor may tell you that you have the flu. This would be an evaluation. However, if he or she tells you to go home and get plenty of rest and fluids, he or she is then giving you a way to get better which is a form of assessment.

The table below identifies skills associated with assessment.

Table 13.1

| Assessment Skills | | |
|---|---|---|
| **Developing an Assessment** | **Conducting an Assessment** | **Reporting an Assessment** |
| setting criteria | introspecting | presenting feedback |
| assuring validity | reflecting | complimenting |
| assuring completeness | applying criteria | accepting feedback |
| creating a measurement system | measuring against a standard | |

When studying for an exam, by using good assessment techniques, you can discover ways to study more effectively and at the same time, determine your level of understanding. You could make lists of concepts you need to learn better, and those you *know* you understand. Students who do well in college are almost always good self-assessors. They are able to analyze their work and understand what to keep and what to change so their academic product is of the highest quality.

## Assessment and Self-Assessment

In principle, assessment and self-assessment are identical. However, with self-assessment, the assessor and assessee are the same person. While very similar, the difference between the two processes can be significant. For most people, they find it more difficult to self-assess themselves than to assess someone else.

To point this out more clearly, suppose you are asked to look at a snapshot and let the photographer know (1) what makes the picture good and (2) what the photographer could do to improve the next snapshot. What would you look at? You may notice the focussing and centering of the picture. Now suppose the snapshot is of you! Your assessment may be completely different unless you keep in mind what *you* look like in the snapshot is *not* the only important issue.

## Profile of a Quality Assessor

Below are some of the attributes and characteristics that are associated with people who are good assessors.

A quality assessor...

- is willing to use evidence to make informed decisions,
- is objective,
- is comfortable receiving and giving feedback for improvement,
- is aware that nothing is so perfect that it cannot be improved,
- has the ability to multitask, and
- can focus on what to observe.

A description of different levels of assessor performance is presented at the end of this chapter.

## Assessment Methodology

The Assessment Methodology provides a framework for making structured assessments. The four main stages of the assessment process are (1) set up the assessment, obtain shared purpose from the assessee and the assessor; (2) design the assessment, establish important criteria; (3) perform the assessment, collect and analyze quality data; and (4) report the assessment, provide feedback in a constructive manner.

Table 13.2

| | **Assessment Methodology** |
|---|---|
| 1. Develop guidelines for the assessor to follow when assesssing a performance. | Both the assessee and assessor should:<br><br>a. Define the purpose of the performance.<br><br>b. Define the purpose of the assessment.<br><br>c. Determine what is appropriate to be assessed.<br><br>d. Agree on what should be reported and how it should be reported (for the assessment/feedback report). |
| 2. Design the methods used for the assessment. | Both the assessee and assessor should:<br><br>a. Inventory a list of possible criteria to be used as part of the assessment.<br><br>b. Choose the criteria from the list in (Step 2a) which best meet the previously established guidelines (Step 1).<br><br>c. Determine an appropriate factor (or set of factors) for each of the chosen criterion (Step 2b) which will be used to assess the assessee's performance.<br><br>d. Determine the appropriate scale for each factor (Step 2c) which will be used to determine or measure the quality of the assessee's performance. |
| 3. Collect information during the performance. | The assessor should:<br><br>a. Set up a system to complete and collect information pertaining to the factors.<br><br>b. Measure the collected information against the established factors using the determined scales.<br><br>c. Document the assessee's strengths, areas for improvement, and insights which will be shared with the assessee.<br><br>d. Offer feedback during the performance, if appropriate and agreed upon beforehand, with the assessee. |
| 4. Report the findings to the assessee. | The assessor should:<br><br>a. Share the assessment report with the assessee. This includes information gathered during the performance and how it relates to the criteria, along with feedback for improving future performances.<br><br>b. Analyze a performance that is believed to be poor or of low quality. Determine what part is due to the information collected, the criteria chosen, and/or the performance itself. |

# Discussion of the Assessment Methodology

**Develop guidelines for the assessor to follow when assessing a performance.**

The first step in setting up an assessment is to define the purpose for the performance and the purpose for the assessment. With this information, the person being assessed (assessee) can better determine what is important to assess, and the person doing the assessment (assessor) is equipped to give correct and appropriate feedback.

After determining these two purposes, the two parties should collaborate to determine what is appropriate to assess. This depends on the nature of the activity being performed, the skill of the person performing that particular activity, the level of assessment skill on the part of the person assessing, and the assessor's knowledge of the activity/content the assessee is performing. Finally, the assessee and assessor must decide on the form and content of the assessment report, what the report should include and how it should be reported.

**Design the methods used for the assessment.**

In designing a method for assessment, both parties should collaborate to generate a list of possible criteria that could be used by the assessor to give feedback to the assessee. From this list, both should agree and select the most important criteria that best meet the guidelines from the first step in the methodology. In most cases, this list should contain no more than four criteria. For each chosen criterion, determine appropriate factors to assess the performance and the appropriate scale to measure or determine the quality of each chosen factor. Note that in some cases where the assessment is more narrowly focused, the criterion may be manageable enough without defining factors.

One of the keys to learning how to assess is to start simple. Often the evidence you collect for analyzing quality can be measured on a basic scale. For example, if you are asked to assess an oral presentation, one of the factors could be "eye contact." A veteran assessor might collect evidence by determining the eye contact on a scale of 1 to 10. However, a novice assessor could use a scale of {*none, some, lots*}. Both scales elicit information to create constructive feedback.

**Collect information during the performance.**

While the assessee is performing, the assessor must collect information based on the chosen criteria and factors. It is important for the assessor to also be noting: (1) the strong points of the assessee's performance (things done well ) and *why* they were considered strong, (2) the areas in which the assessee's performance can improve, along with *how* the improvement could be made, and (3) any insights that might help the assessee. By including this additional form of feedback, the final reporting back to the assessee can take the form of an assessment rather than just an evaluation.

In some cases, rather than waiting for the final assessment report, the assessee may ask the assessor for feedback during the performance, called "real-time" feedback. If appropriate to the situation, and agreed upon prior to the start of the performance, the assessor may offer feedback (to the assessee) during the performance. For example, a basketball coach may give feedback to a player during a game but it is more difficult for an orchestra conductor to give feedback to musicians during a concert.

**Report findings to the assessee.**

The final step of the methodology is for the assessor to provide the report to the assessee. The assessment report documents the information collected during the performance, and provides a discussion on how it relates to each criterion. The agreed upon factors and scales should be integrated into the assessment discussion. An assessment report also includes feedback about how the assessee can improve future performance with references to particular skills. A suggested format requires the assessor to provide information on strengths, areas to improve, and insights made during the assessee's performance.

When a performance has not gone well from the perspective of the assessor, it can typically be attributed to the poor quality of one or a combination of the following:

1.  the performance of the assessor,

2.  the information collected (leading to the wrong evaluation), or

3.  the criteria (inappropriately chosen criteria).

Finally, the assessee may offer feedback about the assessor's performance so that the assessor can improve his or her assessment techniques in the future.

## SII Method of Assessment

The SII Method of assessment is a form of assessment that requires the assessor to focus on three main items: **S**trengths, areas for **I**mprovement, and **I**nsights gained. The SII Method can be used in most any assessment situation.

**Strength** — identifies the ways in which the performance was of high quality and commendable; also includes a statement as to why particular strengths were considered most important.

**Area for Improvement** — identifies what changes can be made in the future (between now and the next assessment) to improve performance; also includes mention about how changes can be implemented most effectively.

**Insight** — identifies what new and significant discoveries or understandings were gained concerning the learning process; i.e., what did the assessor learn that others might benefit from hearing or knowing.

*An insight can be described as...*

- something valuable you learned for the first time.
- something you now begin to understand that you did not understand before.
- something you recognized that you hadn't noticed before.
- something that you perceive is significant.
- an awareness of something important.

## Examples of Designing an Assessment

Consider the following example to help you understand the assessment process. Within the given scenario, examples are given for criteria, factors, and scales.

**Scenario**: Gloria Adams is a sophomore in college who plans to major in chemistry. She is given a laboratory assignment to do at home for the General Chemistry class she is taking. She asks her aunt, who is a chemical technician at a major chemical firm, to assess her performance in completing the laboratory assignment and in understanding how the lab supports the material she is learning in the classroom.

**Purpose of performance:** to complete a laboratory homework assignment

**Purpose of assessment:** to help Gloria improve her laboratory technique

**Criterion:** uses appropriate measuring techniques

**Factor 1:** can replicate mass measurements on balance during the experiment

**Scale:** performs without mistakes, sometimes spills the liquid, sometimes leaves the liquid in the container, doesn't know how to use the balance

**Factor 2:** can weigh material correctly during the next laboratory session

**Scale:** the grade the instructor gives Gloria for her laboratory performance in measuring

**Criterion:** understands how the results of the experiment support the theory

**Factor 1:** correctly analyzes the laboratory results which will be used in the laboratory report

**Scale:** is either {*correct* or *incorrect*}

**Factor 2:** can explain how the hypothesis is linked to the theory and how the hypothesis is supported by the experiment

**Scale:** the grade received on the next chemistry quiz

## Another Example

Consider a situation where the performance of a salesperson is being assessed (refer to Table 13.3).

Initially, a larger criteria list (with six criteria) is generated. Each criterion has factors associated with it. The factors are measured using scales. In this example, the three sample qualitative scale values are presented to represent different levels of performance (*excellent*, *good*, and *fair*). The numerical values for the scales are fictional and are provided simply for example purposes.

From this large list, the assessor must narrow the focus (in agreement with the salesperson) to come up with a smaller "criteria list." Normally factors and scales are determined only for those criteria chosen for the final criteria list.

Table 13.3

| Criterion | Factor | Scale | | |
|---|---|---|---|---|
| | | Excellent | Good | Fair |
| Diligence | Number of hours worked per week | 50 | 40 | 35 |
| | Number of phone contacts made for future appointments per week | 30 | 15 | 8 |
| | Number of sales presentations made per week | 10 | 5 | 2 |
| Productivity | Number of sales made per week | 5 | 2 | 1 |
| | Amount of revenue per week | $50k | $20k | $10k |
| | Ratio of sales presentations to sales made | 2 to 1 | 3 to 1 | 5 to 1 |
| Self-growth | Number of sales seminars attended per year | 4 | 2 | 1 |
| | Quality of time management | Excellent | Good | Fair |
| | Honesty and ethics | Excellent | Good | Fair |
| Appearance | Neatness and cleanliness | Excellent | Good | Fair |
| | Business attire, clothing | Excellent | Good | Fair |
| Knowledge base | Quality of a sales presentation | Excellent | Good | Fair |
| | Knowledge of products | Excellent | Good | Fair |
| | Knowledge of market and competitor's products | Excellent | Good | Fair |
| Follow through | Quality of the follow-up service after the sale | Excellent | Good | Fair |
| | Repeat business, % of customers who buy again | 75% | 50% | 25% |

# Performance Levels for an Assessor

You can learn more about assessment and what makes a person a quality assessor by studying the five levels of assessor performance. The descriptive sentences distinguish assessor performance with respect to interpreting information, giving feedback, comfort in using and applying the process, and selecting criteria.

**Level 5        Sage**

- Correctly interprets the key performance areas, and clearly describes the strengths, areas for improvement, and insights in all contexts.

- Relates the performance issues to the assessee in a way that can transform the quality of the performance.

- Expresses the report in future oriented language leading to a specific plan of action.

- Seeks assessment opportunities in any context and models the use of the skill for assessment across various contexts.

- Removes personal values and biases.

**Level 4        Mentor**

- Usually interprets the key performance areas, and usually describes the strengths, areas for improvement, and insights in familiar and some unfamiliar contexts.

- Consistently provides specific, supported feedback that helps the assessee to grow.

- Uses real-time assessment to improve immediate performance.

- Seeks assessment opportunities, and models good assessment techniques within a particular context.

**Level 3        Guide / Coach**

- Often interprets the key performance areas, and describes the strengths, areas for improvement, and insights best in familiar contexts.

- Identifies and provides helpful feedback on prominent performance issues.

- Conducts intermittent assessments, and formulates insights that are valuable to future performance.

- Appropriately selects performance criteria, and recognizes the specific context of application.

### Level 2     Learner / Player

- Sometimes interprets the key performance areas, and sometimes appropriately describes the strengths, areas for improvement, and insights.

- Provides superficial feedback on obvious performance.

- Exhibits a mechanical approach by completing assessments by following the steps but without appreciating any future value.

- Can use given performance criteria to assess within a specific context.

### Level 1     Novice

- Offers ambiguous strengths, areas for improvement, and insights, which would seldom lead to meaningful improvement.

- Offers unsupported feedback, which misses many important performance issues.

- Engages in little or no assessment, and cannot identify growth opportunities.

- Is unable to recognize appropriate performance criteria in any context.

- Is biased in every aspect and is oblivious to or unaware of the "affect" of the assessee.

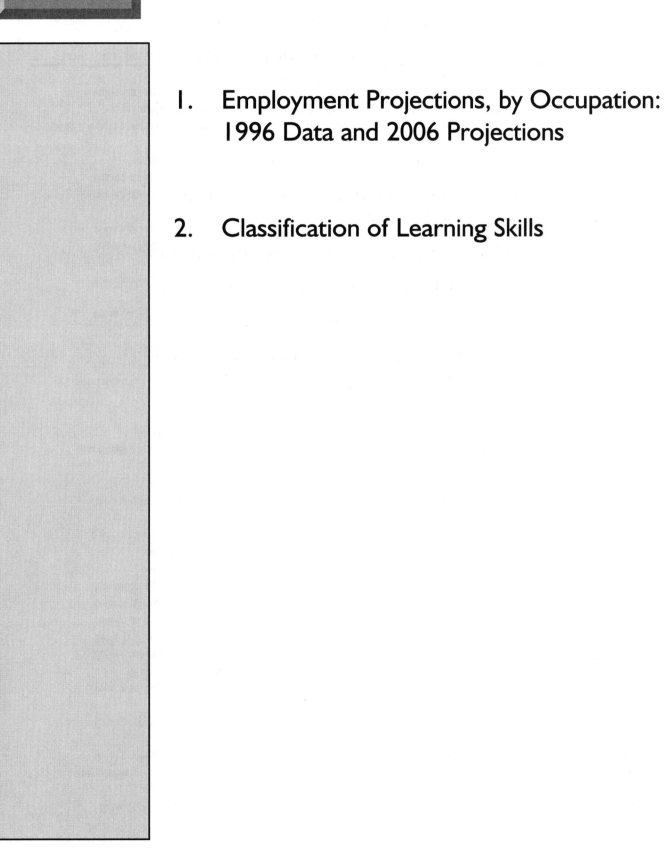

# Appendix

1. Employment Projections, by Occupation: 1996 Data and 2006 Projections

2. Classification of Learning Skills

# Employment Projections, by Occupation: 1996 and 2006

## (in thousands, except percent)

### Largest Job Growth

| Occupation | Employment | | Change | | Education and training |
|---|---|---|---|---|---|
| | 1996 | 2006 | Number | Percent | |
| Cashiers | 3,146 | 3,677 | 530 | 17 | Short-term on-the-job training |
| Systems analysts | 506 | 1,025 | 520 | 103 | Bachelor's Degree |
| General managers and top executives | 3,210 | 3,677 | 467 | 15 | Work experience plus Bachelor's Degree |
| Registered nurses | 1,971 | 2,382 | 411 | 21 | Associate's Degree |
| Salespersons, retail | 4,072 | 4,481 | 408 | 10 | Short-term on-the-job training |
| Truck drivers light and heavy | 2,719 | 3,123 | 404 | 15 | Short-term on-the-job training |
| Home health aides | 495 | 873 | 378 | 76 | Short-term on-the-job training |
| Teacher aides and educational assistants | 981 | 1,352 | 370 | 38 | Short-term on-the-job training |
| Nursing aides, orderlies, and attendants | 1,312 | 1,645 | 333 | 25 | Short-term on-the-job training |
| Receptionists and information clerks | 1,074 | 1,392 | 318 | 30 | Short-term on-the-job training |
| Teachers, secondary school | 1,406 | 1,718 | 312 | 22 | Bachelor's Degree |
| Child care workers | 830 | 1,129 | 299 | 36 | Short-term on-the-job training |
| Clerical supervisors and managers | 1,369 | 1,630 | 262 | 19 | Work experience in a related area |
| Database administrators, computer support specialists | 212 | 461 | 249 | 118 | Bachelor's Degree |
| Marketing and sales worker supervisors | 2,316 | 2,562 | 246 | 11 | Work experience in a related area |
| Maintenance repairers, general utility | 1,362 | 1,608 | 246 | 18 | Long-term on-the-job training |
| Food counter, fountain, and related workers | 1,720 | 1,963 | 243 | 14 | Short-term–on-the-job training |
| Teachers, special education | 407 | 648 | 241 | 59 | Bachelor's Degree |
| Computer engineers | 216 | 451 | 235 | 109 | Bachelor's Degree |
| Food preparation workers | 1,253 | 1,487 | 234 | 19 | Short-term on-the-job training |
| Hand packers and packagers | 986 | 1,208 | 222 | 23 | Short-term on-the-job training |
| Guards | 955 | 1,175 | 221 | 23 | Short-term on-the-job training |
| General office clerks | 3,111 | 3,326 | 215 | 7 | Short-term on-the-job training |
| Waiters and waitresses | 1,957 | 2,163 | 206 | 11 | Short-term on-the-job training |
| Social workers | 585 | 772 | 188 | 32 | Bachelor's Degree |
| Adjustment clerks | 401 | 584 | 183 | 46 | Short-term on-the-job training |
| Cooks, short order and fast food | 804 | 978 | 174 | 22 | Short-term on-the-job training |
| Personal and home care aides | 202 | 374 | 171 | 85 | Short-term on-the-job training |
| Food service and lodging managers | 589 | 757 | 168 | 28 | Work experience in a related area |
| Medical assistants | 225 | 391 | 166 | 74 | Moderate on-the-job training |

# Employment Projections, by Occupation: 1996 and 2006
## (in thousands, except percent)

### Fastest Growing

| Occupation | Employment | | Change | | Education and training |
|---|---|---|---|---|---|
| | 1996 | 2006 | Number | Percent | |
| Database administrators, computer support specialists | 212 | 461 | 249 | 118 | Bachelor's Degree |
| Computer engineers | 216 | 451 | 235 | 109 | Bachelor's Degree |
| Systems analysts | 506 | 1,025 | 520 | 103 | Bachelor's Degree |
| Personal and home care aides | 202 | 374 | 171 | 85 | Short-term on-the-job training |
| Physical and corrective therapy assistants/aides | 84 | 151 | 66 | 79 | Moderate on-the-job training |
| Home health aides | 495 | 873 | 378 | 76 | Short-term on-the-job training |
| Medical assistants | 225 | 391 | 166 | 74 | Moderate on-the-job training |
| Desktop publishing specialists | 30 | 53 | 22 | 74 | Long-term on-the-job training |
| Physical therapists | 115 | 196 | 81 | 71 | Bachelor's Degree |
| Occupational therapy assistants/aides | 16 | 26 | 11 | 69 | Moderate on-the-job training |
| Paralegals | 113 | 189 | 76 | 68 | Associate's Degree |
| Occupational therapists | 57 | 95 | 38 | 66 | Bachelor's Degree |
| Teachers, special education | 407 | 648 | 241 | 59 | Bachelor's Degree |
| Human services workers | 178 | 276 | 98 | 55 | Moderate on-the-job training |
| Data processing equipment repairers | 80 | 121 | 42 | 52 | Post-secondary vocational training |
| Medical records technicians | 87 | 132 | 44 | 51 | Associate's Degree |
| Speech-language pathologists and audiologists | 87 | 131 | 44 | 51 | Master's Degree |
| Dental hygienists | 133 | 197 | 64 | 48 | Associate's Degree |
| Amusement and recreation attendants | 288 | 426 | 138 | 48 | Short-term on-the-job training |
| Physician assistants | 64 | 93 | 30 | 47 | Bachelor's Degree |
| Respiratory therapists | 82 | 119 | 37 | 46 | Associate's Degree |
| Adjustment clerks | 401 | 584 | 183 | 46 | Short-term on-the-job training |
| Engineering, science, and computer systems managers | 343 | 498 | 155 | 45 | Work experience plus Bachelor's or higher |
| Emergency medical technicians | 150 | 217 | 67 | 45 | Post-secondary vocational training |
| Manicurists | 43 | 62 | 19 | 45 | Post-secondary vocational training |
| Bill and account collectors | 269 | 381 | 112 | 42 | Short-term on-the-job training |
| Residential counselors | 180 | 254 | 74 | 41 | Bachelor's Degree |
| Instructors and coaches, sports and physical training | 303 | 427 | 123 | 41 | Moderate on-the-job training |
| Dental assistants | 202 | 278 | 77 | 38 | Moderate on-the-job training |
| Securities and financial sales workers | 263 | 363 | 100 | 38 | Bachelor's Degree |

Source: U. S. Bureau of Labor Statistics, *Monthly Labor Review*, November 1997.

# Classification of Learning Skills

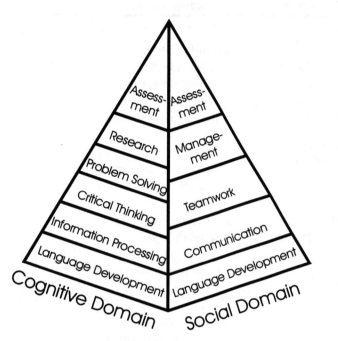

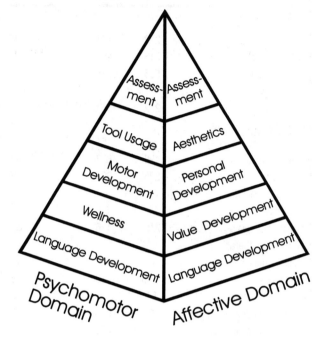

## Cognitive Domain

Information Processing, Critical Thinking, Problem Solving & Research

| Information Processing Skills | | | |
|---|---|---|---|
| Collecting Data | Generating Data | Organizing Data | Retrieving Data |
| observing/recognizing | predicting | outlining | reading |
| skimming | experimenting | categorizing | brainstorming |
| recording | surveying | systematizing | remembering |
| listening | estimating | sorting | reviewing |
| memorizing | | translating | using information systems |
| sensing | | | |

| Critical Thinking Skills | | | | | | |
|---|---|---|---|---|---|---|
| Applying Knowledge | Modeling | Reasoning | Analyzing | | Synthesizing | Creativity |
| transferring | visualizing | evaluating | interpreting | using deduction | combining | being open minded |
| contextualizing | exemplifying | using induction | deconstructing | identifying function | summarizing | divergent thinking |
| generalizing | abstracting | identifying consequences | parallel processing | identifying rules | defining rules | lateral thinking |
| using metaphors | building analogies | inferring/ logical thinking | identifying similarities | identifying learning needs | designing systems | inquiring/ questioning |
| | simplifying/ concretizing | | identifying differences | evaluating appropriateness | recognizing contradictions | making and ignoring assumptions |
| | | | making assumptions | determining the quality of data | making connections/ convergent thinking | questioning assumptions/ challenging |
| | | | | | integrating prior knowledge | |

| Problem Solving Skills | | | |
|---|---|---|---|
| Setting up the Problem | Structuring the Problem | Solving the Problem | Assessing Problem Solution(s) |
| identifying the problem | partitioning | reusing problem solutions | understanding context |
| defining the problem | sequencing | integrating solutions | validating |
| identifying key issues | defining knowns | applying prior knowledge | ensuring solution robustness |
| identifying assumptions | defining unknowns | | documenting |
| | | | generalizing problem solution(s) |

| Research Skills | | |
|---|---|---|
| **Identifying Knowledge Needs** | **Discovering** | **Peer Review** |
| making hypotheses | creating linkages | presenting a paper |
| identifying learning requirements | designing experiments | peer reviewing a paper |
| identifying missing knowledge | testing hypothesis | accepting peer review |
| evaluating existing paradigm | drawing conclusions | |
| recognizing the need for a new paradigm | finding counter examples | |
| | sharing ownership of ideas | |
| | structuring a new paradigm(s) | |

## Assessment & Evaluation, and Language Development Skills

| Assessment and Evaluation Skills | | | |
|---|---|---|---|
| **Designing an Assesment** | **Conducting an Assessment** | **Evaluating** | **Reporting an Assessment** |
| setting criteria | applying criteria | making judgements | presenting feedback |
| creating a measuring system | introspecting | rewarding | complimenting |
| assuring validity | reflecting | punishing | accepting feedback |
| assuring completeness | measuring against a standard | | |

| Language Development Skills | | | | |
|---|---|---|---|---|
| **Building Vocabulary** | **Decoding Communication** | **Understanding Syntax** | **Identifying Semantics** | **Identifying Context** |
| defining | pattern recognition | word recognition | recognizing meaning | identifying cultural background |
| practice and usage | recognizing symbols | proper use of sentence structure | recognizing connotations | identifying historical background |
| | assigning meaning | proper use of grammar | using rhetoric | |

# Social Domain
## Communication, Teamwork & Management

| Communication Skills | | | |
|---|---|---|---|
| **Creating the Message** | **Presenting the Message** | **Receiving the Message** | **Effective Use of Form** |
| articulating an idea | selecting the appropriate time | attending | conversing |
| choosing the medium | selecting the appropriate place | rephrasing | debating |
| defining purpose | using appropriate verbal elements | retaining | informing |
| generating credibility | using appropriate nonverbal elements | checking perception | persuading |
| defining outcomes | using graphics effectively | feeding back | public speaking |
| structuring the message | | reading body language | interviewing |
| | | | writing with technical detail |

| Teamwork Skills | | |
|---|---|---|
| **Team Building** | **Team Maintenance** | **Performing in a Team** |
| defining team roles | negotiating | following |
| commitment to a group | compromising | collaborating |
| planning | supporting | cooperating |
| team goal setting | politicking | performing within a role |
| | attending to group needs | group decision-making |
| | resolving conflict | |

| Management Skills | | | | |
|---|---|---|---|---|
| **Managing Organzations** | | **Managing Systems** | **Leadership** | **Managing Resources** |
| motivating | evaluating performance | designing | leading | utilizing resources: |
| hiring | facilitating change | implementing | mentoring | effectively |
| firing | delegating authority | modifying | performing by example | efficiently |
| | | | | within a budget |
| marketing | building consensus | networking | accepting challenge | |
| promoting | creating a productive environment | | | |

# Affective Domain
## Value Development, Personal Development & Aesthetic Development

| Value Development Skills | | | | |
|---|---|---|---|---|
| **Valuing Self** | | **Valuing Others** | | **Valuing Institutions** |
| building self-esteem | trusting self | caring | being nonjudgmental | valuing history |
| following convictions | attending to personal needs | sharing | forming shared values | valuing tradition |
| committing to self | identifying personal values | respecting | desiring to serve others | valuing principles |
| desiring self-expression | maintaining a sense of wonder | empathizing | committing to others | |
| establishing an ethical code | | appreciating diversity | practicing family values | |

## Personal Development Skills

| Self Management | Emotional Management | | Social Management |
|---|---|---|---|
| preparing | recognizing emotions | being courageous | giving |
| planning individual action | taking risks | being confident | self sacrificing |
| focusing | responding to success | being competitive | loving |
| persisting | responding to failure | responding to humor | following manners |
| managing time | coping | managing frustration | citizenship |
| managing curiosity | managing dissonance | managing worry | being courteous |
| setting personal goals | being patient | maintaining balance | volunteering |
| setting priorities | being assertive | grieving | obeying laws |
| managing personal finances | being nurturing | self motivating/ self-starter | parenting |
| | using intuition | expressing emotions appropriately | following social conventions |
| | asking for help | | service-mindedness |

## Aesthetic Development Skills

| Self Expression | | Cultural Appreciation |
|---|---|---|
| drawing | producing humor | appreciating music |
| dancing | producing music | appreciating art |
| cooking | creative writing | desiring to travel |
| singing | imagining | culinary appreciation |
| acting | innovating | |
| photographing | inventing | |
| story telling | dressing | |

# Psychomotor Domain
## Wellness, Motor Development & Tool Usage

| Wellness Skills | |
|---|---|
| **Maintenance** | **Renewal** |
| eating a healthy diet | recreating |
| exercising | relaxing |
| maintaining hygiene | managing stress |
| sleeping | |

| Motor Development Skills | |
|---|---|
| **Physical Development** | **Motor Integration** |
| developing strength | being versatile |
| developing spatial orientation | being coordinated |
| developing postural awareness | being dexterous |
| developing sensory acuity | being balanced |
| developing endurance | being precise |
| tolerating pain | using the appropriate speed |
| developing flexibility | being accurate |

| Tool Usage Skills |
|---|
| **Using Information Processing Tools** |
| using computers |
| using the Internet |
| using laboratory devices |

# Index